James Barber, Christian Büschges, Dianne Violeta Mausfeld, Britta Sweers (eds.)
Remixing the Hip-Hop Narrative

Popular Music

James Barber, born in 1986, is a PhD student at the Institute of Musicology at Universität Bern. Addressing the Jamaican cultural influence on US hip-hop in New York (1970s-1990s), his thesis focuses on the historical circularity of Jamaican and African American popular music and cultural practice, and proliferating interactions between New York reggae and hip-hop practice in the 1980s and 1990s especially.

Christian Büschges, born in 1965, is professor of Iberian and Latin American history at the Institute of History at Universität Bern, and director of the Center of Global Studies. Büschges completed his doctorate in history at Universität Köln and was professor of history at Universität Bielefeld. His research focuses on Latin American and global history, especially on questions of identity politics, ethnicity, and social movements.

Dianne Violeta Mausfeld, born in 1983, is a research fellow at the Center for Inter-American Studies at Universität Bielefeld. She obtained her PhD in History at Universität Bern in 2022. Her research interests center around US hip hop, Chicano and Latino history and popular culture, and Pan-American history and culture.

Britta Sweers, born in 1969, has been professor of cultural anthropology of music at the Institute of Musicology at Universität Bern since 2009 and was also director of the University's Center for Global Studies (2016-2020). Her research interests include the transformation of traditional musics in a global context, global popular music, nationalism and music, as well as soundscape studies.

James Barber, Christian Büschges, Dianne Violeta Mausfeld, Britta Sweers (eds.)

Remixing the Hip-Hop Narrative

Between Local Expressions and Global Connections

[transcript]

Published with the support of the Swiss National Science Foundation.

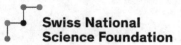

Bibliographic information published by the Deutsche Nationalbibliothek

This work is licensed under the Creative Commons Attribution 4.0 (BY) license, which means that the text may be remixed, transformed and built upon and be copied and redistributed in any medium or format even commercially, provided credit is given to the author.

Creative Commons license terms for re-use do not apply to any content (such as graphs, figures, photos, excerpts, etc.) not original to the Open Access publication and further permission may be required from the rights holder. The obligation to research and clear permission lies solely with the party re-using the material.

First published in 2024 by transcript Verlag, Bielefeld
© James Barber, Christian Büschges, Dianne Violeta Mausfeld, Britta Sweers (eds.)

Cover layout: Jan Gerbach, Bielefeld
Cover illustration: Chavdar Grigorov
Copy-editing: James Barber, Khalifa Bokhammas, Dianne Violeta Mausfeld
Proofread: James Barber, Khalifa Bokhammas
Printed by: Elanders Waiblingen GmbH, Waiblingen
https://doi.org/10.14361/9783839470527
Print-ISBN: 978-3-8376-7052-3
PDF-ISBN: 978-3-8394-7052-7
ISSN of series: 2747-3066
eISSN of series: 2747-3074

This volume is dedicated to the memory of David Buschmann (1989–2018) and Victor da Souza Soares (1985–2020), two dearly missed friends and colleagues who left us too soon. David and Victor were both important contributors to the development of various stages of the "Hip Hop as a Transcultural Phenomenon" project between 2018 and 2020.

Contents

Acknowledgments
James Barber, Christian Büschges, Dianne Violeta Mausfeld,
and Britta Sweers 9

Preface
James Barber, Christian Büschges, Dianne Violeta Mausfeld,
and Britta Sweers 11

Remixing the Hip-Hop Narrative
Introduction
James Barber, Christian Büschges, Dianne Violeta Mausfeld,
and Britta Sweers 17

Epistemological Quandary
Why Hip-Hop Scholars Must Ground Their Transcultural Arguments
in the Work of Fernando Ortiz
Terence Kumpf 47

Hip Hop Becomes Mainstream
or, How to Commodify Multicultural Listeners
Amy Coddington 77

"Double the Struggle"
Chicano/Latino Hip Hop in *The Source* Magazine
Dianne Violeta Mausfeld 105

"Where the Rhymes at?"
How Contemporary Artists are Transforming Notions of Liveness in Hip Hop
Kevin P. Green 133

YEEK!
Atlanta Hip-Hop Dance and the Subversion
of Expressing "Your Energetic Explosive Klimax"
Kevin C. Holt 159

Identity Transgressions as Transgressions of the Art Form
The Case of Frank Ocean
Martina Bratić 185

Afro-Cosmopolitanisms
Discourses on Race and Urban Identities in Brazilian Hip Hop
Eliseo Jacob 209

"Ich lebe für Hip Hop"
German Hip-Hop Music, Cultural Hybridities, and the "Berlin Moment"
Martin Lüthe 235

Producing Hip-Hop Culture and Identity
How a Youth Recording Studio Supports Well-Being
Bronwen Low and Édouard Laniel-Tremblay 259

**Chronicling New York Reggae and Hip Hop's Crossroads,
and Community Media as Historical Archives from the Ground Up**
James Barber 289

Contributors 323

Acknowledgments

James Barber, Christian Büschges, Dianne Violeta Mausfeld, and Britta Sweers

As editors of this volume and members of the research project "Hip Hop as a Transcultural Phenomenon," we would first like to thank the Swiss National Science Foundation for funding the project as a whole, and by extension the present volume. Further gratitude is in order to the University of Bern, for providing the team with a valuable institutional infrastructure and positive environment in which to carry out much of the work and study that has gone into this project. In particular, we are thankful to both the Institute of Musicology and the Institute of History, Department for Iberian and Latin American History, along with the University of Bern's Walter Benjamin Kolleg, and the extensive support they provide to young researchers. An acknowledgement is also due to Roman Kunzmann for his collaboration to an earlier draft of the research project. For the general organization and management of the project, whether in terms of resources, conference and event organization and all-round moral support, a huge thanks are in order to Keith Cann-Guthauser for his tireless efforts and dedication to the project. We extend further gratitude to student assistant Rea Vogt for her invaluable efforts in countless aspects of the project's organization. On the creative side of this volume, special thanks go out to our copy-editor Khalifa Bokhammas, and illustrator and multimedia artist Chavdar Grigorov, who is responsible not only for the book's cover image, but also produced a multitude of wonderful images for the "Hip Hop Transcultural" conference that took place in October 2021 at the University of Bern.

Preface

James Barber, Christian Büschges, Dianne Violeta Mausfeld, and Britta Sweers

This book is the outcome of a research project that in one form or another has been in the works for more than a decade. Original ideas and discussions leading up to the project first manifested at the University of Bielefeld (Germany) in 2009, bringing together historians Christian Büschges and Sebastian Knake, and Wilfried Raussert from literary and cultural studies. In 2016, these early sketches were then taken up by and expanded upon considerably by Christian Büschges and ethnomusicologist Britta Sweers at the University of Bern. In 2018, the culmination of this decade-long process was realized through the Swiss National Science Foundation-funded research project "Hip Hop as a Transcultural Phenomenon. Jamaican and Latin American cultural signifiers in US Hip Hop (New York and Los Angeles, c.1970s–1990s)."

The empirical basis of the project was made up of two doctoral research case studies, focusing on New York and Los Angeles, led by James Barber and Dianne Violeta Mausfeld, respectively. Both candidates brought with them their individual experiences and expertise on hip hop, as long-time fans into the mix, besides research interests in other areas of popular music. Barber completed his undergraduate studies in Sociology and an MA in Global Studies, while Mausfeld has a background in Latin American and North American Studies. In addition, Barber has been heavily involved in the reggae and sound system scene in the UK, and later in Germany, since his teenage years, and also active as a part-time music event promoter, vinyl enthusiast, reggae 'selector' and DJ, and attendee at countless musical festivals, concerts, club nights, and raves since the early 2000s. Mausfeld's very first concert experience was a show in her hometown Hamburg in the mid-1990s from local group Fettes Brot. It was during a high school stay in the Houston area in 2000/2001, however, when she really fell in love with rap music, being exposed to the sound of the "Dirty South" by DJ Screw, Mystical, Ludacris, and UGK. The research team was completed by student assistants Céline Arnold and Rea Vogt, and the tireless efforts of Keith Cann-Guthauser, master organizer and good soul of the Department of Iberian and Latin American History who oversaw all the administrative and infrastructural aspects of the project's coordination. Thus, the project brought together inputs from professors, doctoral and MA students, and other staff members from a wide range of nationalities and cultural backgrounds.

The case studies within the project sought to address the diasporic presence of Caribbean and Latin American communities in the US, in New York on the East Coast and Los Angeles on the West Coast, respectively, between the period of the mid-1960s up to the mid-to-late 1990s. Both Barber's research in New York and Mausfeld's research in LA were at the beginning of the project framed in terms of how cultural signifiers related to these communities, be they religious symbols, musical practices, musical genres and examples adopted by the hip-hop DJ and producer, production techniques and technology, lyricism, fashion, style, and aesthetics, and how these have intersected with the creation and development of hip-hop culture and practice. Building on this initial analytical framework, both studies evolved into independent research projects that were continuously shaped through fieldwork, archival work, and presentations and exchanges with colleagues at academic workshops and conferences.

Barber highlights reggae's reception in New York following the "second mass migration of the Jamaican working class" (Patterson 1994: 107) to the US beginning in 1965, highlighting the Jamaican contributions and influences to early and evolving New York hip-hop culture. In addition, he examines the wider West Indian and pan-Caribbean currents that shaped reggae's initial reception in New York, and eventual dialogue and fusion with hip-hop culture and practice. The height of these overlaps led to the development of an overlooked subgenre of New York reggae and hip-hop fusion, generally recognized to have emerged across the 1980s through to the mid-1990s, and sometimes referred to as "raggamuffin hip-hop" (Marshall and Foster 2013: n.pag.). In this volume, Barber presents a snapshot of his time spent in New York in Spring 2022, vividly describing musical events he participated in and the significance of the grassroots archives of two crucial actors he connected with. He highlights the significance of their materials to researchers, academic and otherwise, in representing the underground music sub- and multicultures of reggae and hip hop, and the intersections between the two, in New York.

At the project's other pole, Mausfeld traces the history of the "Chicano hip hop" subgenre in Los Angeles, highlighting the imprint Mexican American urban culture has had on West Coast hip hop at large. Like Barber, her chapter in the volume is based on ethnographic interviews she conducted during extensive research stays in LA, as well as a critical analysis of a wide range of issues of the pioneering US hip-hop magazine *The Source* that she came across during archival research between 2019 and 2023. The research team and editors of this volume are delighted to feature aspects of both projects in this edited collection. Kick-started by the conference "Hip Hop Transcultural: Constructing and Contesting Identity, Space, and Place in the Americas and Beyond"[1] in October 2021, the volume has been in the works for several years, and we are grateful and thankful to all our contributors and fellow conference participants who have put forward some excellent and thought-provoking examples of hip-hop culture in and between hip hop's local center(s) and global 'margins.'

As a vital part of the umbrella project "Hip Hop as a Transcultural Phenomenon," the conference was originally scheduled for the Fall of 2020 and, like so many other conferences, workshops, archive- and

---

1   Further information on the conference and the project can be retrieved on the website of the Institute of History of the University of Bern: https://www.hist.unibe.ch/forschung/forschungsprojekte/hip_hop_as_a_transcultural_phenomenon/index_ger.html.

fieldwork trips (not to mention wider everyday impacts) was deeply affected by the COVID-19 pandemic. These events also acutely affected the individual research projects and fieldwork stays undertaken by Barber and Mausfeld, which in both cases became somewhat suspended in time. After further postponing the conference several times to the Fall of 2021, as traveling was still difficult and academic life was largely taking place in online or hybrid spaces, it was decided to host the conference in an online format. An earlier call for papers had already yielded a highly promising range of proposals, enabling the organizers to bring together a stellar line-up of prominent hip-hop scholars from a variety of fields, universities, countries, and backgrounds. The conference united these perspectives together with those of contemporary hip-hop practitioners, archivists, enthusiasts, educators, and researchers, with many participants belonging to one or more of these camps. Despite the online format, the conference presented a platform for lively and enriching discussions about the ways hip hop has manifested and is being studied around the globe.

Conference keynotes were provided by P. Khalil Saucier, professor of Critical Black Studies at Bucknell University, and Martin Lüthe, assistant professor of American Studies at Freie University Berlin, approaching the transculturality of hip hop from different national and regional perspectives, reflecting a diverse range of viewpoints and opening up a transatlantic dialogue to set the tone for proceedings. Originally selected as a keynote speaker, pioneering hip-hop studies scholar Murray Forman was eventually unable to participate in this capacity, but attending the conference as a participant enriched the panel discussions with his expert inputs and humor. We were equally delighted to connect with J. Griffith Rollefson's hip-hop research project, "CIPHER: The International Council for Hip Hop Studies," based at the University College Cork, Ireland.[2] The team's roundtable featured a freestyle performance by Orphelia McCabe, which fittingly concluded the conference and reminded everyone just how much we had missed live music and perfor-

---

2   Further information can be found on the project website: https://globalcipher.org/.

mance during the pandemic. It also brought to the fore the importance of bringing together hip-hop academics and artists, a subject taken up further by several authors in this volume.

The present edited volume includes chapters by authors who presented their work at our conference in 2021, with some based on the authors' original presentations, and others bringing new issues to the table that nonetheless still fit within the locus of "Remixing the Hip-Hop Narrative." Although she was eventually unable to contribute a chapter to this volume, a special shout-out to Tasha Iglesias as it was her conference paper entitled "Disrupting the Narrative: Exploring the Latin Influence on the Foundation of Breakin'" that in part inspired the title for this collection. Furthermore, Iglesias' and Travis Harris' (2022) statement was also drawn upon when considering the argument in favor of the capitalization of hip hop in line with foundational Bronx MC and hip hop's "Teacha" KRS-One's original call. The ideas outlined in this text stimulated debate as to our own position in this regard, not solely as hip-hop aficionados and researchers, but also as editors that are somewhat bound to observe accepted grammatical, linguistic, and stylistic standards (however much we may also take issue with these conventions ourselves). While we undoubtedly support KRS-One's position as a central hip-hop authority and indeed cornerstone of the culture, and Harris' and Iglesias' position in following this, after much debate, for the purposes of editorial consistency we have decided to compromise by using the term in lower-case, unhyphenated. We also discussed the fact that while KRS One's claims certainly stand, where does that leave other music cultures such as reggae and salsa, as just two examples? They too, are nowadays established music genres, but like hip hop, their foundations are grounded in everyday, lived music *cultures*. Perhaps in this case we might move to suggest that for both consistency, and equal respect for all BIPOC and marginalized music cultures, repeatedly sidelined and underrepresented within broader popular music histories, that all such examples be capitalized in line with KRS One's, Harris' and Iglesias' calls.

Remixing the Hip-Hop Narrative
Introduction

James Barber, Christian Büschges, Dianne Violeta Mausfeld, and Britta Sweers

Hip hop's fiftieth birthday celebrations in 2023 reflected commemorations of a culture and movement truly global in its proportions, a status that the culture had begun to achieve as early as the 1980s. From its origins to present, hip hop is a culture that combines elements of uniformity with (trans)local and (trans)national symbols and expressions. We see this, for example, in hip hop's emergence in the 1970s, in the musical genres that early hip-hop DJs and pioneers Kool Herc and Grandmaster Flash delved into in search of the elusive "break," including the Latin and Caribbean music of boogaloo and salsa. This applies equally in the musical wellspring that hip-hop producers dived into when developing early sampling techniques and hip-hop productions going into the 1980s.

According to the element of emceeing, hip-hop MCs developed their lyrical arsenals drawing on and developing certain lyrical tropes, pioneering, and adapting stylistic features into their own rapping styles. Introducing new language and everyday slang from the streets into their repertoire, rappers, much like the reggae *deejays*, or toasters[1], before them on Kingston's reggae sound systems, narrated a diverse range of themes, stories, and narratives relating to their lived, or otherwise imagined, experience of everyday life in the streets of New York City—hip

---

1   In Jamaican and reggae sound system parlance, a toaster or a deejay is an MC, not to be confused with the DJ (disk jockey). Cf. also Barber's chapter in this volume for further details on Jamaican sound system culture and the deejay.

hop being central to this everyday experience. Emceeing is an art form importantly anchored in the performative aspect of its "liveness," a term Kevin Green discusses in this volume in relation to a historical view of the development of emceeing and perspectives surrounding authenticity and 'realness' in rappers' live performances, freestyling, and battle rap culture. The meanings and connotations attached to live emceeing and performance, have of course shifted over time, however, sparking further debate within the hip-hop community on subjects of authenticity and the significance of "keeping it real." In addition, Green touches on the hegemonic and counter-hegemonic ideas, discourses, and debates that contribute to the very understanding of 'realness.' From within hip hop's founding communities, to the global hip-hop nation, lively public debate and discourse continue to stake claims for what is (and what isn't) *real* hip hop. In this sense, these notions are constantly scrutinized and re-defined within the culture, community, and through hip-hop practice.

In its originary communities and the US in general, hip hop is widely perceived as a predominantly Black and African American subculture, defined in cultural terms by the Black American experience. Hip hop "is black American music" grounded in "black American aesthetics," Perry (2004: 10, 12) states, which reflects an African American "centrality" as Ogbar (2002: 12–13) and others have reiterated. On the flipside, discussions at the academic, journalistic, and community levels all reflect vibrant, and sometimes controversial debates surrounding the presence and founding contributions to hip-hop culture from individuals of a diverse range of nationalities, ethnicities, and racial backgrounds in The Bronx, New York City, and beyond. Renowned hip-hop scholar Raquel Rivera (2003), for example, has explored the significance of Puerto Rican contributions to early New York hip hop, highlighting iconic figures in breakdance such as Crazy Legs and the Rocksteady Crew, and pointing out that many of the artists in the first hip-hop film *Wild Style* (1982) were of Latinx and Puerto Rican descent. Furthermore, as Barber details in his chapter, when considering the Jamaican contributions to hip-hop culture, according to the theory of reggae's late or delayed reception in New York, as Jamaican sociologist Orlando Patterson (1994) and American musicologist Wayne Marshall (2006) note, it is important to reinstate the idea that reggae would take some time to "percolate" (2006: 215) into hip-hop practice. This is not to say that Jamaican, West Indian, and Caribbean influences have been fully explored and represented within hip hop's originary years either, however. When looking at the intersections between hip hop and reggae sound system and dancehall culture, or as Perry puts it their "crossroads moments" (2004: 15), a notion Barber addresses further, we should in fact be paying attention to the overlaps between these two gargantuan music cultures beyond framing this in terms of claims to "originalism" (ibid.: 9–37). Further attention is still required regarding reggae's reception in hip-hop culture and practice in the ongoing evolution of both music cultures across New York and US hip hop's Golden Age, from the early 1980s through to the mid-1990s.

In short, from its very beginnings up to the present, hip hop has consistently engaged with, repurposed, and integrated diverse actors, musical elements, cultural traditions, and practices. The entanglements of different cultures and diasporas on the evolution of hip hop as a music and a cultural movement in the US, and beyond, is a core part of what this volume seeks to illuminate. Highlighting some examples of the manifold cultural variations and exchanges that have created and constantly transformed hip hop, and helped to spread it within the US and beyond, the book asks how "cultural signifiers" bound by social, ethno-racial, gender, cultural, and spatial categories are being (re-)negotiated in hip hop. While concentrating on the Americas, the volume likewise includes articles that focus on other world regions, further reflecting hip hop's transnational and transregional entanglements.

Hip Hop in Academia

Hip-hop studies is a multi- and inter-disciplinary field that has grown considerably in recent years, encompassing research areas as diverse as musicology, ethnomusicology, history, sociology, and cultural studies. From the perspective of these different disciplines, hip-hop studies incorporate a wide range of research foci, addressing issues of globalization, technology, pop culture, linguistics, geography, identity politics, race and ethnicity, electoral politics, and a variety of other phenomena relating to hip hop and wider contemporary culture (Watkins 1998). The field of hip-hop studies is often cited as having been shaped by the publication of *That's the Joint! The Hip-Hop Studies Reader* in 2003, edited by Murray Forman and Mark Anthony Neal, which brings together almost twenty-five years of hip-hop scholarship, criticism, and journalism. Nonetheless, hip-hop studies emerged as a distinct academic discipline even earlier, when in the mid-1990s Tricia Rose's (1994) seminal text *Black Noise* sparked an overdue reminder that academia had still not given hip hop the attention it deserved. Another early example in the field, Houston A. Baker's (1993) *Black Studies, Rap, and the Academy*, urged African American studies departments to take hip hop seriously and include it in their curricula, a call that given hip-hop culture's recognition in a wide range of US and international teaching practice, pedagogy, and youth work is by now evidently well advanced. Édouard Laniel-Tremblay and Bronwen Low contribute a case study on the effects of hip-hop pedagogy at a youth recording studio in Quebec in this volume, demonstrating that this is a prevalent issue for academia, education, and youth work alike.

In the early 2010s, hip-hop studies evolution reached another peak with the creation of the *Journal of Hip Hop Studies* (JHHS), a publication committed to documenting "critically engaged, culturally relevant, and astute analyses of Hip Hop" (JHHS website n.d.). Topics addressed by the JHHS include the history of hip hop's emergence and evolution, identity politics of the 'hip-hop nation,' technologies of production, debates surrounding 'street authenticity,' race, class, and gender, aesthetics of revolutionary politics, hip hop as a cultural industry, and otherwise. The journal speaks to the relevance of hip hop in academia and has been a mirror of the most relevant topics in the field, in the US especially, for over a decade. Since 2020, intellect has published the *Global Hip Hop Studies* journal (GHHS), which focuses on "research on contemporary as well as historical issues and debates surrounding hip hop music and culture around the world" (GHHS website n.d.) and like the JHHS, is peer-reviewed and available as an open access publication. On the occasion of the fiftieth anniversary of hip hop, producer Greg Schick and hip-hop scholar Sina A. Nitzsche co-edited a "Special 'Hip Hop Atlas' Double Issue" with contributions by hip-hop scholars, educators, and artists from all five continents (Nitzsche and Schick 2023). The Board of Editors of the GHHS reads like a who's who of hip-hop studies, including scholars that we were lucky enough to have in attendance at our conference in late 2021, such as Murray Forman and J. Griffith Rollefson, and, in the case of Amy Coddington, contributors to this collection.

Thirty years after *Black Noise*, the list of significant hip-hop scholarship is far too extensive to be elaborated on in full here. Jeff Chang's (2005) *Can't Stop, Won't Stop: A History of the Hip-Hop Generation*, Nelson George's (2005) *Hip-Hop America*, and Jeffrey O.G. Ogbar's (2007) *Hip-Hop Revolution: The Culture and Politics of Rap*, among others, are crucial examples in the canon, and must-reads for any hip-hop scholar. William Eric Perkins's (1996) essay collection *Droppin' Science: Critical Essays on Rap Music and Hip Hop Culture* is another notable contribution, as it includes a variety of works from by now well-established contributors to the field such as Juan Flores, Robin D.G. Kelley, and Tricia Rose who had already addressed issues like Latinx agency in hip hop, the politics of gangster rap on the West Coast, and the "Institutional Policing of Rap Music," respectively. A great number of works by hip-hop scholars include forewords or commentaries by renowned artists, as for instance Michael Eric Dyson's (2007) collection of essays *Know What I mean?*, framed by contributions from Jay-Z and Nas. The former speaks to the importance of hip-hop scholars such as Dyson, calling him "the most brilliant interpreter of hip hop culture we have" (Jay-Z 2007: x). Jay-Z also speaks to the importance of hip-hop scholarship by people of color with similar socioeconomic backgrounds as the hip-hop practitioners themselves, such as Dyson, which brings us to the subject of our own positionality as White European researchers in hip-hop studies.

While the transnational fluidity of hip hop might explain the fascination of the culture outside of its original contexts, including those in comparably privileged positions, it has also shifted hip-hop-related discourses to an academic context. Due to the impact of cultural studies with its often highly abstract theoretical concepts, related academic debates have been shaped by a specific, complex language, hereby easily running into danger of excluding the voices of the founding individuals and communities who built hip-hop culture. The underlying question of who can conduct research on hip hop under these circumstances was openly addressed by Norwegian hip-hop researcher Kjell Andreas Oddekalv (2022: 115–122). Calling himself a reflective performer, he pointed to his uncomfortable position of undertaking a theoretical musical analysis of hip hop from a privileged position as a White European male researcher: "I am also a (or one could say 'yet another') White cis-male academic writing about Black music, another position which requires reflection, as does the profound *non-Americanness* of my specifically Norwegian and more generally European background, as regards both hip-hop culture and academic disciplinary traditions" (original emphasis). The transparency of Oddekalv's stance is also apparent when he describes his analytical approach as "cultural appropriation," further stating that "hip-hop does in no way need academia" (ibid.: 115) and reiterating the notion of his participation as "a guest in the culture" (ibid.: 116).

While hip hop might not need academia, it could be that academia actually needs hip hop to better understand, as the articles of this volume aim to illustrate, the general positionality of cultural (academic included) production and reflection, as well as the need for communication and translation across different cultural contexts and codes. Studying hip hop as an outsider may open up new perspectives and differentiated ways of approaching sociocultural issues that have been an underlying, yet not always visible theme (at least to outsiders) in US popular culture, and culture more generally. The study of hip hop strongly contributes to a deeper understanding of the mechanisms of globalization and transcultural processes, and the complexity of many theoretical concepts of culture that have been at the core of academic and popular debate in recent decades. The central issue is respect towards the founding protagonists and communities of hip hop, which is also evident in Oddekalv's (2022) statement that Black music does not require analysis by White means (e.g. music theory) to be respected and appreciated. The authors in the present collection represent a mixture of hip-hop scholars from varying backgrounds and positionalities. Those authors whose chapters detail personal contact and exchange with artists, architects, and archivists of hip hop, and Black and minority popular music history more generally, would all concur that the recognition and respect for the founding communities of these cultures is itself a pre-condition of even beginning to establish a research relationship with members of these musical communities in the first place. This is further a condition foremost of ethical scholarship, but second of meaningful representations of those cultures and communities, whether as insiders or outsiders. One thing that is certain is that hip hop has exerted such a deep and multifaceted impact on all levels of society, that its study matters to us all.

Situating Hip Hop Between Local Expressions and Global Connections

Buzzwords like "hybrid," "transcultural," and "multiethnic" are used excessively in hip-hop studies (and indeed elsewhere), often without contextualizing these concepts according to their wider development within the field of cultural studies. In many cases, 'transcultural' can simply mean "involving, encompassing, or extending across two or more cultures" (Merriam Webster n.d.) or "across all cultures of the world" (Collins Dictionary n.d.). But in fact, there is a rich scholarship on transculturality, as Terence Kumpf's contribution shows. His critique of transculturality concepts in hip-hop studies and academia at large sets the conceptual tone of this edited volume. Kumpf makes the case that Fernando Ortiz's original concept of transculturality, as observed and developed in Cuba, can be a fruitful approach for hip-hop scholars. The author raises his objection to the dearth of acknowledgement for the fundamental originator of transculturality, who he argues has been largely swept under the rug in wider analyses of culture in the academic literature. Additionally, Kumpf's chapter provides an overview of the literature engaging in discourses surrounding hybridity and transculturality in hip hop and beyond.

Jaspal Naveel Singh (2022) is one of relatively few hip-hop scholars who in part does base his work, *Transcultural Voices: Narrating Hip Hop*

Culture in Complex Delhi, on Ortiz, among others. Singh's understanding of transculturation is deeply informed by Pratt (1992) and questions of appropriation; he prioritizes "formulas of appropriation rather than appropriating forms" and thus moves beyond Pratt's binary of "usage" and "ownership" of culture in contact zones (Singh 2022: 13). Transculturation can thus be understood as "a multitude of voices and narratives that are circulated and negotiated to make meaning of the self and the other, in unfinished ways" (ibid.). In this sense, the present volume aims to contribute new voices and narratives to the canon of hip-hop studies that has neglected substantive acknowledgement of the stories, artists, and musical productions on the margins of the more dominant and popular narratives of hip-hop history.

Following the celebration of hip hop's fiftieth birthday in 2023, the story of the emergence of hip-hop culture and its beginnings in the early 1970s in the South Bronx, New York City, its' connections to the African American community, Black struggle, resistance, and the Black Power Movement, alongside the emergence and evolution of the four elements were widely commemorated. While these central aspects of hip-hop history and culture are by no means disputed, hip hop must likewise be considered from its very beginnings as being drawing upon and representing strong transnational and hybrid cultural currents. Hip-hop practice has also drawn heavily on musical and cultural symbols from outside of the United States, for example, from various Caribbean and Latin American communities and cultural practices (Rivera 2003; Chang 2005; McFarland 2008). Despite solid scholarship on the Latinx and particularly Puerto Rican involvement in the creation of hip hop, these claims are often disputed by critics who consider hip hop a solely African American practice, with Mausfeld referring to this recurring debate in her chapter.

In recent years, the African Caribbean heritage of numerous hip-hop pioneers such as DJ Kool Herc, Grandmaster Flash, and Afrika Bambaataa has received more attention. The importance of Jamaican popular music practice on the emergence of hip hop is at once recognized, yet rarely substantiated or explored beyond a surface level—which in many cases, for example, begins and ends with an acknowledgement of Kool

Herc's foundational contributions. Barber takes up aspects of these connections in his chapter, with such debates already periodically gaining further momentum (and indeed backlash) in recent years in comments from hip-hop luminaries such as MC Busta Rhymes and producer Pete Rock, among others, who have reiterated the centrality of these connections. As Barber shows in his chapter, part of the complexity of this subject is that many individuals with African Caribbean ancestry did not reveal—in many cases actively concealed—this cultural heritage in the early period of hip hop, and therefore were simply identified as Black or African American. Going into the 1980s, Jamaican and Caribbean culture would undergo "shifting significations" (Marshall 2006: 213–221) in New York, further permeating into hip hop and wider African American popular music culture and practice.

We aim to highlight examples of ethnic diversity in the founding stages of hip hop in the US, as well as the magnitude of cultural influences that have informed the culture ever since. When referring to ethnic or racial categories, we are conscious that these are both scientific terms as well as social and political categories of everyday use, and in no way can we take them for granted or suggest that they are "real" or fixed (Büschges 2019; 2015). Following sociologists Pierre Bourdieu (1985) and Rogers Brubaker (2004), we focus particularly on the social and political use of these terms, as representations of the social world and categories of identity politics. To fully understand the ethno-racial and sociopolitical dynamics within hip-hop culture, it is essential to employ a multidimensional perspective, including, for instance, musical influences and entanglements, Black American, Latinx, and African Caribbean diasporic cultural traditions, social discourses, etc.[2] The im-

---

[2] There are manifold possibilities to refer to ethno-racial identities in the Americas. Due to regional differences, personal preferences—of the authors or their interview partners—and differences in source materials, the authors in this volume use diverging terminologies for people of Latin American and Caribbean descent in the US, such as Latin, Latina/o, Hispanic, or Latinx. Likewise, elsewhere in the volume authors use variations for people of African diasporic descent in the Americas, including African Caribbean, Afro-Latino, Afro-Caribbean, Afro Cuban, and Afro-Brazilian.

portance of diasporic elements and the creative embeddedness of these different cultural strands in US hip hop is unquestionable, despite the difficulties in sometimes framing or representing these within existing hegemonic or dominant narratives. Since the term 'culture'—and its derivatives—is a notoriously difficult term to define, we want to clarify that we deploy the term according to a set of interacting systems, and symbolic references, that perpetuate cultural practices over time (Ember and Ember 1990). Similarly, historian Peter Burke's (2009: 5) definition of culture incorporates "attitudes, mentalities and values and their expression, embodiment or symbolization in artefacts, practices, and representations."

Hip hop combines elements of uniformity with local symbols and expressions regarding musical forms, lyrics, performances, and social content. A close reading of these symbols, or rather "cultural signifiers," can be a good place to start in disentangling these transcultural contributions in hip hop. Here, 'symbol' is understood in the broadest sense, following biological anthropologist Terrence W. Deacon's (2011) definition that refers to "spoken utterances, inscriptions, or other culturally generated meaningful artefacts and actions created specifically for representational purposes." The idea of the "cultural signifier" introduced earlier, is partly rooted in Charles Sanders Peirce's concept of semiotics that similarly highlights the element of "representation." Peirce (1955: 99) stresses that "the sign"[3] (which he terms *"representamen"*) "stands to somebody for something in some respect or capacity." Thus, "the sign" or "signifier" unfolds its full potential in dialogue with its "addressees"—in this case hip-hop audiences, fellow artists etc.—who are able to understand, interpret, and identify with it, and, by extension, with the culture it represents (ibid.). All these expressions provide a good opportunity to similarly reflect on transcultural and global perspectives on hip hop, and the question of how these fusions of diverse cultural traditions, practices,

---

[3] In contrast to a symbol, it does not entail a "'natural' affinity, which is to say, [an] intrinsic, perceptible, resemblance to what it signifies" (Weber 2016: 113).

and symbols emerge, and the new forms of expression yielded by these intersections.[4]

The theory of "globalization as hybridisation" put forward by sociologist Jan Nederveen Pieterse (2004) is crucial to understand this phenomenon. His theory argues that cultural globalization does not simply involve a dominant culture infiltrating another 'weaker' culture, rather, it is a series of processes that involve cultural hybridization. Similarly, sociologist Roland Robertson (1995) articulates the theory of "glocalization," stating that globalization of culture does not necessarily lead to the homogenization of and, implicitly, destruction of local cultures. The processes of global homogenization and heterogenization are "mutually implicative" (Robertson 1995: 27) because the global has a local, diversifying dimension, and there is a mutual relationship between the local and the global (ibid.: 34). Robertson's argument refers to cultural interaction, which takes place when a cultural practice is accepted and then assumed in another cultural context. As Eliseo Jacob elaborates in his chapter, Afro-Brazilian hip-hop artists felt a pan-African identification with the Black Power Movement and Black American hip-hop artists in the US, owing to the similarities in the historical and political struggles they faced in societies built on slavery and structural racism. In combining universally Afrocentric themes, with specific local and cultural issues, Afro-Brazilian hip-hop artists have forged a hip-hop scene that is nonetheless unmistakably Brazilian.

Globalization has further changed musical production and its relation to, and perception of, shifting understandings of space and time, as Connell and Gibson (2003) suggest. "Music nourishes imagined communities, traces links to distant and past places," and emphasizes that all human cultures have musical traditions, however differently these have been valued (ibid.: 271). The impact of transcultural and diasporic musical traditions on the development of hip hop in the US is especially

---

4   While our understanding of "cultural signifiers" is loosely based on linguists Charles Sanders Peirce (semiosis, 1955) and Ferdinand de Saussure (*signifier/significant*), we do not only apply it to language, but to a variety of cultural expressions that could be audio-visual, musical, material, culinary, geographical etc.

visible in the subsequent creation of distinct strands of hip hop, such as Latino rap and Chicano rap, addressed by scholars such as Juan Flores (1996), Raquel Rivera (2003), Pancho McFarland (2008; 2013), and Jason Nichols and Melissa Castillo-Garsow (2016). These currents, whether being created in the US or in Latin America, suggest a sense of belonging to the Mexican, Puerto Rican, Dominican etc. diasporas, much like Anderson's "imagined communities" (2006 [1983])—a phenomenon that can be found in hip-hop communities from Germany to Brazil, even if they do not share the same countries of origin, as Martin Lüthe and Eliseo Jacob demonstrate in this volume. The concept of "diaspora" according to Brubaker (2005: 3), can be applied "to an ever-broadening set of cases: essentially to any and every nameable population category that is to some extent dispersed in space." Along similar lines, Robert Fox (1999: 369) points out that etymologically diaspora suggests "a scattering which is also a sowing," the dispersion of a people, their implantation in a new area, and a "harvesting" of a new culture. This "dispersion" was accelerated through migration flows and globalization, both of which have contributed to the creation of hip hop and its subsequent global dissemination.

Social-cultural anthropologist Arjun Appadurai (1993: 274) reinforces Robertson's idea of "glocalization," outlined above, arguing that "at least as rapidly as forces from various metropolises are brought into new societies they tend to become indigenized in one or another way." He contends that when a culture becomes transnational, the process of localization is likely to be involved. Thus, the process of developing a transnational culture is more complex than the idea of a uniform global culture implies. Appadurai further argues that "the new global cultural economy has to be seen as a complex, overlapping, disjunctive order, which cannot any longer be understood in terms of existing center-periphery models (even those which might account for multiple centers and peripheries)" (ibid.: 275). The absence of a center of cultural globalization, along with the inner dynamics of any culture or cultural practice, suggests the potential of flows, as cultural forms seem to circulate in multiple ways. The relationship between transnational and local cultures is particularly interesting when examining hip hop as a transcultural phenomenon. Because as Peter Burke (2009: 41) points out, the crux of Fernando Ortiz' transculturation concept is the reciprocity of cultural influences, that do not abide to hierarchies; a "two-way" process, rather than "the notion of one-way 'acculturation.'" Thus, globalization in the cultural realm operates in multiple directions and is likely to involve cultural interaction, appropriation, and hybridization.

Thus, as hip hop has spread nationally and globally, its manifestations in different regions and cultural contexts have renegotiated the boundaries between different locations of musical and cultural production. The assumption of New York as the "only" center of hip-hop production—despite its undisputed status as "the Mecca," not only within the US but worldwide—resulted in the by now infamous East Coast/West Coast beef during the 1990s when West Coast gangster rap became commercially successful and demanded to be taken seriously. In the late 1990s, the southern metropoles of Houston, Atlanta, New Orleans, Memphis, and Miami—the so-called "Dirty South"—developed its own sound that uniquely mirrored their environment and became just as commercially successful as New York hip hop. Several authors question and 'remix' some of these established assumptions and narratives in this volume. As Kevin C. Holt shows in his chapter, Atlanta also gave birth to the dance style "YEEK"—little known beyond the borders of the ATL, but with an origin story that fits the bill of hip-hop culture as "making something from nothing"; an expression of creativity in the context of urban abandonment and racial profiling. Miami was the cradle of the "Crossover" format, as Amy Coddington argues in her chapter, that spread to radio stations across the US in the late 1980s. She highlights the importance of radio for the commercialization of hip hop, but also points out the pitfalls of alleged "colorblindness" and ethnic marketing of hip hop on the airwaves in the "Magic City."

Outside of the US, from region to region, different hip-hop hubs have emerged, establishing themselves as more than just "peripheries" on hip-hop's global map. As hip hop conquered the world during its "Golden Age," it was catapulted to new heights of commercial and mainstream success, with local hip-hop scenes emerging on every continent. While these often emulated US hip hop at first, they soon developed their own unique (trans-) national, regional and (multi-) cultural manifestations of the form, incorporating local and international language(s), adding or repurposing new slang, musical influences, and dance practices. All of this, is of course brought about by contact between individuals from different cultural backgrounds and contexts in global urban centers especially, part of a process in which culture and music evolve and adapt (Baumann 2004). In Alan Light's *VIBE History of Hip-Hop*, Greg Tate (1999: 393) refers to hip hop as "trans-historical... obliterating a clear connection between time periods and musical styles. Hip hop is transstylistic and even trans-musical as well, since any sound can be rendered hip hop-able." This kind of cultural diffusion is of course not new and has affected the development and evolution of popular music cultures from their beginnings until now. In the late capitalist age of information overload experienced in the last decades especially, related processes and, thus, also broader categories like 'fusion music' or 'hybrid music' have become even more dominant. Rap music is probably the most significant global example of this development. In addition, the transcultural flows of hip hop allow it to move within and beyond national borders. As the Australian linguist Alastair Pennycook (2007: 5) states in this regard, "[h]ip-hop is a culture without a nation. Hip-hop culture is international. Each country has its own spin on hip-hop."

Global Hip-Hop Cultures: Adaptation and Cultural Appropriation

The global hip-hop nation as it stands today, though still hopefully centrally related—or at least aware of and paying its respects to—the culture's physical and spiritual home and the New York neighborhoods that it first emerged from, has spread, first, across the US to establish other substantial national, and later international, hubs. In these centers, the culture has flowed in from the source, been taken on, repurposed, fused, and splintered off into new forms and expressions of rap music and hip-hop culture. Having been strongly influenced by pre-digital mass media, movies, MTV, as well as stationed (often African American) GIs, German hip hop was also a central expressive means of the migrant youth generation, including groups such as Advanced Chemistry, who despite this would eventually move away from rapping in English, to choosing to rap in German, thus representing their cultural and linguistic identity as individuals born and raised in Germany (Elflein 1998; Yakpo 2004). Martin Lüthe's paper in this volume, for example, looks at the history of German hip-hop culture's emergence and the transatlantic relationship with its role model, that is also reflected in collaborations that address police discrimination, among other commonalities between artists from both sides of the Atlantic. Less political variants, as seen in the German context with groups like Die Fantastischen Vier or Fettes Brot, coexisted with groups who considered rap political activism such as Advanced Chemistry and Main Concept (Uschmann and Kleiner 2022).

Elsewhere, Jacob and Mausfeld in their respective chapters illustrate how Brazilian hip hop from the Metropoles of Brazil and Chicano rap, originally emerging in Los Angeles, express similar social critiques as African American artists from New York to Los Angeles. At the same time, both examples reflect their own narratives specific to notions of ethnic, racial, and linguistic identity, racism, and discrimination experienced within their communities. While many other US and global expressions of hip-hop culture have followed on in this spirit and tradition of narrating subjects of injustice, racism, and critique of social conditions and marginalization, highlighting the revolutionary, political potency of hip hop's foundations as in Chuck D and Public Enemy's call to "Fight the Power," a multitude of other interpretations use hip hop as a platform to express a myriad of causes, experiences and reflections for artists who step into the cipher. The lyrics and language of an MC, the sample choices of the hip-hop producer, the fashion, style and adopted symbols of MCs, b-boys and b-girls, and graffiti artists, all represent different angles on what is being expressed, by who, and to who, in hip-hop culture.

While remembering hip hop's center, we should also remember the various sources of inspiration the culture has taken from outside the US, many of which were instrumental in articulating aspects of the various political, social, and cultural issues that the culture reflects (this cultural 'bricolage' being fundamental to the aesthetic of rap music and hip-hop culture). Sources of inspiration from which hip-hop culture and practice have drawn upon, and which other music cultures themselves adapt and repurpose, is not clearly demarcated. Throughout the various styles and forms that hip hop's inherent prolific productivity yields, an abundance of authenticity claims may arise, which can be complex and even problematic (Gilroy 1991; Hodgman 2013; Ochmann 2014). However complex the notion of the 'authentic' might be, being "authentic" (Claviez, Imesch, and Sweers 2020) and "keeping it real" is vital to hip-hop culture (cf. Barker and Taylor 2007). As Ogbar (2002: 1) notes, "[a]uthenticity, however defined or imagined, has always been central to the culture." Hip-hop authenticity and claims to realness may highlight aspects of style (fashion, dress, and adoption of particular symbols), language, attitude, performance, and dance from across the global hip-hop nation, to a greater or lesser extent associated or dissociated from developments in US hip hop, combining elements of tradition and/or innovation.

In light of the utmost importance of these, and wider related debates about authenticity and cultural appropriation, it is necessary to first offer some points of reflection from the editors of this volume, pertaining to our own positionality and standpoint on the subject. Following in the footsteps of Kjell Andreas Oddekalv's reflections on being a White Norwegian rap scholar introduced earlier, it is important to note that above all, we as researchers, while coming to the research from a perspective of hip-hop enthusiasts, are very much "guests" in hip-hop culture. Oddekalv's (2022: 116) stance is informed by comments he cites from Akil the MC, member of the "legendary rap crew" Jurassic 5, who states that, even being from LA, "I am a guest in the culture of Hip Hop because I am not from where Hip Hop originated (The Bronx, New York)." Oddekalv adopts this same position as a guest in the culture, "with the extra added difference that unlike Akil The MC, I am not African American." Akil the MC's sentiment is echoed elsewhere when, for example eminent hip-hop scholar Imani Perry (2004) highlights "Teacha" KRS One's suggestion that you can't understand the origins of hip hop, and where it's coming from, if you've never stepped foot in The Bronx. The importance of these considerations neither escape the editors of this volume, as we too recognize that we are guests in the house of hip hop.

Some of these authenticity-related discourses would, for example, in part frame the recurring debate in hip hop centered on White US-American rapper Marshall Bruce Mathers III aka Eminem, although here, the issue of street credibility as a factor of authentication, was clearly decisive. As Bonsu Thompson (2020) concisely summarized in the online magazine *Black Level*:

> In his early days, Eminem was to hip-hop what Black folks have been to America. He's from the bottom—reared on the side of 8 Mile Road where poverty was life—and was raised by a culture that doggedly oppressed his talent, dreams, and purpose. Like brave Black men pre-Civil War, his calling to battle was met with mobbish resistance. When allowed to join predominantly Black ciphers, he was marginalized. Until he began rhyming, that is. "It was always a White Men Can't Jump situation every open mic," says Bizarre, Em's childhood friend and fellow member of rap group D12. "Then, after the first 10 bars, they'd start changing their minds."

Thompson's authentication related back to a longstanding 'beef', lyrically and personally, between Eminem and MC Lord Jamar (Lorenzo Dechalus), which re-emphasized that "White people are guests in the house of hip-hop that black people built" (Jones 2020) when Eminem finally acknowledged this statement in 2020. Yet, the fragility of this situation became apparent when the debate stirred up again following the release of the *Elvis* biopic movie (2022). In "The King and I" (feat. CeeLo Green), the fourth single from the film's soundtrack, Eminem compared himself to Elvis by pointing to similar experiences of being in-between Black and White cultures and of having been successful with Black genres that were, as Eminem openly emphasized in the lyrics, "stolen." However, the rap line of having likewise been called "king" subsequently provoked major criticism, although Eminem repeatedly rejected having made the claim himself. Rather, as was also stated in the lyrics, it had come from the outside (Beame 2022). These debates are significant precisely because they point to the issue of the past and ongoing racism, discrimination, and marginalization faced by BIPOC groups highlighted throughout, discriminated and exploited by White hegemonic structures. These structures have dominated many directions of the global flows of the music industry, not to mention central social and political structures.

Similarly, the practice of cultural appropriation also directly relates to hegemonic power imbalances (Rogers 2006). Cultural appropriation is, as outlined in the *Encyclopedia Britannica*, generally defined as an "adoption of certain language, behavior, clothing, or tradition belonging to a minority culture or social group by a dominant culture or group in a way that is exploitative, disrespectful, or stereotypical" (Kendall 2022). In addition, as Kitwana (2006) illustrates, the line between appreciation and cultural appropriation is very thin. For instance, adopting hip-hop style and dress can either be a form of honoring the culture, or of appropriation, e.g. when specific symbols are just used for entertainment or commodification. It could also be summarized as the opposites of respect versus fetishism, or stereotypes versus a deeper understanding. Beyond the question of legitimization, a further central issue has thus been the respect factor—of understanding the deeper sociopolitical factors behind this music culture and genre to which this volume likewise wants to contribute further insights, taking into account that, according to the codes of hip-hop culture, and the streets and neighborhoods from which it emerged, it is a question of 'keeping it real.'

While the Eminem case clearly illustrates the importance of understanding and acknowledging the post-colonial and post-slavery context of African American history regarding the emergence and development of hip hop in the United States, the study of hip hop on a global scale is determined by a diverse range of other historical and sociopolitical realities. One important contribution to answering this dilemma and envisioning new and nuanced ways of approaching hip hop from this perspective is developed by author, singer-songwriter, and scholar Raquel Z. Rivera (2003: 15) who has pointed out that "[h]ip hop is a fluid cultural space, a zone whose boundaries are an internal and external matter of debate. A profoundly diverse, translocal, multiethnic and multiracial cultural phenomenon."[5] Rivera thus emphasizes the idea of a "hip hop zone" rather than a "community" or "nation" (ibid.), a notion that could be tied in to Mary Louise Pratt's concept of a "contact zone" (Pratt 1991) where cultures meet and clash. Consequently, if cultural adaptation is understood as a natural and positive process of creativity, the revelation of hegemonic, abusive, or ridiculing acts as forms of negative cultural appropriation, as well as actively including and highlighting the role of previously disadvantaged groups, constitute central steps in re-balancing and decolonizing historical representations of these processes and the cultural appropriation debate at large.

The Scope of this Book

An ongoing question for the editors of this volume, then, is how do we conceptually frame the dynamics of the local, national, and global spread and interactions of hip hop? As discussed above, the process of cultural globalization does not necessarily imply cultural homogenization. Rather, the result has been a process of cultural 'glocalization' and cultural hybridization, in the sense of a blending of different cultural elements (Yazdiha 2010), where cultures continuously interact with and interpret each other to produce hybrid cultural forms. As Arjun Appadurai (1993) argues, neither centrality nor peripherality of culture exist in the context of cultural globalization. We should perhaps instead think of the idea of *multiple* centers and peripheries. The discussion of transnational and translocal cultural flows in hip hop presented up to now, also reflects the notion that these flows, fusions, and mergings, however fleeting or sporadic, are not only bi-directional or reciprocal, but can often branch off in multiple directions. One important consideration in this regard, is the question of how global adaptations outside

---

5   See also Dennis, Christopher. 2014. "Locating Hip Hop's Place within Latin American Cultural Studies." *alter/nativas Latin American Cultural Studies Journal* 2 (Spring): 1–20. https://alternativas.osu.edu/en/issues/spring-2014/essays1/dennis.html.

of hip hop's physical, originary communities, rooted in Black, African American culture and historical experience, are to be viewed according to the discourses of cultural appropriation, and recent historical events such as the overdue emergence of the Black Lives Matter movement that started in 2013 and came to global visibility after the death of George Floyd in 2020. Furthermore, where do the debates, and discourses emerging from these events sit in relation to wider identity and cultural hybridity discourses presented (and indeed critiqued) in this volume and elsewhere?

The contributions of this book address the fluid and hybrid nature of hip hop's musical and cultural production in different spatial, social, and political contexts, while also reflecting critically on academic approaches to hip-hop culture, and the challenges and blind spots these different approaches face, including reflections on the central failings of White, Western scholarship depicted by Oddekalv (2022), and their claims to an overarching and universal applicability. Such discourse has obscured many important concepts already influential in their shaping of modern postcolonial discourses, including the concept of transculturality, which was first developed outside of a Western context. In the chapter "Epistemological Quandary: Why Hip-Hop Scholars Must Ground their Transcultural Arguments in the Work of Fernando Ortiz," *Terence Kumpf* introduces this collection by casting a deeper look at the writings of Cuban politician, anthropologist, and ethnomusicologist Fernando Ortiz who strongly shaped discourses on transculturalism in the 1940s. Kumpf, however, argues that Ortiz has been widely negated by cultural theorists, illustrating how we might revive his ideas and apply them to studies of hip hop moving forward.

The following three chapters not only illustrate how transculturalism and hybridity manifested themselves within different media formats, but also within different cultural contexts in the US. *Amy Coddington* in particular addresses the multicultural adaptation of hip hop with her chapter "Hip Hop Becomes Mainstream: or, How to Commodify Racial Hybridity." Focusing on the ethnic orientation of "Cross Over" radio formats in Miami during the 1980s and 1990s, Coddington's analysis of the local radio industry exemplifies the complexity of "commodifying racial hybridity" in an ethnically divided city that came together on the airwaves in a shared appreciation for rap music. *Dianne Violeta Mausfeld* also presents a historical analysis of mass media in her discussion of the representation of Chicano and Latino hip-hop artists in East Coast-based hip-hop publications in her piece "'Double the Struggle': Chicano/Latino Hip Hop in *The Source* Magazine." In the context of the East Coast-West Coast 'beef,' Mausfeld examines the often assumed alliance between Latino artists in the US and finds that they were rarely featured in major hip-hop publications during the 1990s. *Kevin P. Green* asks "Where the Rhymes at?,'" examining "How Contemporary Artists are Transforming Notions of Liveness in Hip Hop" in his exploration of how and why the use of performance tracks in hip hop has become acceptable, though nonetheless subject of spirited debate between the old and new generations of the US hip-hop community. Unpacking the ways in which artists construct themselves as consumable brands, and how this is mediated by fans through television, social media, and interaction on streaming platforms, Green's chapter illustrates how the practice of using performance tracks has been a natural conclusion to hip hop's transformation from countercultural entity to mainstream fixture over the last two decades.

The performative aspect of hip-hop culture, including the themes of dance, the body, and physicality, is further explored by *Kevin C. Holt* who takes us on a historical journey to Atlanta showing how racial and spatial segregation, discrimination against Black youth, and skating rinks contributed to the evolution of the local dance form YEEKing that emerged during the 1980s. In his chapter "YEEK! Atlanta Hip-Hop Dance and the Subversion of Expressing 'Your Energetic Explosive Klimax,'" Holt shows how yeeking became an embodied language of resistance that allowed African Americans to fight for their presence in public spaces. *Martina Bratić*'s "Identity Transgressions as Transgressions of the Art Form: The Case of Frank Ocean" focuses on the work of one artist singlehandedly challenging boundaries of expression from within hip-hop culture. Exploring the unique artistic world of African American artist Frank Ocean, Bratić highlights Ocean's navigation and critique of heteronormative values within hip hop and popular music culture at large, illustrating how the artist has not only opened up new spaces for gender debates and discourse in hip hop, but in doing so has developed new forms of artistic expression and production in the process.

The last four chapters add case studies of global and transnational entanglements, analyzing how central sociopolitical and sociocultural aspects have become reference points for hip-hop cultures outside the US. However, and this is also central to the idea of transculturalism and cultural hybridity, these contributions illustrate how these elements were adapted into the respective cultures—and vice versa. In "Afro-Cosmopolitanisms: Discourses on Race and Urban Identities in Brazilian Hip Hop," *Eliseo Jacob* addresses the global role of hip hop in expressions of racial inequality. Given that Brazil features the largest population of African descent outside of the African continent, hip hop plays a central role in the reaffirmation of the ethnic identity of marginalized groups within an urban context. *Martin Lüthe* contributes another global perspective in his analysis of the transculturality of the German "Straßenrap" (street rap) scene in Berlin from the 1990s onward in "'Ich lebe für Hip Hop': German Hip-Hop Music, Cultural Hybridities, and the 'Berlin Moment.'" His detailed overview of German hip-hop history shows that the influence of US hip-hop on local artists changed over time, and that the stylistic emancipation from "the motherland" gains importance with every new generation of hip-hoppers. The experience of racialized youth discrimination and marginalization is also a central feature in *Bronwen Low and Édouard Laniel-Tremblay*'s case study "Producing Hip-Hop Culture and Identity: How a Youth Recording Studio Supports Well-Being." The authors' study of a community-based recording studio in Montreal, Canada, shows how hip hop can become a means of creating alternative spaces of belonging, which also intersects with the central importance of an acquisition of related performance and production skills. In the final article, *James Barber* brings us back to the source of hip-hop culture in his piece "Chronicling New York Reggae and Hip Hop's Crossroads, and Community Media as Historical Archives from the Ground Up." Barber presents a selected outline of the significance of reggae and Jamaican sound system and dancehall culture in New York after 1965, drawing on aspects of his ethnographic research in New York and the work of two central archivists of reggae and hip-hop culture established in the 1980s and 1990s respectively, to illuminate the underrepresented intersections, dialogue, and historical reciprocity between these two gargantuan global music cultures in hip hop's source and beyond.

Discography/ Videography

Ahearn, Charlie, dir. *Wild Style*. 1983; Merenberg: ZYX Music, 2009, DVD.
Public Enemy. *Fight the Power*. Motown Records, 1989, vinyl.

References

Anderson, Benedict. 2006 [1983]. *Imagined Communities: Reflections on the Origin and Spread of Nationalism*. London: Verso.
Appadurai, Arjun. 1993. "Disjuncture and Difference in the Global Cultural Economy." In *The Phantom Public Sphere*, edited by Bruce Robbins, 269–295. Minneapolis: University of Minnesota Press.
Baker, Houston A. 1993. *Black Studies, Rap, and the Academy*. Chicago: The University of Chicago Press.
Barker, Hugh and Taylor, Yuval. 2007. *Faking It: The Quest for Authenticity in Popular Music*. New York: W.W. Norton.
Baumann, Max Peter. 2004. "The Charango as Transcultural Icon of Andean Music." *Trans. Revista Transcultural de Música* 8. https://www.sibetrans.com/trans/article/192/the-charango-as-transcultural-icon-of-andean-music.
Beame, Abe. 2022. "Elvis' Complicated Relationship To Hip-Hop." *Okayplayer*, June 27, 2022. https://www.okayplayer.com/originals/elvis-hip-hop-public-enemy-eminem-masta-ace.html.
Bhabha, Homi. 2004. *The Location of Culture*. London: Routledge.
Bourdieu, Pierre. 1985. "The Social Space and the Genesis of Groups." *Theory and Society* 14 (6): 723–744.

Brubaker, Roger. 2004. *Ethnicity without Groups*. Cambridge/London: Harvard University Press.

Brubaker, Roger. 2005. "The 'Diaspora' Diaspora." *Ethnic and Racial Studies* 28 (1): 1–19.

Burke, Peter. 2009. *Cultural Hybridity*. Cambridge: Polity Press.

Büschges, Christian. 2019. "Ethnicity." In *The Routledge Handbook to the History and Society of the Americas*, edited by Olaf Kaltmeier et al., 259–269. London: Routledge.

Büschges, Christian. 2015. "Politicizing ethnicity – ethnicizing politics. Comparisons and entanglements." In *Ethnicity as a Political Resource: Conceptualizations across Disciplines, Regions, and Periods*, edited by University of Cologne Forum "Ethnicity as a Political Resource," 107–116. Bielefeld: transcript.

Castillo-Garsow, Melissa, and Jason Nichols, eds. 2016. *La Verdad: An International Dialogue on Hip Hop Latinidades*. Columbus: Ohio State University Press.

Chang, Jeff. 2005. *Can't Stop Won't Stop: A History of the Hip-Hop Generation*. New York: Picador.

Claviez, Thomas, Kornelia Imesch, and Britta Sweers. 2020. "Introduction." In *Critique of Authenticity*, edited by Thomas Claviez, Kornelia Imesch, and Britta Sweers, viii–xix. Wilmington, DE: Vernon Press.

Collins Dictionary. n.d. "transcultural." Accessed January 11, 2024. https://www.collinsdictionary.com/de/worterbuch/englisch/transcultural.

Connell J.; Gibson, C. 2003. *Soundtracks: Popular Music, Identity and Place*. London: Routledge.

D'Anjou, Cyan. "Out of Line: On Hip Hop and Cultural Appropriation." *Medium*, June 22, 2020. https://medium.com/@cyandanjou/out-of-line-on-hip-hop-and-cultural-appropriation-1c060e6801e9.

Deacon, Terrence W. 2011. "The Symbol Concept." In *Oxford Handbook of Language Evolution*, edited by Maggie Tallerman and Kathleen R. Gibson, 393–405. Oxford: Oxford University Press.

Dyson, Michael Eric. 2007. *Know what I mean? Reflections on Hip-Hop*. New York: Basic Civitas.

Elflein, Dietmar. 1998."From Krauts with Attitudes to Turks with Attitudes: Some Aspects of Hip-Hop History in Germany." *Popular Music* 17 (3): 255–65. http://www.jstor.org/stable/852956.

Ember, Carol R., and Melvin Ember. 1990. *Cultural Anthropology*. New Jersey: Prentice Hall.

Flores, Juan. 1996."Puerto Rocks: New York Ricans Stake Their Claim." In *Droppin' Science: Critical Essays on Rap Music and Hip Hop Culture*, edited by William Eric Perkins, 85–105. Philadelphia: Temple University Press.

Forman, Murray, and Marc Anthony Neal, eds. 2004. *That's the Joint! The Hip-Hop Studies Reader*. New York: Routledge.

Fox, Robert. 1999. "Diasporacentrism and Black Aural Texts." In *The African Diaspora: African Origins and New World Identities*, edited by Isidore Okpewho, Carole Boyce Davies, and Ali A. Mazrui, 367–378. Bloomington: Indiana University Press.

García-Canclini, Néstor. 1989. *Culturas híbridas: Estrategias para entrar y salir de la modernidad*. Mexico: Grijalbo.

George, Nelson. 2005. *Hip Hop America*. London: Penguin Books.

Gilroy, Paul. 1991. "Sounds Authentic: Black Music, Ethnicity, and the Challenge of a 'Changing' Same." *Black Music Research Journal* 11 (2): 111–136.

Global Hip Hop Studies (Journal). "Aims & Scope." Accessed January 12, 2024. https://www.intellectbooks.com/global-hip-hop-studies.

Hodgman, Matthew. 2013. "Class, Race, Credibility, and Authenticity within the Hip-Hop Music Genre." *Journal of Sociological Research* 4 (2): 402–413. http://dx.doi.org/10.5296/jsr.v4i2.4503.

Iglesias, Tasha, and Travis Harris. 2022."It's 'Hip Hop,' Not 'hip-hop.'" *Journal of Hip Hop Studies* 9 (1): 8. https://doi.org/10.34718/c8gm-6j27.

Jay-Z. 2007. "Intro." In *Know what I mean? Reflections on Hip-Hop* by Michael Eric Dyson, ix–xii. New York: Basic Civitas.

Jones, Damian. 2020. "Lord Jamar hits back at Eminem over his response to claims white rappers are "guests" in hip-hop." *New Musical Express online*, February 24, 2020. https://www.nme.com/news/mus

ic/lord-jamar-hits-back-at-eminem-over-his-response-to-claims-white-rappers-are-guests-in-hip-hop-2613962.

Journal of Hip Hop Studies. n.d. "About." Accessed January 7, 2024. https://scholarscompass.vcu.edu/jhhs/about.html.

Kendall, Emily. "Cultural Appropriation." *Encyclopedia Britannica*. Published October 14, 2022. https://www.britannica.com/topic/cultural-appropriation.

Kitwana, Bakari. 2006. *Why White Kids Love Hip-hop: Wangstas, Wiggers, Wannabes, and the New Reality of Race in America*. London: Civitas Books.

Kjell Andreas Oddekalv. 2022. "On Being a White Norwegian Analysing Rap." *Danish Musicology Online Special Issue* 2022: 115–122.

Marshall, Wayne. 2006. "Routes, Rap, Reggae: Hearing the Histories of Hip-Hop and Reggae Together." PhD diss., University of Wisconsin-Madison.

Marshall, Wayne, and Pacey Foster. 2013. "Hearing Raggamuffin Hip-hop: Musical Records as Historical Record." *Ethnomusicology Review*, October 1, 2013. https://ethnomusicologyreview.ucla.edu/content/hearing-raggamuffin-hip-hop-musical-records-historical-record-wayne-marshall-and-pacey.

McFarland, Pancho. 2008. *Chicano Rap: Gender and Violence in the Postindustrial Barrio*. Austin: University of Texas Press.

McFarland, Pancho. 2013. *The Chican@ Hip Hop Nation: Politics of a New Millennial Mestizaje*. East Lansing: Michigan State University Press.

Merriam Webster. n.d. "transcultural." Accessed January 11, 2024. https://www.merriam-webster.com/dictionary/transcultural.

Miller, Monica, Daniel White Hodge, Jeffrey Coleman, and Cassandra Chaney. 2014. "The Hip in Hip Hop: Toward a Discipline of Hip Hop Studies." *Journal of Hip Hop Studies* 1 (1): 6–12. https://doi.org/10.34718/71Z9-7Z58.

Nederveen Pieterse, Jan. 2004. *Globalization and Culture: Global Mélange*. Lanham, MD: Rowman & Littlefield Publishers.

Nitzsche, Sina A., and Greg Schick. 2023. "Mapping the Global Hip Hop Nation at 50: Introducing the 'Hip Hop Atlas' Special Issue." *Global Hip Hop Studies* 3 (1–2): 3–9. https://doi.org/10.1386/ghhs_00064_2.

Ochmann, Matthäus. 2014. "The Notion of Authenticity in International Hip-Hop Culture." In *Hip-Hop in Europe: Cultural Identities and Transnational Flows*, edited by Sina Nietzsche and Walter Grünzweig, 423–446. Berlin: Lit.

Ogbar, Jeffrey O.G. 2007. *Hip-Hop Revolution: The Culture and Politics of Rap*. Lawrence, KS: University Press of Kansas.

Patterson, Orlando. 1994. "Ecumenical America: Global Culture and the American Cosmos." *World Policy Journal* 11 (2) (Summer 1994): 103–117. https://www.jstor.org/stable/40468616.

Peirce, Charles Sanders. 1955. *Philosophical Writings*, edited by Justus Buchler. New York: Dover.

Pennycook, Alastair. 2007. *Global Englishes and Transcultural Flows*. London: Routledge.

Perkins, William Eric, ed. 1996. *Droppin' Science: Critical Essays on Rap Music and Hip Hop Culture*. Philadelphia: Temple University Press.

Perry, Imani. 2004. *Prophets of the Hood: Politics and Poetics in Hip Hop*. Durham, NC: Duke University Press.

Pratt, Mary Louise. 1991. "Arts of the Contact Zone." *Profession*: 33–40. http://www.jstor.org/stable/25595469.

Pratt, Mary Louise. 1992. *Imperial Eyes: Travel Writing and Transculturation*. London: Routledge.

Rabaka, Reiland. 2013. *The Hip Hop Movement: From R&B and the Civil Rights Movement to Rap and the Hip Hop Generation*. Plymouth: Lexington Books.

Raussert, Wilfried, and John Miller Jones, eds. 2008. *Traveling Sounds: Music, Migration, and Identity in the U.S. and Beyond*. Berlin: Lit.

Rivera, Raquel Z. 2003. *New York Ricans from the Hip Hop Zone*. New York: Palgrave Macmillan. https://doi.org/10.1057/9781403981677.

Robertson, Roland. 1995. "Glocalization: Time-Space and Homogeneity-Heterogeneity." In *Global Modernities*, edited by Mike Featherstone, Scott Lash, and Roland Robertson, 25–44. London: Sage Publications. https://doi.org/10.4135/9781446250563.

Rogers, Richard A. 2006. "From Cultural Exchange to Transculturation: A Review and Reconceptualization of Cultural Appropriation." *Com-*

munication Theory 16 (4): 474–503. https://doi.org/10.1111/j.1468-2885.2006.00277.x.

Rose, Tricia. 1994. *Black Noise: Rap Music and Black Culture in Contemporary America*. Middletown, CT: Wesleyan University Press.

Singh, Jaspal Naveel. 2022. *Transcultural Voices: Narrating Hip Hop Culture in Complex Delhi*. Bristol/ Blue Ridge Summit, PA: Multilingual Matters. https://doi.org/10.21832/9781788928144.

Tate, Greg. 1999. "15 Arguments in Favor of the Future of Hip Hop." In *The VIBE History of Hip Hop*, edited by Alan Light, 385–394. New York: Three Rivers.

Thies, Sebastian, and Josef Raab. 2009. "E Pluribus Unum? Interdisciplinary Perspectives on National and Transnational Identities." In *E Pluribus Unum? National and Transnational Identities in the Americas*, edited by Sebastian Thies and Josef Raab, 1–23. Münster: Lit; Tempe: Bilingual Press.

Thompson, Bonsu. 2020. "How Eminem Conquered Black Music (and White Privilege) With 'The Marshall Mathers LP.'" *Level*, May 22, 2020. https://www.levelman.com/the-6-worst-cities-to-spend-memorial-day-weekend-ranked-18f52dfc3ede/.

Uschmann, Oliver, and Marcus S. Kleiner. 2022. "Rückenprobleme: Die Narrative der Straße und ihre Krise im deutschsprachigen Gangsta-Rap." In *HipHop im 21. Jahrhundert: Medialität, Tradierung, Gesellschaftskritik und Bildungsaspekte einer (Jugend-)Kultur*, edited by Thomas Wilke and Michael Rappe, 25–53. Wiesbaden: Springer.

Watkins, S. Craig. 1998. *Representing: Hip Hop Culture and the Production of Black Cinema*. Chicago: University of Chicago Press.

Watkins, S. Craig. 2005. *Hip Hop Matters: Politics, Pop Culture, and the Struggle for the Soul of the Movement*. Boston: Beacon Press.

Weber, Samuel. 2016. "11. Culture as sign/signifier/signifying." In *Sprache– Kultur– Kommunikation / Language– Culture– Communication: Ein internationales Handbuch zu Linguistik als Kulturwissenschaft / An International Handbook of Linguistics as a Cultural Discipline*, edited by Ludwig Jäger et al., 112–117. Berlin/ Boston: De Gruyter Mouton. https://doi.org/10.1515/9783110224504-013.

Yakpo, Kofi. 2004. "'Denn ich bin kein Einzelfall, sondern einer von vielen': Afro-Deutsche Rapkünstler in der Hip-Hop-Gründerzeit." Accessed 15 April, 2020. Bonn: Bundeszentrale für politische Bildung. https://www.bpb.de/gesellschaft/migration/afrikanische-diaspora/59580/afro-deutsche-rapkuenstler.

Yazdiha, Haj. 2010. "Conceptualizing Hybridity: Deconstructing Boundaries through the Hybrid." *Formations. The Graduate Center Journal of Social Research* 1 (1): 31–38.

Epistemological Quandary
Why Hip-Hop Scholars Must Ground Their Transcultural Arguments in the Work of Fernando Ortiz

Terence Kumpf

Abstract *Hip hop, particularly outside the United States, has been characterized as a transcultural phenomenon since the late 1990s. While many scholars have contributed to this engaging, and still emerging, academic discourse, no one has done so in a principled manner. As Nadja Gernalzick and Gabriela Pisarz-Ramirez have shown, cultural critics and commentators across the humanities have thoroughly neglected Fernando Ortiz, the Havana-born cultural anthropologist who coined the term transculturation nearly 60 years ago. Understood as an epistemological quandary, this chapter seeks solutions. Which aspects of Ortiz's thinking can help us properly explain hip hop as a transcultural force? Moreover, how can his materialist analytical mode, which I call Ortizian dialectics, strengthen analyses of identity, hybridity, and place in hip hop? To what extent does his neoculturation concept confirm hip-hop scholars and practitioners who have trumpeted the culture's 'newness' for decades? Finally, what reasons might there be for overlooking Ortiz, and what remedies must researchers conjure and apply to cure this intellectual malady?*

Introduction: Ethical Scholarship, *bitte*!

In the preface to *Transmediality and Transculturality*, Nadja Gernalzick and Gabriela Pisarz-Ramirez (2013) pulled back the curtain to make an astonishing revelation. Up until that time, no one researching, lecturing, or writing about literature, culture, or the arts as transcultural phenomena in the English or German-speaking worlds had rooted their scholarship in the work of Fernando Ortiz, the Havana-born lawyer, ethnomusicologist, and polymath who coined the term *transculturación* to explain the complex socioeconomic and cultural changes Cuba had undergone since European colonial contact. "Many of the scholars applying the concepts of transculturation, transculturality, and transculturalism to various contexts outside of Latin America today," they write, reference Mary Louise Pratt's *Imperial Eyes: Travel Writing and Transculturation* "while eliding that the term transculturation was coined by Ortiz in 1940, long before Pratt's study" (xvi). They further assert that if "Pratt's appropriation of the term transculturation had been more true [*sic*] to the comparativist spirit [her study] professes, Ortiz's work in her book might not have been relegated to a single footnote" (ibid.). In effect, Pratt lifted a term Ortiz had coined in correspondence with Yale University's Bronislaw Malinowski in the 1940s (Reichardt 2018: 68–9) and placed it like a plundered New World jewel atop what eventually became a widely cited book.

Similarly, scholars in the German-speaking world uncritically relied on a series of articles philologist Wolfgang Welsch penned in the 1990s, whom Gernalzick and Pisarz-Ramirez assert also did not "consider the history of the term as it relates to Ortiz's writings" (xxi). Instead, Welsch counterfactually speculated in a short conference paper from 1991 that Nietzsche may have been the originator of the concept (Welsch 1994). Similarly, media theorist James Lull, whose *Media, Communication, and Culture: A Global Approach* has been influential in hip-hop scholarship in Germany, defines transculturation as "a process whereby cultural forms literally move through time and space where they interact with other cultural forms and settings, influence each other, produce new forms, and change the cultural settings" (2000: 242). Missing from this definition are two crucial elements: human agency—after all, cultural forms do not move themselves—and a reference. What is the origin of Lull's authoritative-sounding definition? It is impossible to say because he provides no citation. Failing to reference the originator of the concept, let alone apply his ideas, constitutes a major breach in intellectual integrity, particularly among scholars with careers based, at least in part, on their introduction of the term transculturation to the English and German-speaking worlds. Can we get some ethical scholarship, please?

Transcultural Hip-Hop Studies: State of the Field

In hip-hop studies, this type of transgression would be akin to talking hip-hop history without acknowledging the early contributions of Robert Ford Jr. or Nelson George, two young music journalists who chronicled New York City's nascent hip-hop scene for *Billboard* magazine in the late 1970s. Their observations were vital for outsiders to understand what was happening on the ground. While Ford went on to produce rapper Kurtis Blow, he also mentored Russell Simmons, the co-founder (together with Rick Rubin) of Def Jam Records (Caramanica 2020). More recently, Nelson George, who has published and spoken on hip-hop culture for decades, consulted on the short-lived Netflix series *The Get Down* (2016–17), a fictionalized retelling of the rise of hip hop in The Bronx in the 1970s. Since George and Ford reported on working-class culture from the streets, neglecting them would be an affront to the working-class people who spawned the culture. Doing so, however, would paradoxically remain true to the spirit of hip hop. After all, The Sugarhill Gang lifted rhymes from Grandmaster Caz's little black book for their surprise breakout hit "Rapper's Delight" (Chang 2005: 131). Regardless of hip hop's penchant for 'taking' or 'borrowing,' neglecting predecessors is not cool.

As a doctoral student in 2015, I was stunned when I stumbled across Gernalzick and Pisarz-Ramirez's revelation because I, too, had published and given conference talks about hip hop as a transcultural force without considering Ortiz. In my defense, I assumed my predecessors had done their homework, but that is no excuse. In retrospect, I recall feeling a twinge of pain like the one Marcellus Wallace (Ving Rames) referred to in *Pulp Fiction* (1994) when Wallace, an underworld crime boss, instructs Butch (Bruce Willis), a washed-up prize-fighter, to ignore pride on the night of the fight Wallace has paid him to throw. I took a step back and dusted myself off. Surely someone must have consulted Ortiz, I thought, so I scanned the indexes of the three major works in hip-hop studies with articles that forward transcultural arguments.

Alastair Pennycook namedropped Ortiz in *Global Englishes and Transcultural Flows* (2007), but, like Pratt, he only gives him a single shout-out in the footnotes without applying any of his ideas. Neither the editors nor the contributors to the discipline-defining *Global Linguistic Flows: Hip Hop Cultures, Youth Identities, and the Politics of Language* (2009) cite Ortiz or work through his ideas. The same applies to the editors and contributors to *Hip-Hop in Europe: Cultural Identities and Transnational Flows* (2013). As South Bronx rapper KRS-One famously asked, "Why is that?" Shaken but not deterred, I scanned the bibliographies of all the books, articles, and essays I had collected on hip hop in Germany and the United States, the scope of my research. Alas, no one had referenced Ortiz, including me. The point is not to name and shame but simply this: Yo, let's keep it real.

What does that mean in scholarship? To read, think critically, ask questions, and to write, talk, and challenge one another to extend our collective knowledge with the utmost integrity possible. I also think it means not to be afraid to admit when one has made a mistake. So I'm going to keep it real right now: I should have known better. As early as 2008, Christoph Schaub, a German literary scholar, had sounded the alarm on the casual use of the adjective 'transcultural' in hip-hop scholarship (247, footnote 1). Could it be there was no firm politically stable understanding of the term, as Schaub noted, because no one had bothered to work through Ortiz's ideas? As Marwan M. Kraidy points out, the trend throughout the 1990s was to blend (2005: 1). Had 'transcultural' simply become a synonym[1] for terms like heterogeneity and 'glocalization' (Robertson 1992), cultural hybridity (Bhabha 1994), polycultural (Rose 1994), syncretism and pluralism (Potter 1995), tricultural (Ickstadt 1999), multiculturalism (Mitchell 2001), or postmulticultural (Chang 2006: 4)? By neglecting Fernando Ortiz, particularly through the cavalier use of a term he coined, hip-hop scholars have opened a major epistemological quandary. If we want to remedy this lack of intellectual integrity and transparency in transcultural hip-hop studies, we must bring Fernando Ortiz and his thoughts on transculturation into the cipher. Which aspects of his landmark work *Cuban Counterpoint: Tobacco and Sugar* can better enable us to understand and explain hip hop as a transcultural phenomenon?

In this chapter, I want to do three things. First, I want to focus on one small passage from the opening pages of his book to show how we might proceed. Second, I want to consider another of Ortiz's coinages, neoculturation, which he devised to describe new cultural forms that arise from transculturation, particularly how hip-hop scholars, and even producers, often characterize hip hop as a 'new' cultural form. As brief as these observations may be, I hope they encourage researchers to return to Ortiz's seminal work to harvest and apply his thinking with greater transparency. In the third and final part of this article, I speculate why Ortiz may have been overlooked, which includes careerism, cultural chauvinism, western propaganda, and institutional resistance. Above all, it is my hope that these three interventions will stimulate a spirit of reassessment and deeper inquiry and reflection among hip-hop researchers, critics, and commentators so that our work may become more rigorous, accountable, and reputable.

---

1 Prof. Dr. Ulla Haselstein of the John F. Kennedy Institute for North American Studies (FU Berlin) torpedoed my graduate school dreams with this deceptively disarming question when I interviewed for a position at the Graduate School in early 2013. I didn't have an answer for her then, and it took me another couple of years to appreciate the thrust of her inquiry. Shout-out!

Counterpoints: This/That, and More

Ortiz examined sugar and tobacco, Cuba's main agricultural exports, to explain the complex changes European colonization had wrought on the island. Through a dialectical materialist method indebted to Marx and Engels (via Hegel), the genius of Ortiz's approach are the metaphorical analogies he unfolds to reveal a plethora of contradistinctions.

> Sugar and tobacco are all contrast. It would seem that they were moved by a rivalry that separates them from their very origins. One is a gramineous plant, the other a solanaceous; one grows from cuttings of stalk rooted down, the other from tiny seeds that germinate. The value of one is in its stalk, not in its leaves, which are thrown away; that of the other is its foliage, not its stalk, which is discarded. Sugar cane lives for years, the tobacco plant only a few months. The former seeks the light, the latter shade; day and night, sun and moon. The former loves the rain that falls from the heavens; the latter the heat that comes from the earth. The sugar cane is ground for its juice; the tobacco leaves are dried to get rid of the sap. Sugar achieves its destiny through liquid, which melts it, turns it into a syrup; tobacco through fire, which volatizes it, converted into smoke. The one is white, the other dark. Sugar is sweet and odorless; tobacco bitter and aromatic. Always in contrast! Food and poison, waking and drowsing, energy and dream, delight of the flesh and delight of the spirit, sensuality and thought, the satisfaction of an appetite and the contemplation of a moment's illusion, calories of nourishment and puffs of fantasy, undifferentiated and commonplace anonymity from the cradle and aristocratic individuality wherever it goes, medicine and magic, reality and deception, virtue and vice. Sugar is she [sugar cane, *la caña de azúcar*]; tobacco is he [*el tabaco*]. Sugar cane the gift of the gods, tobacco of the devils; she is the daughter of Apollo, he is the offspring of Persephone. (Ortiz 1995: 6)

Sugar? Tobacco? Hip Hop? The dissimilarity of these subjects is perhaps one reason scholars have not linked to Ortiz directly. Yet the way he teases out metaphorical difference along binary opposition is instructive. For it is from these counterpoints that he began to develop a theory to explain complex sociocultural change—first in Cuba, but potentially in the United States, where, in the 1965 revision of his book, he suggested transculturation might also be taking place (ibid.: 103). What happens if we apply Ortiz's analytic calculus to the term hip hop itself?

Though explanations about its origins vary, the prevailing story maintains that Keith "Cowboy" Wiggins of Grandmaster Flash and The Furious Five playfully pitted 'hip' and 'hop' against each other to tease a friend who had decided to join the military (JayQuan 2005). Soon after, influential early MC Lovebug Starski popularized it (Caramanica 2018). Yet Ortiz's dialectic allows us to approach the term in at least one novel new way while staying true to Cowboy Keith's playful, jesting spirit. Where smoking necessitates burning to release tobacco's intoxicating chemicals (and was once considered 'hot' or 'cool'), tobacco becomes a corollary for 'hip.' Likewise, sugar, which provides people with short bursts of energy, becomes a stand-in for 'hop.' In an Ortizian sense, hip hop can be understood as a 'cool' and/or 'hot' cultural 'energy' which, like Cuban tobacco and sugar, has swept the globe and animated people of all faiths, colors, and creeds. Framed in a slightly different manner, the rhymes that intellectually intoxicate us are the smoke; the music that physically propels us is the sugar. While these analogies may seem facile, are they that far off the mark? Hip hop gets us high and gets us dancing. 'Music the sugar, rhymes the smoke' is one result of an initial application of what we might call Ortizian dialectics.

Nor should we stop there. His dialectic helps to unfold hip hop's numerous internal logics, which, following the impressive array of abbreviations H. Samy Alim put forward in *Roc the Mic Right: The Language of Hip Hop Culture* (2006), one might call Hip Hop Logic (HHLg). Typically framed as opposites, these orientations include, but are not limited to

- Regions (uptown/downtown, East/West Coast, domestic/foreign)
- Markets (commercial/independent, charts/underground)
- Styles (hard/soft, conscious rap/party music)
- Rivalries (gangs/crews, beefs and battles)
- Sexuality (hetero/homo, straight/gay)

- Status (super stars/nobodies)
- Values (dissing/respect)
- Authenticity (real/fake)
- Race (Black/White)
- Class (rich/poor)

and so on. Why does hip hop do this? Does hip-hop duality simply flow from, and thus appeal to, human mortality, i.e. birth and death? Does it stem from capitalism and the drive to enrich oneself as much as possible à la 50 Cent's *Get Rich or Die Tryin'* (2003), or does hip-hop duality arise, as Paul Gilroy reminded us, from the unfinished business of overcoming the "Manichean dynamic" of "black and white" (1993: 1–2), which still shapes, and plagues, western democracies? Perhaps hip-hop duality originates in how the world's great religions frame morality within conceptualizations of right and wrong, good and evil, heaven and hell, or the sacred and profane (Miller and Pinn 2015: 4). Perhaps these dualities are extensions of the electro-analogue era (on/off) or, further still, the age of advanced digital silicon computing (I/O, input/output). After all, the original hip-hop DJs utilized faders (A/B) to move back and forth between the percussive breaks on two different—though ultimately the same—records to keep the beat going. A/B faders further empowered hip-hop DJs to blend disparate forms of music to fashion more musically complex breakbeats. In truth, hip-hop duality may stem from these and still other binary figurations but resuscitating and applying Ortiz's 'counterpoints' to hip hop with transparency invites us to scrutinize some of the culture's core assumptions with renewed candor, vigor, and creativity.

Why would Ortiz begin with contradistinctions? For one, binaries allow for ease of categorization, understanding, and, ultimately, identification. Yet while it is easy to imagine oneself as this or that, it takes concerted effort to be this *and* that: to find the courage required to imagine oneself, and others, outside the status quo—that is to say, to think 'beyond the binary' and become something more. By formulating his transculturation concept within such figurations to explain how Cuba had become something different, Ortiz seemed to suggest that we move beyond them. Importantly, he carried out his dialectical analysis fifty years before the 'trend to blend' became the rage in the 1990s. Has hip hop undertaken a similar project? After all, hip-hop DJs have been blending disparate musical forms long before academics, to quote James Brown, urged us to 'get on the good foot.'

A cursory glance at some of the biggest names in hip hop reveals that binaries are well suited for creative exploitation. For as much as Chuck D's booming bass voice defines Public Enemy, Flavor Flav, the group's hype man, is a jester persona whose countervailing treble voice bolsters the seriousness of Public Enemy's Black cultural politics. Similarly, West Coast gangsta rap by Ice-T, N.W.A, and Cypress Hill emerged when chart hits by MC Hammer, DJ Jazzy Jeff and the Fresh Prince, Tone Lōc, and Vanilla Ice flourished. Acclaimed rapper Tupac Shakur was as renowned for his contemplative, philosophical nature as for his hardcore street smarts. The Notorious B.I.G. could be tough and cuddly, but Christopher Wallace was also known as Biggie Smalls. (Ortiz: "Always in contrast!") Nor has this creative 'split' been strictly limited to the United States. In Germany in the early 1990s, Die Fantastischen Vier (The Fantastic Four) released chart-friendly pop rap akin to early output by The Beastie Boys while Heidelberg's Advanced Chemistry dished out blistering social critiques (Elflein 1998). Binaries, it seems, are the 'sugar and smoke' of creativity. In retrospect, Keith "Cowboy" Wiggins hit upon genius. Had he chosen other vowels, we might not be talking about hip hop but 'hep hup.' Hep means cool (hep cats), and hup is often deployed as an interjection (Hup! Hup! Hup!) to get soldiers moving. Hep hup is the only other possible formulation that captures the spirit of Cowboy Keith's retort.

Could hip hop—which is Black first, everything else second—be transcultural at its core? If we understand transculturation to be inherently Black, then hip hop, even in the United States, could be more accurately understood as a transcultural phenomenon. Understanding hip hop in this way might help advance the project of Black liberation to overturn the persistent, despicable racism that props up White supremacist societies—certainly in the United States, but also anywhere else racism rears its ugly head, including Cuba, which was a deeply White supremacist society under Spanish colonial rule. Can we understand transculturation as inherently Black? We may if we return to Ortiz and apply his thinking honestly. As he reminds us repeatedly in the first half of his book, West African slaves were pressed into the brutally harsh working conditions of Cuba's sugar plantations while migrant Spanish laborers did the considerably less demanding work of tobacco cultivation. As in the United States, racist ideology ordered Cuban society into strict hierarchies so Europeans could get rich and, in terms of labor, get off easy. In my reading of *Cuban Counterpoint*, transculturation could, and perhaps should, be part and parcel of Black culture. For that to be the case, however, scholars must carefully work through Ortiz's concepts if we are to have any chance of applying them in a politically meaningfully way.

Neoculturation: Nueva, Nouveau, Nieuwe, Neu, New, Nü?

As Gernalzick and Pisarz-Ramirez remind us, Ortiz coined transculturation "to replace the concepts of deculturation and acculturation which focused on the transition of one culture into another more powerful one" (2013: xiv). He did not, however, abandon those concepts entirely, perhaps because he empathized with the people who experienced the savage cruelty of transculturation in the colonial era. Ortiz argued that

> the word *transculturation* better expresses the different phases of the process of transition from one culture to another because this does not consist merely in acquiring another culture, which is what the English word *acculturation* really implies, but the process also necessarily involves the loss or uprooting of a previous culture, which could be defined as deculturation. In addition, it carries the idea of the consequent creation of new cultural phenomena, which could be called neoculturation. (ibid.: xiv–xv)

While there is much to unpack in the above quote, especially if we want to locate "the Black" in transculturation (not to mention sympathize with people who lost their languages, cultures, and histories after imperial systems bent on domination robbed them of life, liberty, and their innate right to human dignity), I want to focus on Ortiz's notion of neoculturation, which casts a long shadow over hip-hop culture. Before we apply it to hip hop, however, we must consider how Ortiz derived it from his observations of colonial Cuba.

To explain neoculturation, Ortiz visually recounted how indigenous cultures across the Americas inhaled finely ground tobacco into the nose through bifurcated tubes (Ortiz: 111–133). Where artifacts found in various locations over time were similar, yet different, Ortiz suggested that these implements evinced the rise of the new, i.e. the adoption of a heretofore unknown cultural practice in other locales by different people using similar utensils albeit with slight modifications. It is an astute observation. In essence, a kind of *Tabaklust* (tobacco craze) drove innovation. Yet it was not only indigenous Americans who fell under the plant's intoxicating spell. Tobacco, Ortiz wrote, "ran through the world like wildfire" to become "adopted by the Europeans on the other side of the Atlantic, thus giving rise to a profitable trade" (ibid.: 183). Where indigenous Americans sniffed tobacco through tubes, Europeans pinched and snorted snuff. Like some connoisseurs in the Americas, Europeans preferred smoking, which led to the proliferation of pipes, all of which were the same in function, similar in form, and more-or-less stylized with ornate designs. Furthermore, this desire to enjoy tobacco led to the development of cigarettes, another innovation. Add to that vaporizers and crystal-clear cotton mallow rolling papers, and the drive to innovate continues today. In each case, a new vehicle is developed to deliver tobacco's highly sought-after nicotine buzz.

Just as this explains the spread of tobacco out of Cuba into colonial America and across the Atlantic to Europe, so too does it help to understand the spread and development of hip-hop culture. In terms of music, the link to the Caribbean is not Cuba *per se* but Jamaica. DJ Disco Wiz, an early innovator in New York City, attests that Bronx-based DJs "had powerful 'Jamaican bass bottoms,' large speakers custom-built by Bronx-dwelling immigrants from the island" (Katz 2012: 26). As agents of cultural transfer, these individuals brought the sound system to The

Bronx and continued developing it. DJ Kool Herc, who reportedly had the most powerful system, organized competitions known as battles not unlike Kingston's famed sound system clashes (ibid.). Furthermore, the "shout outs, boasts, and disses of microphone-wielding DJs and MCs that evolved into rap [were] similar to the sound system practice of 'toasting'" (ibid.). Through people, some of whom were migrants (but also US-born citizens), rap music developed from street-based Jamaican music-making practices, and early hip-hop DJs eventually infused the percussive rhythms of funk breakbeats with a variety of musical genres, including Latin music and rock. None of this history is new, but since developments in The Bronx occurred across countries and cultures, hip hop in the United States seems to have arisen through a process of transculturation, at least according to Ortiz's formulation of the principle. This underscores why we must explicitly apply his thinking if and when we argue that hip hop is a transcultural phenomenon.

Just as the spread of ornate insufflation tubes and pipes for smoking demonstrate neoculturation, so too has hip hop been adopted and adapted, two words which help us get around the pejorative term appropriation. New styles of rap music—often similar, sometimes different, and always more-or-less stylized—have developed on both sides of the Atlantic and all over the world. Nor is it an exaggeration to argue that hip hop exemplifies Ortiz's neoculturation concept. Scholars have emphasized its 'newness' for decades. For example, Justin A. Williams writes that

> the fundamental element of hip-hop culture and aesthetics is the overt use of preexisting material to new ends. Whether it is taking an old dance move for a breakdancing battle, using spray paint to create street art, quoting from a famous speech, or sampling a rapper or a 1970s funk song, hip-hop aesthetics involve borrowing from the past. When these elements are appropriated and reappropriated, they become transformed into something new, something different, something *hip-hop*. (2013: 1)

The utilization of 'past forms' is not unlike adopting and adapting existing methods to consume tobacco. Both reflect the human impulse to make cultural practices from other people and places meaningful elsewhere. As with the creation of ornate pipes, stylized forms of rap music with lyrics in various languages and sounds culled from an array of musical sources achieve essentially the same result as their American counterparts: they pump people up, get them dancing, and give them a wicked buzz. Music the sugar, rhymes the smoke.

Consider how Mark Katz characterizes hip-hop dance, which he describes as a "new, exciting style of dance [that] could not have flourished without the invention of the disc jockey" (2012: 15). He further asserts that "a rich, new art form came into being" through collaboration (ibid.: 16). New terminology such as b-boying, b-girling, popping and locking (the US West Coast influence), and breaking soon appeared to describe new dances based on moves inspired from various Afro and Latin American dance traditions as well as the dramatic kicks and leg sweeps prominent in the martial arts films of the 1960s and 70s (Banes 2004: 18). Hip hop, Katz concludes, "is a unique art form and cultural phenomenon" (2012: 23). Outside the US, hip hop is commonly referred to as a transcultural art form. Does its uniqueness, or newness, justify the transcultural label even in the United States?

Further evidence of hip hop's neocultural dimensions is seen in the practices of its founding DJs. Kool Herc, Grand Wizard Theodore, Grandmaster Flash, and Afrika Bambaataa pioneered techniques. Herc was one of many Jamaicans who brought sound system culture to The Bronx; Theodore is credited with inventing the scratch; Flash perfected Herc's breakbeat methodology and Theo's scratching technique; and Afrika Bambaataa is celebrated for imparting hip hop with musical eclecticism (George 2004: 50). Not unlike people who fashioned tools to imbibe tobacco, hip hop's founding DJs learned from and taught each other, even while protecting their secrets. With origins in the Caribbean and innovation in The Bronx, one could assert, following Ortiz, that their activities brought about the transculturation of New York City, the United States, Germany, Europe, and anywhere else hip-hop deejaying and rapping have been adopted and adapted. Hip hop in The Bronx in the mid-to-late 1970s can be understood as transcultural *and* Black because its founding figures engaged in behaviors and practices which adhere to Oritz's neoculturation principle.

There are other ways to locate the 'new' in hip hop's utilization of past forms. Following the groundbreaking scholarship of Juan Flores and Raquel Z. Rivera, Katz traces hip hop's musical antecedents to include funk, salsa (and other forms of Latin music), disco, and various 'urban influences,' all of which were prevalent in The Bronx (2012: 30). The "Latino influence on hip-hop," he writes, "is deeper and more pervasive than the contributions of any individuals" because "Latin music, particularly, from Cuba and Puerto Rico, has been part of the Bronx soundscape since the 1940s" (ibid.). Moreover, mashups of Latin and African American music had been common there since the 1950s (ibid.), with salsa and hip hop sharing a "predilection for hard-driving syncopations and percussive breaks" (ibid.: 31). In retrospect, these rhythmic similarities functioned as a kind of 'membrane' to bridge and fuse communities and cultures. Interrelation, interaction, and collaboration among diverse people in The Bronx evince a 'synergizing effect,' which gave rise to the new cultural form we now know as hip hop. Katz's passing reference to Cuba further warrants introducing Ortiz to the hip-hop studies cipher because he devoted considerable effort to understanding the development of African musical instruments across the Caribbean (Lapidus 2005: 237). Including sound system technology, these instruments and the music they enabled eventually made it to New York City to inform hip hop—the blueprint, so to speak.

Scholars are not the only people who emphasize hip hop's newness. Many of the producers Joseph G. Schloss interviewed for *Making Beats: The Art of Sample-based Hip-Hop* (2004: 30) draw attention to newness. Recounting his experiences as an emerging producer, Prince Paul claims that he couldn't "describe the whole feeling of how it was, because everything was so new and so fresh." Steinski, a producer respected for his mid-80s sampling experiments released on Tommy Boy Records (ibid.: 88), states that "one of the best things about hip-hop" is "that there's a lot of room in it for new shit, for anomalous shit, for all kinds of stuff" (ibid.: 10). Following Russell A. Potter, Schloss notes that producers took "musical sounds, packaged for consumption" and remade them "into new sounds through scratching, cutting, and sampling" (ibid.: 31). Schloss further emphasizes, following Tricia Rose, that the looping of breakbeats led to an entirely "new aesthetic" (ibid.: 31–2), where sampling and looping created "a radically new way of making music" (ibid.: 33). Just as DJs fashioned 'new' compositions by isolating and looping percussive breaks from vinyl records, the advent of digital samplers "greatly expand[ed] the creative horizons of the modern composer" (ibid.: 34). To underscore this point, Schloss notes that Public Enemy and their production team, The Bomb Squad, "were self-consciously breaking new ground" which, in turn, was "an inspiration to other producers" (ibid.: 40). The Bomb Squad radically altered hip-hop production, and producers who have drawn inspiration from them are hardly relegated to the United States. Many artists in Germany emulated The Bomb Squad's approach in the 1990s. In an Ortizian sense, The Bomb Squad fashioned pipes ('bombs' or 'bomb tracks') to inspire people elsewhere to devise their own. Numerous producers following their lead in countries all over the world helps to explain, in part, why Public Enemy occupies such an esteemed position in the global hip-hop pantheon.

The 'new' is so lauded in sampling culture that producers often gain credibility for reusing old records in new ways, which Schloss argues "can alert the thoughtful producer to new strategies and techniques" (ibid.: 85) to drive innovation. While all musicians irrespective of genre strive to break new ground to distinguish themselves, when respected figures such as DJ Shadow contend that hip hop "should be understood as an *omnigenre*, a genre of music that includes all others" (Katz 2012: 24), we should pause, reflect, and ask deeper questions. If hip-hop DJs have been pioneering methods and technologies, and producers and beatmakers have been blending elements from a variety of musical traditions since the 1970s, could hip-hop music be transcultural at its root, even in the United States? If so, what does that hold for the country and Black cultural politics?

The importance of the new is not merely the view of scholars or artist-practitioners but of fans. One may assume—safely, I think—that hip hop 'blew up' in The Bronx, New York City, and across the United States because its sound and style caught people by surprise and thrilled them. The same holds true elsewhere. In the German context, Horst Tonn has stressed rap's novelty, writing that the early years of hip hop

> are in retrospect associated with pioneering improvisation and a vaguely felt sense of the emergence of something radically new. At the same time, the attraction to Hiphop [sic] was intuitive and very personal. Some of the early Hiphoppers [sic] describe their first encounters with the culture in terms of epiphanic moments, of a sudden revelation or an intuitively perceived affinity. 'Energy' is the most frequently used term when they describe their immediate first responses to Hiphop [sic] culture. (2004: 278)

The new rap language, a hot new high: music the sugar, rhymes the smoke. The widespread use of the adjective 'fresh' to describe beats, rhymes, fashion, dance, and graffiti further evidences hip-hop culture's predilection for newness. That young people, according to Tonn, felt part of something 'radically new' confirms that 'fresh' cultural forms were emerging in Germany, first, through the reception of rap music (Strick 2008) and, later, through entirely new forms of music via adoption and adaptation—which, again, helps us sidestep the pejorative term 'appropriation.' After all, hip hop's founding figures appropriated music from various sources to forge breakbeats. While Timothy S. Brown (2006) has described young people in Germany who responded intuitively to rap music as the (African-)Americanization of German culture, their receptiveness invokes acculturation (as per Ortiz's transculturation model) as well as H. Samy Alim's notion of a "Global Hip Hop Nation." If hip hop constitutes the neoculturation of Germany both prior to and after the Fall of the Berlin Wall, the same must hold true across the United States; otherwise, why did hip hop spread like wildfire? Since people in the American south, Midwest, and West Coast caught the East Coast hip-hop bug in the late 1970s and early 1980s, apprehending hip hop as a neocultural—and, thus, transcultural—form in the United States seems long overdue.

Beyond personal taste, one might understand the resistance to hip hop in the US as a backlash against the 'African-Americanization' of a White supremacist society. Thanks to funk, soul, disco, R&B, jazz, the blues, and ragtime before it, that process had been occurring for nearly 100 years before hip hop got going in The Bronx. If Ortiz's speculation that transculturation was also happening in the United States is accurate, then people who dismiss hip hop as an 'illegitimate' form of music may be revealing their reluctance to accept profound cultural changes, i.e. the hip-hop revolution. Isn't hip hop's wide appeal and commercial success one of the reasons given for why Barack Obama was able to become president? It may have also been why Bill Clinton, another Democrat, was able to play saxophone on *The Arsenio Hall Show*. While a large portion of the country gave Obama a mandate to govern (as well as to bomb numerous countries around the world), his rise to political prominence incensed a significant portion of the US population. Though I have not done the research, I suspect that Obama's detractors were not hip-hop aficionados. But perhaps they were. People are oftentimes stuttering contradictions.

Why Has Ortiz Been Neglected: A Minor Oversight, or Something More?

Fernando Ortiz's *Contrapunteo cubano* was published in 1940. Translated into English in 1947, he expanded it in 1965 to add, as Dagmar Reichardt has noted, the entire second half of the book, including the term transculturation, which he did not expound upon at length. Why would Ortiz introduce the concept but not develop it? Given how he added the term just four years before his death, two answers might be his advanced age and the desire to establish a lasting contribution to the then emerging discipline of postcolonial studies. Given that Ortiz lived through electrification and witnessed the advent of radio, two devastating world wars, and other technological advancements, e.g. transistors, atomic energy, satellite communications, and the beginnings of modern computing, he may have envisioned greater changes on the horizon. For example, the production of reliable low-cost electronics in Japan and Taiwan via transnational capitalism, which got underway in the 1960s, has been a boon to hip-hop culture. Today, China is at the fore. While Ortiz was expanding his book, the US Congress passed Public Law 89–236 ("Immigration and Nationality Act of 1965"). To what extent did that legislation influence the families of Kool Herc and Grandmaster Flash to emigrate to The Bronx from Jamaica and Barbados, respectively, and to what extent did Ortiz envision the impact people of the Caribbean would continue having on the United States? Given hip hop's massive social, cultural, and economic impact (both 'at home' and abroad), these questions strike me as sensible. Since they arise when we introduce Ortiz to hip-hop studies, why has he been overlooked?

Mary Louise Pratt caused a sensation when she introduced the term transculturation in *Imperial Eyes* in 1992. Her book quickly 'blew up' in adjacent disciplines and has been widely cited. Duke University Press reissued *Cuban Counterpoint* in 1995, almost surely as a response. Today, Pratt is Professor Emerita at NYU, which raises a question: how could an eventual professor of Spanish and Portuguese Languages and Literatures overlook Ortiz's seminal work in translation, but especially in Spanish? To be fair, the world today is very different from the late 1980s and early 90s. With more information at our fingertips than ever before, scholars and hip-hop artists have benefited immensely from the digital revolution. But is that a legitimate excuse or explanation?

Pratt is not alone. Wolfgang Welsch's most compelling article on transculturality went to press in 1999. In it, he helpfully delineates slippery terms like multicultural, intercultural, and transcultural, yet Ortiz does not inform Welsch's concept of transculturality, which is strange given how both men discuss deculturation and acculturation at length. Heinz Ickstadt, an Americanist at the Free University of Berlin, explicitly described the stylized Turkish German rap music of Aziza A as transcultural in a short article published in the same year. With no mention of Ortiz, Ickstadt also got caught up in the trend to blend, which may speak to the profound impact Cornel West's essay "The New Cultural Politics of Difference" (1990) had on American Studies and African American Studies. The worst offender, however, is James

Lull, who defines transculturation as though he developed the concept himself. Why have these scholars, many of them distinguished and now retired, done this? Is it laziness, dishonesty, or something else? Like most sectors, higher education and publishing are about distinguishing oneself and making a mark—many marks, in fact—if someone hopes to have a career. Perhaps the explanation is that simple: make a name for yourself to get a chair in the Ivory Tower and RSVPs to the best parties. Write it down and move on.

Lest you think I am some flippant contrarian, I fully admit that these scholars expanded my intellectual horizons immensely. Pratt's concept of the contact zone is intriguing, and Sina A. Nitzsche (2012) has compellingly applied it to hip hop in Germany to argue that *Wild Style*, *Style Wars*, and *Beat Street* opened a 'medial contact space' in the mid-1980s which allowed young people in East and West Germany to imaginatively connect with hip hoppers on the US East Coast. To bolster Nitzsche's argument, the Anglicized German verb *connecten* remains meaningful in leftist German hip-hop circles today. Thanks to globally distributed extraction-production networks that have provided audio-visual technologies over the last half century, the medial space Nitzsche describes was not only transatlantic but transnational. Was it also transcultural? A transparent application of Ortiz's ideas might shed light on that question.

Why did Mary Louise Pratt only give Ortiz one reference in her footnotes? Perhaps she sought to shift the focus away from men and Eurocentrism. She is free to do so, of course, and I support such efforts *im Allgemeinen*, but if some disciplines in the humanities have devoted themselves to unwinding colonial transgressions, and Pratt plucked Ortiz's neologism from *Cuban Counterpoint* and tucked it in her satchel like a dusky New World jewel, excuse me, but isn't that an example of a Eura American exploiting pre- and post-revolutionary Cuba for personal gain? If true, the decision to do so was as much a prelude to 50 Cent's *Get Rich or Die Tryin'* as it is an example of vulture capitalism *par excellence*. Even though she is not responsible for hip-hop scholars choosing not to review Ortiz's work or apply his thinking, Pratt's intellectual negligence should not be explained away as a mere oversight, innocent or otherwise. In the end, she seems to have set a trend.

There may be other explanations. The relationship between the West and Cuba has been strained since the 1959 revolution, and certainly well before that. As a US citizen I sometimes need to remind myself that Cuba is just 90 miles off the coast of Florida. Again, I defer to KRS-One: "Why is that?" Because anti-communist propaganda defined the Cold War and propaganda works. Repeated ad nauseam it stunts minds and thwarts inquiry. *Cuba is communist! A Soviet satellite, the Evil Empire! Fidel Castro is the devil incarnate, Mephisto in the flesh!* Such efforts continue today with the villainization of Hugo Chávez, Venezuela's former president, or Nicolas Maduro, its current head of state. These shenanigans make Cuba feel as though it were on some distant planet, and it might as well be. For even after a brief period of rapprochement under US President Barack Obama I still cannot legally travel there as a US citizen. Have we avoided Ortiz due to latent cultural prejudices we are not even consciously aware of? If so, then decolonizing our minds will entail more than clever sloganeering. As Margaret Kimberley (2022) noted following Queen Elizabeth II's death, we must reject the forms of conventional wisdom too often passed off in the press, both popular and academic, if we are to have any hope of liberating ourselves from the persistent, pernicious impulses of colonialism in the present.

Finally, there may be institutional resistance. Routledge, an imprint of Taylor & Francis, published Pratt's *Imperial Eyes*. Routledge also put out Alastair Pennycook's *Global Englishes and Transcultural Flows* and the influential collection *Global Linguistic Flows* edited by Alim, Ibrahim, and Pennycook. Indeed, Routledge has brought out many titles devoted to hip hop. In a practical sense, we would be nowhere without that publishing house's commitment to the culture, but let's not be naïve: even in academic publishing hip-hop titles offer tantalizing prospects for profits. But for whom? I pitched a book proposal that seeks to unwind these issues to Taylor & Francis and got stonewalled through two peer reviews before I finally gave up. How far would any publishing house go to get to the bottom of its own ethically questionable scholarship?

Nevertheless, these titles and many other books and articles profoundly shaped my thinking when I first encountered them as a graduate student at the John F. Kennedy Institute for North American Studies in Berlin in the late 2000s. Danny Hoch's scintillating contribution to *Total Chaos* (2006) touches upon many of the dynamics that fueled the rise of the Global Hip Hop Empire. While Hoch does not characterize hip hop as transcultural, introducing Ortiz and building upon the insights of previous scholars, none of whom have worked through or applied his thinking, could help us do just that. It is apparent following Gernalzick and Pisarz-Ramirez's revelation, however, that the humanities (and hip-hop studies) has got itself in an epistemological bind. It is my hope that this collection, for which I am grateful to contribute, begins to address this deficiency. If we are to have any hope of properly maintaining and developing this field with the rigor it deserves, then we must revisit Ortiz's metaphoric dialectic, resuscitate his thoughts on transculturation, and determine the extent to which they can invigorate the hip-hop studies toolkit. Given these revelations, such an effort must be undertaken with candor, vigor, and full transparency. Anything less would still be hip hop, but going above and beyond might be "DY-NO-MITE!," as J.J. often quipped in the 1970s TV show *Good Times*.

Conclusions: "To Ortiz or Not to Ortiz, That is the Question" (12-inch Remix)

Like sugar and tobacco in Cuba, hip hop has profoundly changed the Americas, Europe, and the world. Fernando Ortiz's term for that process—transculturation—offers untapped potential to pursue new lines of inquiry. His metaphoric dialectic opens doors, but he also makes valuable insights on a range of issues including economics, capitalist production, commerce, and culture, which could be of service to hip-hop studies. Hip-hop researchers who want to run the transcultural jewels, to paraphrase Killer Mike and El-P, must apply Ortiz's ideas if we wish to have intellectual integrity in this discipline.

Like the United States, Cuba was subjected to brutal White supremacy. West African people were pressed into the harsh work on sugar plantations while Spaniards got off easy with tobacco cultivation. While these historical facts must be delicately addressed, we need not get bogged down in dour-faced seriousness. Staying true to hip hop's playful attitude and its penchant for dissing and respect, we can simply get busy. In time, hip-hop researchers might refer to Fernando Ortiz as Big Daddy Fern or DJ El Dorado à la Transcultural. Perhaps most importantly, locating "the Black" in his transculturation model could do much to secure Black liberation and equality, which has clear implications for us all, regardless of whether, or perhaps especially because, some people still need convincing.

Cuban Counterpoint is a rich text that has been sorely underutilized. It takes time and considerable effort to appreciate Ortiz's insights let alone connect them to a late-20th century pop cultural phenomenon. Like Shaolin Fantastic (Shameik Moore) in *The Get Down*, I had to roll up my sleeves and get to work. According to that retelling of hip-hop history, Shaolin did not master the art of the breakbeat overnight. There were many stops, starts, missteps, and failures before he unlocked its secrets and eventually perfected and advanced it. As Nelson George has noted, Joseph Saddler, who later fashioned himself as Grandmaster Flash, was a technologically gifted teenage Barbadian immigrant in The Bronx "fascinated by records and audio circuitry" (2004: 45). In the German context, Irina Schmitt (2005) has characterized young people who followed the lead of early US hip hoppers as a 'transcultural avant-garde.' Even in the United States, hip hop is understood as working-class culture. It is already widely understood as a migrant, or migrating, culture in the German-speaking world. Why can't it be that in the US, particularly in lieu of the Great Migrations, which were by no means unproblematic, including despicable episodes of racist terror that forced Black flight northward? Given how Ortiz accounted for the horrors of colossal change in colonial Cuba, the rise of hip hop in the United States might be better understood as a process of transculturation. As a cursory glance at any pre-Columbian map of North America will attest, the development of United States *and* hip hop occurred across regional, cultural, racial, ethnic, class, and linguistic borders. This suggests that we might have to consider the United States to be a neocolonial society. Since hip hop projects American values around the world and gets people dancing, does that make hip hop neocolonial art?

As someone who grew up in the working-class milieu of a rural western New York b(l)ackwater, I admire the perseverance the writers of *The Get Down* imparted on Shaolin Fantastic. As an analogue for anyone who not only endeavors to learn but innovate, Shaolin is a compellingly flawed character who nevertheless did the work. If Ortiz's neoculturation principle explains the rise and spread of new cultural forms, then the producers of *The Get Down* may have inadvertently told the story of the transculturation of the United States. It is, of course, a matter of perspective. Was hip hop born in The Bronx, or did it start in Jamaica? Did it start in Jamaica, or did Cuba play a role some decades, and even centuries, prior? If tracing origins to understand the influence West African people have had on our world is 'your thang' (Salt-N-Pepa a la Ortiz: "Always in contrast!"), that story runs 400 years deep. While transculturation may have been happening much longer than we'll ever know or truly understand, that doesn't mean we should not try. Though his focus was Cuba, transparently applying specific elements of Ortiz's model to other national contexts could help us draw a plethora of infinitely deeper connections to Mama Africa. The people whose destructive and creative energies coalesced in colonial Cuba eventually radiated upwards into the Americas to cross the Atlantic and wash over Europe and much of the world. What stops us from pursuing the implications of those historical facts today?

Is it a reluctance to undermine the project of Black cultural politics and its on-going push for socioeconomic justice and equality? Has too much been invested in explaining hip hop, like other forms of music, literature, and culture, as Black? It has been thirty years since Stuart Hall (1993) intervened to ask what the "Black" is in Black popular culture. Since then, many scholars have helped us better understand the influence of Latinas and Latinos on early hip hop culture. Do we shy away from deeper reflection of Hall's question because we don't want to open a pandora's box that might shake cultural narratives to their foundations? All we must do is introduce Ortiz to hip-hop studies, transparently apply his ideas, and distill an understanding of transculturation that places Blackness at its core. And why shouldn't we? Ortiz had a deep interest in the broader influence West African people had on Cuba, the Caribbean, and the Americas. Were he alive today, I suspect Ortiz would agree that transculturation is Black first, everything else second—or is it messier than that?

Since the 1990s scholars have written exhaustively about postcolonialism, but did colonialism ever end? Stefan Engel (2003) argues that it morphed into neocolonialism. Again, does that make hip hop neocolonial art? Given how he devised the term neoculturation to explain how new cultural forms emerge, Ortiz might characterize it thusly. Does neoculturation apply to hip hop? Considering the extent to which scholars and producers have described it as new, I see no reason why not. Again, what stops us? Surely hip hop can be Black and more. Indeed, it already is. Hasn't the predilection of producers to infuse rap music with elements from other cultures been one hallmark of their cultural power and the aesthetic allure of hip-hop music? What would the Wu-Tang Clan be without the inspiration its members drew from Asian martial arts culture, which they brilliantly grafted onto Black music thanks to hip hop's open aesthetic disposition? Frankly, I don't want to know. As the saying goes, *Wu-Tang Forever*.

As Mary Louise Pratt wrote in the preface to *Imperial Eyes*, "Intellectuals are called upon to define, or redefine, their relation to the structures of knowledge and power that they produce, and that produce them" (1992: xi). Just two years later, Tricia Rose, the First Lady of Hip Hop Scholarship, reminded us that the "future of insightful cultural inquiry lies in those modes of analyses that can account for and at the same time critique the raging contradictions that comprise daily life" (1994: xii). She continues: "When a comfortable fit between theoretical concerns and the limits of an oppositional practice is revealed, the reason may not be because the practice itself has failed to work in oppositional ways but, instead, that the theory could not in some way account for the conditions that shaped the practice and its practitioners." (ibid.)

Could Ortiz aid us in our efforts to better understand hip hop? By today's standard of advanced academic theory (which, in its worst manifestations, obfuscates rather than elucidates), his thoughts on transculturation are hardly complete. In fact, his prose, which reads like C.L.R. James's *The Black Jacobins*, harkens to a bygone era. At times, however, Ortiz's insights are refreshingly straightforward. But one cannot simply copy and paste from *Cuban Counterpoint* and dash off to the next hot cultural theory to assemble an impressive theoretical scaffolding to get a professorship. If we want to apply Ortiz's insights about 18th and 19th-century Cuba to the digitally interconnected world of the late 20th and early 21st century, his text demands "interpretive study of epic proportions" (Font, Quiroz, and Smorkaloff 2005: xii). Although colonial Cuba and our present-day world are separated by hundreds of years, they are not dissimilar. By Ortiz's account, 19th-century Havana was a rocking place with people from all four corners of the globe. New York City in the 1970s was no different. The same is true of other metropoles, yet people there have been allowed to speak truth to their former colonial overlords. Why is it taking so long for the ghosts of Havana to do the same?

If we want to be taken seriously as individual scholars or collectively as contributors to an emerging field that remains true to the working-class roots from which hip hop sprang (up to and including the workers who assemble music-making technologies in Asia), we must do the work. To riff on Will Smith, do not be afraid to get jiggy with *Cuban Counterpoint*. With his material, philosophical, moral, and political commitments to better understanding Afro-Cuban culture, not to mention his suggestion that transculturation was also underway in the United States, I suspect Big Daddy Fern would approve. Let's roll up our sleeves and get busy, y'all.

References

Alim, H. Samy. 2006. *Roc the Mic Right: The Language of Hip Hop Culture*. New York: Routledge.

Alim, H. Samy, Awad Ibrahim, and Alastair Pennycook. 2009. *Global Linguistic Flows: Hip Hop Cultures, Youth Identities, and the Politics of Language*. London: Routledge.

Banes, Sally. 2004. "Breaking." In *That's The Joint: The Hip-Hop Studies Reader*, edited by Murray Forman and Mark Anthony Neal, 13–20. New York: Routledge.

Bhabha, Homi K. 1994. *The Locations of Culture*. New York: Routledge.

Brown, Timothy S. 2006. "'Keeping It Real' in a Different 'Hood: (African-)Americanization and Hip Hop in Germany." In *The Vinyl Ain't Final: Hip Hop and the Globalization of Black Popular Culture*, edited by Dipannita Basu and Sidney J. Lamelle, 137–150. London: Pluto Press.

Caramanica, Jon. 2018. "Lovebug Starski, Hip-Hop Trailblazer, Is Dead at 57." *New York Times*, February 9, 2018. Accessed October 25, 2021. https://www.nytimes.com/2018/02/09/obituaries/lovebug-starski-hip-hop-dead.html.

Caramanica, Jon. 2020. "Robert Ford Jr., an Early Force in Hip-Hop, Is Dead at 70." *New York Times*, June 5, 2020. Accessed October 25, 2021. https://www.nytimes.com/2020/06/05/arts/music/robert-ford-jr-dead.html.

Chang, Jeff. 2005. *Can't Stop Won't Stop: A History of the Hip-Hop Generation*. New York: St. Marks Press.

Chang, Jeff. 2006. "Roots: Perspectives on Hip-Hop History." In *Total Chaos: The Art and Aesthetics of Hip-Hop*, edited by Jeff Chang, 3–5. New York: BasicCivitas.

Elflein, Dietmar. 1998. "From Krauts with attitudes to Turks with attitudes: some aspects of hip-hop history in Germany." *Popular Music* 17 (3): 255–265. http://www.jstor.org/stable/852956.

Engel, Stefan. 2003. *Twilight of the Gods – "Gotterdämmerung over the 'New World Order'": The Reorganization of International Production*. Essen: Verlag Neuer Weg.

Font, Maurico A., Alfonso Quiroz, and Pamela Maria Smarkaloff. 2005. "Introduction: The Intellectual Legacy of Fernando Ortiz." In *Cuban Counterpoints: The Legacy of Fernando Ortiz*, edited by Maurico A. Font and Alfonso Quiroz, xi–xix. New York: Lexington Books.

George, Nelson. 2004. "Hip-Hop's Founding Fathers Speak the Truth." In *That's the Joint! The Hip-Hop Studies Reader*, edited by Murray Forman and Mark Anthony Neal, 45–55. New York: Routledge.

Gernalzick, Nadja, and Gabriela Pisarz-Ramirez. 2013. "Preface and Comparative Conceptual History." In *Transmediality and Transculturality*, edited by Nadja Gernalzick and Gabriela Pisarz-Ramirez, vi–xxvi. Heidelberg: Universitätsverlag Winter.

Gilroy, Paul. 1993. *The Black Atlantic: Modernity and Double Consciousness.* Cambridge: Harvard University Press.

Hall, Stuart. 1993. "What is this 'black' in black popular culture?" *Social Justice* 20, 1/2 (51–52) "Rethinking Race" (Spring–Summer): 104–111. http://www.jstor.org/stable/29766735.

Hoch, Danny. 2006. "Toward a Hip-Hop Aesthetic: A Manifesto for the Hip-Hop Arts Movement." In *Total Chaos: The Art and Aesthetics of Hip-Hop*, edited by Jeff Chang, 349–63. New York: Basic Civitas.

Ickstadt, Heinz. 1999. "Appropriating Difference: Turkish-German Rap." *Amerikastudien/ American Studies* 44 (4): 571–78. http://www.jstor.org/stable/41157976.

JayQuan. 2005. "Remembering Cowboy Keith." *Five Mic Media*. Accessed February 12, 2021. http://www.furious5.net/cowboy.htm.

Katz, Mark. 2012. *Groove Music: The Art and Culture of the Hip-Hop DJ*. Oxford: Oxford University Press.

Kimberley, Margaret. 2022. "Decolonizing the Mind." *Consortium News*, September 23, 2022. https://consortiumnews.com/2022/09/23/decolonizing-the-mind/.

Kraidy, Marwan M. 2005. *Hybridity, or the Cultural Logic of Globalization.* Philadelphia: Temple University Press.

Kumpf, Terence. 2013. "Beyond Multiculturalism: The Transculturating Potential of Hip-Hop in Germany." In *Hip-Hop in Europe: Cultural Identities and Transnational Flows*, edited by Sina A. Nitzsche and Walter Grünzweig, 207–25. Berlin: LIT.

Lapidus, Benjamin L. 2005. "Stirring the Ajiaco: Changüí, Son, and the Haitian Connection." In *Cuban Counterpoints: The Legacy of Fernando Ortiz*, 237–246. Lanham: Lexington Books.

Lull, James. 2000. *Media, Communication, and Culture: A Global Approach.* Cambridge: Polity Press.

Miller, Monica R., and Anthony B. Pinn. 2015. *The Hip Hop and Religion Reader*. New York: Routledge.

Mitchell, Tony. 2001. "Introduction: Another Root—Hip-Hop outside the USA." In *Global Noise: Rap and Hip-Hop Outside the USA*, edited by Tony Mitchell, 1–38. Middletown, CT: Wesleyan University Press.

Nitzsche, Sina A. 2012. "Hip-Hop Culture as a Medial Contact Space: Local Encounters and Global Appropriations of 'Wild Style.'" In *Contact Spaces of American Culture: Globalizing Local Phenomena*, edited by Petra Eckhard, Klaus Rieser, and Silvia Schultermandl, 173–188. Vienna: LIT.

Nitszche, Sina A., and Walter Grünzweig. 2013. *Hip-Hop in Europe: Cultural Identities and Transnational Flows*. Berlin: LIT.

Ortiz, Fernando. 1995. *Cuban Counterpoint: Tobacco and Sugar*. Trans. Harriet de Onís. Durham, NC: Duke University Press.

Pennycook, Alastair. 2007. *Global Englishes and Transcultural Flows*. London: Routledge.

Potter, Russell A. 1995. *Spectacular Vernaculars: Hip-Hop and the Politics of Postmodernism*. Albany: State University of New York Press.

Pratt, Mary Louise. 1992. *Imperial Eyes: Travel Writing and Transculturation*. London: Routledge.

Reichardt, Dagmar. 2018. "Creating Notions of Transculturality: The Work of Fernando Ortiz and his Impact on Europe." In *Komparatistik: Jahrbuch der Deutschen Gesellschaft für Allgemeine und Vergleichende Literaturwissenschaft 2017*, edited by Joachim Harst, Christian Moser, and Linda Simonis, 67–82. Bielefeld: Aisthesis.

Rivera, Raquel Z. 2003. *New York Ricans from the Hip-Hop Zone*. New York: Palgrave Macmillan. https://doi.org/10.1057/9781403981677.

Robertson, Roland. 1992. *Globalization: Social Theory and Global Culture*. London: Sage.

Rose, Tricia. 1994. *Black Noise: Rap Music and Black Culture in Contemporary America*. Middletown, CT: Wesleyan University Press.

Schaub, Christoph. 2008. "If Black Dante were to meet the Tupac Amaru of Stuttgart's barrio: Political Poetics and Global Society: Contemporary Rap Lyrics in the U.S.A. and Germany." In *Traveling Sounds: Music, Migration, and Identity in the U.S. and Beyond*, edited by Wilfried Raussert and John Miller Jones, 247–63. Berlin: LIT.

Schloss, Joseph G. 2004. *Making Beats: The Art of Sample-based Hip-Hop*. Middletown: Wesleyan University Press.

Schmitt, Irina. 2005. "Germany Speaking? Rap and Kanak Attack, and Dominant Discourses on Language." In *Negotiating Transcultural Lives: Belongings and Social Capital among Youth in Comparative Perspective*, edited by Dirk Hoerder, Yvonne Hébert, and Irina Schmitt, 213–34. Göttingen, Germany: V&R unipress.

Strick, Simon. 2008. "Competent Krauts – Following the Cultural Translations of Hip-hop to Germany." In *Traveling Sounds: Music, Migration, and Identity in the U.S. and Beyond*, edited by Wilfried Raussert and John Miller Jones, 265–288. Berlin: LIT.

Tonn, Horst, 2004. "Rap Music in Germany: How Ethnic Culture Travels." In *Sites of Ethnicity: Europe and the Americas*, edited by William Boelhower, Rocío G. Davis, and Carmen Birkle, 271–286. Heidelberg: Universitätsverlag Winter.

Welsch, Wolfgang. 1999. "Transculturality: The Puzzling Form of Cultures Today." In *Spaces of Culture: City, Nation, World*, edited by Mike Featherstone and Scott Lash, 194–213. London: Sage.

Welsch, Wolfgang. 1994. "Transkulturalität – Die Veränderte Verfassung Heutiger Kulturen: Ein Diskurs mit Johann Gottfried Herder." Published in an expanded form under the title "Transkulturalität – Lebensformen nach der Auflösung der Kulturen." In *Dialog der Kulturen. Die multikulturelle Gesellschaft und die Medien*, edited by Michael Martischnig and Kurt Luger. Vienna: Österreichischer Kunst- und Kulturverlag.

West, Cornel. 1999. "The New Cultural Politics of Difference." In *The Cornel West Reader*, 119–139. New York: Basic Civitas Books.

Williams, Justin A. 2013. *Rhymin' and Stealin': Musical Borrowing in Hip-Hop*. Ann Arbor: The University of Michigan Press.

Hip Hop Becomes Mainstream
or, How to Commodify Multicultural Listeners

Amy Coddington

Abstract *Throughout the 1980s, hip-hop music dramatically increased in popularity in the United States, transitioning from a local trend understood to be primarily made by and for African American youth in New York City to a genre ubiquitously consumed by Americans of all races and ethnicities. In this chapter, I contend that the Crossover format, a commercial radio format that began broadcasting in Miami in the mid-1980s, was central to this transformation. This format, which spread throughout the United States during the second half of the 1980s, played rap songs to appeal to a coalition audience of Black, White, and Hispanic listeners.*

As I argue, these stations challenged the segregated structure of the radio industry, acknowledging the presence and tastes of Hispanic listeners and commodifying young multicultural audiences. The success of this format in turn influenced programming on more traditional Top 40 radio stations, bringing hip hop into the US popular music mainstream. But like many forms of liberal multiculturalism in this era, the racial politics of these stations were complex, as they decentered individual minority groups' interests in the name of colorblindness and inclusion. These stations played a central role in hip hop's growth into the mainstream, but in so doing laid bare the problematic politics of commodifying hybridity.

The final scene in the widely panned 1985 movie *Rappin'* begins with the male lead, Rappin' John Hood, and his crew walking down the street, celebrating their recent success at driving several nefarious characters out of the neighborhood. As the credits roll, each takes a turn clumsily rapping about solving the neighborhood's problems with nothing more than a rhyme. Barely locating the beat, they join together for the song's hook, "We can't stop, won't stop, rockin' that rhythm till we hit the top" (Silberg 1985: 1:26:27). While their rapping may leave something to be desired, the crew certainly looks the part: they fit the demographic profile that hip hop's primary creators and consumers were commonly understood to be in 1985, young men of color.

As the song continues, it becomes clear that it is not just this demographic who can participate in the genre. Walking down the street, Rappin' Hood first sees his White nemesis, Duane. As the backing track transitions from synthesizer-driven R&B to the twangy sounds of a banjo, Duane raps a verse that ironically starts with him demurring that "I may not rap, I may not rhyme, but I got something to say this time" (Silberg 1985: 1:26:37). The beat morphs again and the crew continues down the street to find other members of their multiethnic community who each rap along to an individualized beat that crudely stereotypes their cultural backgrounds: a middle-aged, middle-class Black developer raps along to what sounds like a jazzy muted trumpet, an elderly Jewish woman raps atop a klezmer-inflected clarinet line, and the gyro salesman raps along to a modal harmony shoddily representing some sort of Eastern European folk music. Rapping, here, is some sort of musical common ground. While each member of the community has their own style of music—a clichéd musical representation of their cultural identity—rapping cuts across these differences.

The unifying potential of rap indeed drives the movie's rather flimsy plot. Upon his release from jail, Rappin' John Hood teaches his friends about rap's dual roles as entertainment and political expression. Together, they solve the neighborhood's problems while having fun, a mission culminating in a rapped performance convincing the city council to deny a developer's gentrification project. Here, rap's broad appeal is transformational. The music brings people together, amplifying the concerns of those on society's margins.

And this logic extended beyond the script of a pretty terrible movie. Throughout the twentieth century, scholars and journalists alike have credited Black music's multiracial appeal with reshaping racial attitudes in the United States. From rock'n'roll through Motown and the crossover careers of Whitney Houston and Lionel Richie in the 1980s, Black music's appeal beyond a Black audience has often been interpreted as indicative of social integration more broadly (Goodman and George 1986; Nathan 1988; Weisbard 2014). Hip hop was no different in this regard: shows in the early 1980s brought White and Black audiences together during an era of increasing segregation, the popularity of Run-D.M.C.'s rock/rap hybrid "Walk This Way" has been heralded as a catalyst for substantive social change, and early advocates for the genre such as Bill Adler believed that hip hop could radically reshape the politics of race in the United States by providing a "successful voluntary desegregation plan" (Chang 2005: 245; Edgers 2019).

In this chapter, I look towards the commercial radio industry in the United States to understand how rap's multiracial appeal was commodified. On commercial radio, rap music first thrived on what were called Crossover stations, hit music stations intended for young multiracial and multiethnic audiences. Hip hop, at least on this medium, was targeted at a broad public. But did hip hop's appeal to this coalition audience translate into amplifying the concerns of young people of color or reshaping racial politics in local communities?

While elsewhere I have centered my analysis of the Crossover radio format on the Los Angeles radio market, here I turn to Miami, where the nation's first Crossover station began broadcasting in 1985, to better understand how programming for multicultural audiences impacted local minority-oriented stations and the listeners for whom these stations were intended (Coddington 2023). More than many other places in the country, Miami's radio stations catered to the area's diverse listeners. By the mid-1980s, more than forty stations in the competitive market carved out specific programming niches aimed at the area's White, Black, and Hispanic listeners—around one-quarter of the stations were aimed squarely at the latter two constituencies (Thornton 1986c). Through an analysis of radio station ratings and playlists, combined with the examination of reporting in nationally distributed radio trade journals *Radio & Records* and *Billboard* as well as in the *Miami Herald*, this essay complicates an optimistic reading of rap's multicultural appeal by interrogating whose interests were centered when radio stations played hip hop to bring multicultural listeners together. As Anthony Kwame Harrison and Craig E. Arthur argue, music trade journals offer scholars a particularly rich text to help make sense of the "incorporation of new musical forms into the 20th- and 21st-century world of music commerce" (2009: 310). And, thanks to the digitization efforts of the archivists at www.worldradiohistory.com, these sources are readily available to scholars interested in learning more about how the music industries incorporate new genres and styles. As rap in particular moved from the margins to the mainstream, these sources reveal how the radio industry understood and acted on the genre's multiracial appeal. To ground the discussion, I begin with a short summary of this appeal and an explanation of the structure of the commercial radio industry. From there, I examine the Crossover radio format's emergence in Miami, and analyze the reasons why programmers played rap on this format in the late 1980s. In the final part of the essay, I critique this format for its reluctance to engage with issues important to its local communities of color and for diverting economic power from stations aimed at minority audiences.

Born in The Bronx

From its beginnings, hip hop was made and consumed by a multicultural public (Rose 1994). Its birth in the South Bronx during the 1970s almost guaranteed multiracial and multiethnic participation: over three-quarters of those living in the neighborhood, according to a survey taken a decade earlier, were Black and Puerto Rican residents (Ewoodzie 2017). These populations "lived next door; [they] shared the same cockroaches," and they experienced related types of racial discrimination, governmental negligence, and limited employment opportunities (Rivera 2003: 53). And they had more than just these immediate concerns in common; their lives were similarly shaped, as DJ Davey D notes, by the "legacy of exploitation, oppression and colonization" that has influenced hip hop's style and substance (1999). Jorge Duany clarifies that the Black/White racial binary in the mainland United States has rarely made sense for Puerto Ricans who "have African as well as European backgrounds and range phenotypically across the entire color spectrum from black to brown to white," and many Puerto Ricans in the mainland US were racialized as Black by others, regardless of their specific racial or ethnic background (2016: 164). Both groups were integral participants in hip hop's development, although African American artists participated more often in DJing and MCing while Puerto Rican artists were more active in the breakdancing and tagging scenes (del Barco 1996: 87). Even as African American artists dominated the musical components of hip-hop culture, their funk-derived breakbeats and the rapping delivered over these loops were influenced by Caribbean musical styles (Ewoodzie 2017; Perry 2004; Rivera 2003).

Despite its multicultural roots, rap music has long been considered an African American cultural product (Harrison 2009).[1] While Raquel Z. Rivera notes that the genre's commercialization in the 1980s contributed to the style's "growing African Americanization" (2003: 89), this characterization was evident in its early years. When DJ Charlie Chase started performing in the late 1970s, he remembers being asked "What the fuck are you doing here, Puerto Rican?" (quoted in Rivera 2003: 63). But this sort of gatekeeping did not often apply to the audience, to those purchasing tickets and eventually records. According to Chase, "Hispanics always liked rap, young Puerto Ricans were into it since the beginning. I wasn't the only one who felt the same way about music like that. There were plenty of them, but they didn't have the talent, they just enjoyed it" (quoted in Flores 2004: 73). As the genre moved into New York City clubs in the early 1980s, the audience remained multiethnic and multiracial (Rivera 2003). And while hip hop has maintained its Black identity, its young multiethnic and multiracial appeal extends far past this original scene-based moment.

---

1   Joseph C. Ewoodzie notes that Puerto Rican involvement in hip hop didn't preclude its Blackness; rather, it demonstrated the extent to which "blackness in New York City during the 1970s overlapped with Puerto Ricanness" (2017: 162).

Radio Does Not Just Play Music, Radio Uses Music

When record labels began recording the genre, their primary partner in promoting records—the commercial radio industry—was not all that interested in young multiethnic and multiracial audiences. Commercial radio stations in the United States use music as a tool to divide local audiences into discrete audience segments (divided by race, ethnicity, gender, and age) that the advertising industry is interested in marketing products towards (Coddington 2023). A station's audience determines the rates that it can charge advertisers, who are willing to pay more for non-Hispanic White listeners aged 25 to 54. Despite copious research debunking racist ideas about Black and Hispanic consumers, the advertising industry has long considered Black and Hispanic listeners less preferable (Lopez 1988; Ofori et al. 1999). Due to this advertising industry bias, most commercial radio stations in the early 1980s worked to attract some proportion of White adult listeners (Turow 1997; Keith 1987). To accomplish this, stations played styles of music (such as pop, rock, and country) that they believed White adults liked.

Across the country, stations broadcast similar playlists to appeal to the same types of audiences, and the radio industry groups these stations into what they call formats (Adams and Massey 1994). Some formats are labeled by the terms that listeners use to describe musical styles: Rock and Top 40 stations, for example, are programmed to appeal to a specific subset of non-Hispanic White listeners (White 1997). The names of other formats such as Spanish, Urban, and Adult Contemporary indicate their target audiences.[2] This formatting structure divides

---

2   Throughout, I use the terms *Hispanic*, *Black*, and *White* to accurately reflect the terminology that the radio and advertising industries used during the 1980s and early 1990s. For the sake of clarity, I capitalize all radio format names. For simplicity, I refer to stations programmed primarily for Black audiences as Urban. During the 1980s, many of these stations changed their name from Black to Urban, Urban Contemporary, or Progressive Contemporary to appease companies that were unwilling to advertise their products on stations that called themselves Black (Brackett 2016). Similarly, I refer to stations that played cur-

both local and national audiences into sellable segments. Record companies tend to organize their portfolios similarly to facilitate promoting artists on the radio; while the record industry existed prior to the development of commercial radio, these two industries grew side-by-side throughout the twentieth century, mapping musical artists and genres onto listener demographics and pressuring performers to conform to their mapping (Cepeda 2000; Coddington 2023). The radio industry's organization overtly demonstrates who certain types of music are targeted towards. Genres are not played unless radio programmers—those responsible for determining playlists—think that the style is acceptable to their target audience.

One way that stations can generate additional income is by modifying their playlist in the hope that this will shift their audience profile. In the 1980s, many stations that had up until this point focused on Black listeners sought increased advertising rates by appealing to wider and Whiter audiences, adding songs by White musicians, and changing their presentation to not "be too black musically" (Washington 1985: 10). To indicate the multiracial nature of their audience to advertisers, most of these stations referred to their formatting as Urban or Urban Contemporary (Klaess 2022; Brackett 2016).

"Tri-ethnic" Programming

Beginning in 1985, Miami's WHQT did something similar, programming danceable songs aimed at a young "tri-ethnic" audience made up of Black listeners, "party-going, club-loving Anglos in the community," and Hispanic listeners (Thornton 1985a: 4D). Miami already had contemporary music stations aimed at these three constituencies, including Urban station WEDR, Top 40 station Y-100, and eight Spanish-language stations (Thornton 1986c). But WHQT programmer Bill Tanner considered WHQT distinct from these stations and their associated formats:

---

rent hits as Top 40, although many in the industry also used the format name CHR (Contemporary Hits Radio) (Weisbard 2014).

WEDR's audience was similarly multiracial, but Tanner did not think that his station qualified as an Urban Contemporary station because these were primarily aimed at Black audiences, while WHQT was "heavily targeted at Latins" (Love 1985: 58); Spanish-language stations shared *this* target audience, but they broadcast mostly in Spanish whereas WHQT broadcast in English; and although WHQT played some of the latest pop hits, it played far more dance and R&B music than a typical Top 40 station. Tanner, instead, preferred the format name "dance rock," which to him more aptly described the station's sound, "a cross between a traditional Kansas City [Top 40] and a Chicago Urban station" (Love 1985: 58). In an industry organized by separating listeners of different races and ethnicities onto different stations in the interest of selling advertisements, WHQT stood out for squishing all these demographics back together. It played songs by Black musicians for a mostly non-Black audience, songs by Hispanic musicians for an audience composed of plenty of non-Hispanic listeners, and songs by non-Hispanic White artists they hoped would appeal to non-White audiences.

WHQT's programming was unique within the radio industry, but bringing together this "tri-ethnic" audience was not particularly novel in Miami. In the early 1980s, Miami was primarily made up of the same three groups that WHQT was hoping to attract: most Dade County residents were Hispanic, about 20 percent were Black, and less than 30 percent were non-Hispanic White (Nijman 2010). These groups had specific political interests. In 1980, many Hispanic Miamians of Cuban heritage were concerned with US/Cuba relations as well as the sudden influx of 125,000 Cuban refugees via the *Mariel* boatlift. That same year, Black residents came together over the course of three days to protest the acquittal of four White police officers accused of beating a Black motorcyclist to death in what would be the largest racial uprising prior to the one in Los Angeles in 1992; meanwhile, many non-Hispanic White Miamians focused on maintaining their social and political interests in the face of increased immigration by passing a referendum denying funding to bilingual communication projects. These three groups were physically divided by some of the most pervasive residential segregation in the country (Aranda, Hughes, and Sabogal 2014; Nijman 2010).

Miami's politicians needed to cut across these and other differences to build successful campaigns; they needed to balance the unique priorities of each group while crafting a platform that appealed to everyone. In what was referred to as "the milk-stool strategy," candidates throughout the 1980s won elections by building support among the three "legs" of Miami's stool: Black, Hispanic, and White voters (Fiedler 1987: 1B). Due to the demographic makeup of the area, support from each of these legs was not similarly sized. While many candidates won elections by appealing equally to all three legs, others catered more to the rapidly growing Hispanic population in Miami.[3] And, Tanner did something similar at WHQT; his station's primary target was, as he described them, "upwardly mobile Latin Americans who...[are] on the upper end of the economic scale and love to dance, dress, drive fancy cars, and travel" (Love 1985: 58).

In music industry parlance, WHQT played "crossover music," meaning songs that exceeded the music industry's narrow framework that mapped a performer's race and ethnicity to their musical style and associated audience. Beat and "danceability" were key considerations for admittance onto the station's playlist, but more important was a song's appeal to the demographics the station was interested in (*Radio & Records* 1985a: 6). Like politicians nuancing their platforms to appease the three legs of the milk stool, WHQT's playlist combined styles that Tanner believed might appeal to the station's three target audience groups (Ross 1989b). In the fall of 1985, playlists were composed of R&B songs by Black performers such as Whitney Houston and Stevie Wonder, dance-pop songs by White artists such as Madonna, danceable rock songs by groups like A-ha, freestyle songs by Lisa Lisa and Cult Jam, Latin dance music by Miami Sound Machine, and rap songs by the Real Roxanne, Grandmaster Melle Mel, and Doug E. Fresh (Freeman 1985; *Radio & Records* 1985b). While the station's closest English-language competitors played some of these same artists, they leaned further towards either

---

3   By the late 1980s, some politicians succeeded by appealing to only Hispanic voters plus one other leg, not relying on both Black and White voters (Grenier and Stepick III 1992).

rock or R&B. Top 40 station Y-100 also included songs by Dire Straits and Phil Collins on its playlist, and Urban station WEDR added songs by the Pointer Sisters, Starpoint, and Family to its playlist.[4]

Tanner was not particularly attached to the music he played on WHQT: a 1985 feature reported that the parrot-raising, burgundy Jaguar-driving programmer mainly listened to classical music and Motown hits in his spare time (Thornton 1985b). Perhaps that was one reason why he programmed such a unique mix. By paying attention to what was popular in the clubs, Tanner's playlists exceeded the narrow-minded industry norms expecting musical taste to align with racial and ethnic identity. But these playlists proved popular and influential. While programmers at Top 40 station Y-100 initially scoffed at Tanner playing Jelly Bean Benitez's dance track "Sidewalk Talk," for example, they added it after the song became a hit on WHQT (Love 1985). And these playlists drew in listeners from Y-100 and WEDR; within a few months, it was the sixth-most popular station in the South Florida area (Thornton 1985c).

But Y-100 and WEDR fought back (Thornton 1986a; Ross 1985). Regularly the area's most popular station, Y-100 considered WHQT's success a mere blip in their usual strong ratings. But WEDR, according to Tanner, had been "asleep at the switch and got knocked on its ass" (Washington 1985, 10; Thornton 1985d). WEDR, however, woke back up. Black listeners—despite switching over occasionally to see what the new station was playing—were loyal to the only Urban FM station in the area, which tended to play new releases by Black artists sooner than WHQT or Y-100 did (Thornton 1985d). And, like many other stations in this format, WEDR demonstrated a strong commitment to its Black community: the station assisted listeners in need by pointing them towards government resources, it helped small Black-owned businesses by offering them lower advertising rates, it highlighted local Black artists on its playlists, and it produced Black-oriented news and community affairs programs (Washington 1985).

---

4   These stations reported at least part of their playlists to *Radio & Records*. See, for example "Black/Urban Adds," *Radio & Records*, October 4, 1985, 68; "CHR Parallel One Playlists," *Radio & Records*, October 4, 1985, 84.

WHQT's too-brief moment of glory meant that Tanner was shown the door. In the summer of 1986, the station fired him due to poor ratings (Freeman 1986a). But he quickly found a new position across town at the brand-new station Power 96, which he described as a "rock and rhythm" station (Thornton 1986b: 3E). Like at WHQT, Tanner designed Power 96 to fit between, rather than into, the radio industry's preexisting format categories. The station played pop, dance, and freestyle songs, and the playlists were informed by about forty pages of research compiled each week from telephone surveys, sales figures, and a panel of club-going teens (Freeman 1986c). The station had a close relationship with local venues; its playlist influenced DJs' sets, and the station often began playing songs after hearing them in the clubs (Ellis 1986; Terry 1988).

Like WHQT, Power 96 was aimed primarily at young Hispanic, Black, and White listeners and catered more to its Hispanic listeners than these other constituencies. In comparison to WHQT, Power 96 played more freestyle and club-oriented 12-inch singles aimed at Hispanic listeners by artists like the Cover Girls and Exposé (Terry 1988). In Tanner's own analogy, if WHQT was at 9:00 on a clock, thanks to its dance- and R&B-friendly playlist, and Top 40 station Y-100 was at high noon, Power 96 would fit somewhere in the brunch hour between the two (Freeman 1986a). Tanner thought that this brunch spot represented Top 40 for Miami, due to its large Hispanic population, and that his station's orientation towards this audience made it "not an urban... really, we're more dance than urban" (Freeman 1986b: 15). This distinction was important. As Tanner knew from his stint at WHQT, advertising agencies discriminated against Urban stations (a fact he described as "the shame of the industry"), and reporting as one would decrease advertising rates (Ross 1988a: 10). And within a few months, WHQT shifted their programming to generate higher rates, occupying a slightly later—and less Urban—brunch spot between Power 96 and Y-100 (Denver 1987a).

Becoming a Format

Within the next few years, Power 96 and WHQT would be joined at the brunch table by dozens of other stations throughout the country that programmed music for multiracial and multiethnic audiences. Mostly located in urban areas with sizeable enough Hispanic and Black populations to support this sort of "milk stool" approach, these stations played up-tempo dance, freestyle, R&B, rap, and pop songs—along with enough ballads to provide some balance—for a young, club-friendly audience (Freeman 1987b). Local demographics as well as the nuances of their radio market determined each station's particular balancing of the stool's legs. While Hispanic listeners were most often the "linchpin of each station's success," some stations did well in markets with a smaller Hispanic population, such as New Orleans and Washington, DC (Chin 1987: D3; Freeman 1988). And the distinct cultural backgrounds of their Hispanic listeners also made for "significant programming differences" between these stations (Chin 1987: D3).

This all meant that fitting them into the industry's format structure would be complicated. Their "relating to several ethnic groups instead of one in particular" broke longstanding formatting norms in an industry organized along racial lines (Love and Ross 1987: 44). Indeed, the *Los Angeles Times* proposed that their programming was so "violently different" to necessitate "a whole new category" (McDougal 1987). Most often referred to as either "Churban" stations (combining the industry term for Top 40, CHR, with Urban) or Crossover stations (for their playlists filled with music intended to do just that), these stations were "writing their own rules" in an industry that typically segregated listeners by race and ethnicity onto different formats (Denver 1987a: 47). Few agreed whether they should report to the trade journals as Urban or Top 40 stations. Programmers, acutely aware of advertising industry bias against Urban stations, often insisted they were the latter even though they targeted non-White listeners (Chin 1987). Indeed, Tanner noted that one reason why he was the first in Miami to program this type of station was because others "were scared the station would be labeled as Black" (Love 1985: 58).

By mid-1987, these stations were proving popular enough across the country that the trade journals were forced to act. *Billboard* debuted a new chart, the "Hot Crossover 30," which was intended to not only resolve the format classification question, but also demonstrate the popularity of songs—such as freestyle hits by Nice & Wild and the Cover Girls—that had not previously charted well because their airplay was split between Urban and Top 40 stations (Freeman 1987a).[5] The chart editor described Crossover as a new format, one which was "happening in the country's urban centers" (Freeman 1987a: 83), but designed the chart to acknowledge its relation to pre-existing formats: stations could report only to the "Hot Crossover 30" chart, or those programming closer to traditional formats could also report to the "Hot 100" or the "Hot Black Singles" chart.[6]

These stations often had a young listener base, which was a financial risk. It was clear from the success of the format that there were plenty of young listeners whose needs were not being met by other stations. But English-dominant Hispanic teenagers who were not being served by the Spanish-language stations catering to their parents and young audiences interested in budding club trends were tricky listeners to monetize (Ross 1990a). Making money at a Crossover station was difficult, one programmer claimed, because "the median age of the [Crossover station audience] was 19, and you can't live on that" (Stark 1994: 111). But Bill Tanner insisted Crossover stations' young listeners set musical trends and that older listeners would "com[e] along for the ride" (Denver 1987b: 46). Other stations found financial success by prioritizing the sale of advertisements intended for younger listeners rather than succumbing to the general industry trend of trying for older White audiences (Denver 1988a; 1989a; 1989b).

One of the clearest indications of the format's success, however, was not financial—it was musical. Crossover stations had been breaking

---

5   *Radio & Records* also established a category for these stations, calling them P1A reporters (Denver 1987a).
6   In Miami, WHQT reported exclusively—for a brief time—to the "Hot Crossover 30" chart while Power 96 reported to the "Hot 100" as well, indicating the station's smaller Black listener base (Freeman 1987a).

new music locally and influencing nearby Top 40 and Urban stations for a few years, but the publication of the "Hot Crossover 30" chart increased the geographical reach of their influence. These stations almost immediately began affecting the playlists at Top 40 stations, bringing the sounds of the city to suburban and rural parts of the country (Denver 1988b; Grein 1988). And their influence grew stronger when *Billboard* began printing the Crossover chart close to the Top 40 chart. Programmers looking at the latest hits could not help but witness the growing popularity of artists like Salt-N-Pepa and Club Nouveau, who first experienced success on Crossover playlists (Ellis 1988). Industry observers began wondering whether the influence of these stations was too great, and indeed, in 1990, *Billboard* deemed the "Hot Crossover 30" chart no longer necessary because it had "influenced the Hot 100 Singles chart to such a great extent that a separate chart to break out dance titles is no longer necessary" (*Billboard* 1990b: 84; Denver 1988b).

Rap on Crossover Stations

Looking at the last week of *Billboard*'s "Hot Crossover 30" chart demonstrates one important component of that influence: one-third of the songs on the chart had rapped vocals in them. Some of these songs, like Deee-Lite's "Groove is in the Heart" and C+C Music Factory's "Gonna Make You Sweat," were slamming club-oriented tracks that featured rappers. Others were by new jack swingers and ex-New Edition members like Bell Biv DeVoe and Ralph Tresvant, while MC Hammer's "Pray" and Candyman's "Knockin' Boots" were by more straight-ahead rappers and could be found on *Billboard*'s rap singles chart (*Billboard* 1990a). Regardless of style, all these songs with rapped vocals made their way onto Top 40 stations after showing promise on the Crossover chart.[7]

While Crossover programmers had not initially intended to play rap, they began playing an increasing amount of the genre throughout the

---

7   In most cases, they appeared on the "Hot 100 Airplay" chart a few weeks after debuting on the "Hot Crossover 30" chart.

late 1980s. In Miami, WHQT and Power 96 played rap songs occasionally throughout the mid-1980s, throwing songs by LL Cool J and Tricky T into the mix, but rap was not their focus—dance music was. But stations around the country experienced success when adding rap songs to their playlists. By the time *Billboard* debuted the "Hot Crossover 30" chart in 1987, about seven percent of its songs had rapped vocals. The following year, this percentage doubled, and it continued to grow until 1990 when songs with rapped vocals made up a full third of the chart (Coddington 2023). As the 1990s began, Crossover stations were the most reliable place to find rap songs on the commercial radio dial.

Crossover stations were well suited to play hip hop. Many Urban and Top 40 programmers did not play the style because they claimed their older listeners, who raised advertising rates, did not like it (Ross 1990b; 1990d; Simmons 1985). But Crossover stations' business models were not dependent on appealing to older listeners, which meant that they could play rap without worrying about this demographic tuning out. Instead, they played rap to develop a young multicultural audience.

Many of the rap songs that they played took the musical styles already popular among specific segments of their audience—freestyle, up-tempo R&B, and dance-oriented rock—and added rapped vocals. Freestyle group Sweet Sensation, for example, teamed up with Romeo J.D. in their 1989 song "Sincerely Yours," which featured the female vocalists and rapper discussing faithfulness above a Latin-influenced dance beat and multi-part horn riffs. R&B singer Jody Watley similarly added Eric B. and Rakim to her song "Friends" the same year, and MC Hammer's "Pray" sampled Prince's 1984 song "When Doves Cry," a danceable pop-rock hit that would have easily fit on Crossover playlists had the format existed when it was released.

But rap's appeal extended beyond the target demographics of its backing tracks. Programmers noted that all three of the demographic segments they considered their audience to consist of liked the genre. This was not a guarantee for much of the music these stations played; programmers worried about pleasing all three parts of their audience, whose tastes they believed did not always align. During programming meetings at WHQT, for example, the staff worked to understand every song's demographic reach, "openly discuss[ing] who [they thought] a song would appeal to, and who would be turned off by it" (Love and Ross 1987: 44). A song only made the playlist if the staff thought it could appeal to at least two parts of their "tri-ethnic" audience. Across the country, programmers considered freestyle to be a particularly difficult genre to program. While it developed out of the same African American and Puerto Rican communities from which hip hop emerged, programmers thought that it mainly appealed to Hispanic listeners. Rap, on the other hand, came to be seen as a "common denominator" between the Black and Hispanic segments of Crossover stations' audiences, and programmers began adding dance-oriented rap songs to their playlists (Ross 1990c: 13). As the format's influence grew, these same songs made their way onto Top 40 stations across the country, ushering hip hop into the mainstream.

In Miami, programmers also recognized the genre's unifying nature. Crossover stations in the Magic City did not play much hip hop, but one style seemed to cut across racial and ethnic lines. Programmers found it difficult to simultaneously please two parts of their "tri-ethnic" audience. While Black and Hispanic listeners liked dance music, programmers thought that they did not like the same *kind* of dance music. But according to WEDR programmer Leeo Jackson, one point of agreement was bass, Miami's homegrown style of hip hop, by artists like 2 Live Crew and Gucci Crew (Ross 1988b). And so WEDR, Power 96, and WHQT all played the hottest bass tracks. For Power 96, which leaned further towards a Hispanic audience than these other stations, songs by these artists—which Bill Tanner praised as "a little madness from the street"—were at times the only rap songs on its playlist (*Radio & Records* 1988: 56).

And in a residentially segregated city whose politics were drawn according to the same racial lines that defined its geography, hip hop's ability to physically bring together young multicultural audiences was notable. When MC Hammer came to the Miami Arena in 1990, one columnist at the *Miami Herald* praised the audience as "the Miami many of us adults have given up on: multicultural, multiethnic. Rather, it was who-cares-what-ethnic." After the concert, he noted, many would return to their segregated areas of Miami and "go back to hanging out with their isolated ethnic crowds again." But he hoped that one day "they'll remember only that they all liked the same music and danced the same steps" (Steinback 1990: 1B). The writer's hope was, of course, the promise of hip hop presented in *Rappin'*: a music that could unite factions with diverging interests, offering a fun way of coming together and making the world less divided. And on the radio, Crossover stations used hip hop for precisely this purpose, to bring together diverse audiences. But what was the impact of these stations off the air, within the communities they played rap for?

Commodifying Multicultural Listeners

Crossover stations made space within the radio industry for multicultural audiences, but their positioning did little to challenge the racism inherent to the industry's business model. Indeed, their place within the industry only reinforced its economic status quo, which discriminated against stations formatted for non-White audiences. At the local level, Crossover stations directly competed against Urban and Spanish-language stations, meaning that their growing popularity decreased the audience size and economic power of these other stations. In particular, Crossover stations repackaged the multiracial promise of Urban radio with a Whiter facade, dividing the local multiracial coalition audiences that Urban stations had been working to cultivate since the early 1980s and forcing Urban stations to compete against their more advertiser-friendly format (Ross 1990a, Hammou 2023). The coexistence of Crossover and Urban stations, *Radio & Record* columnists Walt Love and Sean Ross wrote, brought to mind "two separate but not very equal drinking fountains dispensing similar music" (1987: 44).

The competition between Crossover and Urban stations was tight in Miami. Returning to 1987, local gossip indicated that pressure from Crossover competitors would force Urban station WEDR to switch to a Country format (Love 1987). But the station held fast. Its continued success may have had to do with its programming team's recognition of the complex relationship between race, ethnicity, and musical preference. Black programmer Jerry Rushin found that the station's Hispanic listeners "also like the same rhythms we do for the most part," and he understood that it was inaccurate for programmers to simplistically divide non-White audiences into Black and Hispanic segments. "People in other parts of the country," he thought, "don't realize that there are also blacks who were born in a number of Latin American countries." But Rushin was not convinced that the station's success would do much financially for it. Referring to advertisers, he bleakly stated that "[p]eople just want to look the other way when a Black station does well" (Love 1987: 47).

The station had only about a year to see whether its success could generate additional income. In the late Summer of 1988, WHQT recalibrated its programming once again (Ross and Olson 1988). Attempting to fit somewhere between Power 96 and WEDR, the station played "common denominator" rap, R&B, freestyle, and dance music alongside older hits by Black musicians such as New Edition's "Candy Girl" and the Sugarhill Gang's "Rapper's Delight." Programmer Keith Isley wanted WHQT to be "some sort of top-40-type station," but one that played more music by Black performers because he believed that "Black-based music is a lot more mass appeal than just black listeners." New jack swing, rap, and R&B "seem[ed] to cross better to both Anglos and Hispanics than dance music" (Ross 1989a: 19). But the appeal of Black culture only spread so far at the station. Like at many Crossover stations, the station's jocks were all White or Hispanic.

WEDR's ratings tanked, as young Black listeners in particular turned their radio dials away from the Black-operated station to the Crossover station. By 1989, half of WHQT's audience was Black, while almost all the station's staff were White, a disparity that some flyers critical of WHQT posted in nightclubs and flea markets pointed out (Love 1989). WEDR denied any direct involvement with this flyer campaign, but the station began running public service announcements highlighting its commitment to the local Black community, noting that "While others are exploiting our community, we truly do care" (Viglucci 1989: 1B). Commenting on his rival's lack of involvement with the Black community, WEDR programmer Jerry Rushin suggested that "They could hire some black people, other than the janitor" because "Somewhere we have to give something back other than bumpin' and grindin' music." WHQT's response emphasized the colorblind philosophy at the station; general manager Chuck Goldmark claimed that when a job opened, they would not prioritize Black talent and instead would hire any qualified DJ: "We don't care what color they are" (Viglucci 1989: 1B).

But the criticism did seem to affect the station's positioning. Shortly after the flyer campaign, WHQT began reaching out to the local Black community and started reporting to the trade journals as an Urban station (*Billboard* 1989). Perhaps the station's rapid rise to the top of the local market gave it leverage with advertisers, maybe advertisers had already seen through the Crossover label and noticed the station's sizeable Black audience, or maybe the station was simply trying to be more honest about its place within the market. Either way, its rebranding did not change the fact that its staff—on-air and behind the scenes—was mostly White. The station used Black music to appeal to a broad multicultural audience but did not hire staff who reflected the diversity of its playlists. Across the country, Crossover stations did much the same, playing music by artists of color while not increasing economic opportunities for professionals of color within the radio industry.

What's more, Crossover stations were often criticized for their unwillingness to engage with issues important to their local listeners of color (Andrews 1990). Miami's Crossover stations were often wary of discussing contentious local issues that their "tri-ethnic" audience might disagree on, such as the 1990 visit of Nelson Mandela (who had recently made pro-Fidel Castro comments) or the trial that same year of William Lozano, a Hispanic police officer accused of killing two unarmed Black men. Lozano's guilty verdict divided Miami's population along racial and ethnic lines: Black residents celebrated while the Hispanic Officers Association of Miami described the verdict as "a sad, sad day for the people of this city" (Schmalz 1989: A1; Nijman 2010). In some ways, Crossover stations' lack of engagement was a product of trying to appeal to such a multiethnic audience. Goldmark claimed that WHQT "tr[ied] not to exclude anybody" but noted that this attitude limited the sorts of topics his on-air staff could discuss because "a lot of the issues are narrowly targeted" (Andrews 1990: 3). WEDR program director B.J. Barry agreed and considered this limitation a strategic advantage for his station. If WHQT were to make "the commitment to the black community that's necessary to keep blacks listening," he claimed, "it just might offend their white and Hispanic audience" (Love 1989: 47).

And even if Crossover stations had engaged in more contentious issues, programmers were not trained to deal with the intricacies of balancing and mediating these conversations. Even a decade later, and after wholly adopting a hip-hop format after gaining popularity as a Crossover station, New York's Hot 97, for example, was criticized for interviewing a police officer during their public-affairs show about the acquittal of the police officers who killed Amadou Diallo (Johnson 2009). When it came to the music, programmers were often ill-equipped to present hip hop along with its cultural context; many programmers were hired for their audience-building acumen, not their knowledge about the music they played. Like other industries, commercial radio incentivized a programmer's attention to the bottom line rather than educating their listeners or improving their ethical relationships with the world around them.[8]

But ultimately, it was not the programmers but rather the system that denied hip hop the potential to reshape the politics of race in the communities it brought together on the radio. Throughout its decade-long history, the commercial radio industry in the United States has been celebrated for its ability to bring listeners together. Eric Weisbard writes that on Top 40 stations, "music did not just sell out communal impulses; it subsidized new publics, or at least glimpses of social relationships still being cemented" (Weisbard 2014: 264). But it did so within the constraints of its business model, bringing together only the audiences which made stations money. This meant that there was a substantive difference between what Rappin' John Hood's rhymes

---

8   Programmers weren't ethical role models. In 1992, Tanner and some of his colleagues from Power 96 were charged with, and sometimes found guilty of, crimes ranging from driving under the influence to drug possession and child molestation (Due 1992).

could do within his neighborhood and what happened when Crossover stations played rap.

Crossover stations created the conditions for hip hop to be heard regularly on commercial radio stations, making spaces for multicultural audiences to come together to listen to artists of color rhyming over a beat. But the financial imperatives of the industry dictated the terms of hip hop's inclusion. The radio industry incentivized catering to White listeners, meaning that many Crossover stations maintained a distanced relationship to rap's Black identity, obscuring the genre's potential to be a platform for Black artists. Perhaps these stations' popularity among White listeners even demonstrated these listeners' distance from Black culture; as one Black programmer noted, "the shift by white listeners to white radio stations [from Urban stations] for Black music only shows that white people find the connection to Black people to be undesirable" (Martin 1988: 1–2). Crossover stations played a central role in hip hop's growth into the mainstream, bringing the sounds of young Black artists to airwaves across the country. But these stations failed to challenge the discriminatory practices so central to the radio industry's business model, demonstrating just how difficult it would be for the genre to exact lasting social change.

Discography/Videography

Silberg, Joel, dir. *Rappin'*. 1985; New York: MGM/UA Home Video.

References

Adams, Michael H., and Kimberley K. Massey. 1994. *Introduction to Radio: Production and Programming*. New York: McGraw-Hill.
Andrews, Sharony. 1990. "More Listeners Dial WEDR: Station Making Gains Among Blacks." *Miami Herald*, July 8, 1990.

Aranda, Elizabeth M., Sallie Hughes, and Elena Sabogal. 2014. *Making a Life in Multiethnic Miami: Immigration and the Rise of a Global City*. Boulder, CO: Lynne Rienner Publishers, Inc.

del Barco, Mandalit. 1996. "Rap's Latino Sabor." In *Droppin' Science: Critical Essays on Rap Music and Hip Hop Culture*, edited by William Eric Perkins, 63–84. Philadelphia: Temple University Press.

Billboard. 1989. "Black Singles Reporting Panel Updated," September 16, 1989.

Billboard. 1990a. "Crossover Radio Airplay," December 1, 1990.

Billboard. 1990b. "Billboard Drops Crossover Radio Airplay Charts," December 8, 1990.

Brackett, David. 2016. *Categorizing Sound: Genre and Twentieth-Century Popular Music*. Oakland: University of California Press.

Cepeda, María Elena. 2000. "Mucho Loco for Ricky Martin; or the Politics of Chronology, Crossover, and Language within the Latin(o) Music 'Boom.'" *Popular Music and Society* 24 (3): 55–71. https://doi.org/10.1080/03007760008591776.

Chang, Jeff. 2005. *Can't Stop Won't Stop: A History of the Hip-Hop Generation*. New York: Picador.

Chin, Brian. 1987. "Radio's Resurgent Dance Beat Puts Heat in 'Hot' Format." *Billboard*, July 18, 1987.

Coddington, Amy. 2023. *How Hip Hop Became Hit Pop: Radio, Rap, and Race*. Oakland: University of California Press. https://doi.org/10.1525/luminos.165.

Davey D. 1999. "Why Is Cleopatra White?" *The FNV Newsletter* (blog). May 21, 1999. http://www.daveyd.com/fnvmay21.html.

Denver, Joel. 1987a. "CHR—A New Way of Looking at Things." *Radio & Records*, July 31, 1987.

Denver, Joel. 1987b. "Miami Trio Draws Battle Lines." *Radio & Records*, September 18, 1987.

Denver, Joel. 1988a. "Power 96 Extends Lead in Three-Way Battle." *Radio & Records*, February 12, 1988.

Denver, Joel. 1988b. "Urban/Dance Music: Where's the Happy Medium?" *Radio & Records*, March 25, 1988.

Denver, Joel. 1989a. "Teen Titans." *Radio & Records*, October 6, 1989.

Denver, Joel. 1989b. "Teens: Not a Tough Sell." *Radio & Records*, October 13, 1989.

Duany, Jorge. 2016. "Neither White nor Black: The Representation of Racial Identity among Puerto Ricans on the Island and in the U.S. Mainland." In *The New Latino Studies Reader: A Twenty-First-Century Perspective*, edited by Ramón A. Gutiérrez and Tomás Almaguer, 157–84. Oakland: University of California Press.

Due, Tananarive. 1992. "The Power Drain Arrests of 3 DJs Rock a Hot Radio Station." *Miami Herald*, January 2, 1992.

Edgers, Geoff. 2019. *Walk This Way: Run-DMC, Aerosmith, and the Song That Changed American Music Forever*. New York: Blue Rider Press.

Ellis, Michael. 1986. "Hot 100 Singles Spotlight." *Billboard*, October 18, 1986.

Ellis, Michael. 1988. "Hot 100 Singles Spotlight." *Billboard*, September 24, 1988.

Ewoodzie, Joseph C. 2017. *Break Beats in the Bronx: Rediscovering Hip-Hop's Early Years*. Chapel Hill: The University of North Carolina Press.

Fiedler, Tom. 1987. "Anglos Bypassed in Miami Race." *Miami Herald*, October 28, 1987.

Flores, Juan. 2004. "Puerto Rocks: Rap, Roots, and Amnesia." In *That's the Joint! The Hip-Hop Studies Reader*, edited by Murray Forman and Mark Anthony Neal, 73–91. New York: Routledge.

Freeman, Kim. 1985. "Grass Route." *Billboard*, April 13, 1985.

Freeman, Kim. 1986a. "Vox Jox." *Billboard*, July 5, 1986.

Freeman, Kim. 1986b. "Vox Jox." *Billboard*, November 22, 1986.

Freeman, Kim. 1986c. "Out of the Box." *Billboard*, December 13, 1986.

Freeman, Kim. 1987a. "Hot 30 Crossover Chart Tracks New Breed Of Radio." *Billboard*, February 28, 1987.

Freeman, Kim. 1987b. "Crossover Outlets Prove Their Power." *Billboard*, September 5, 1987.

Freeman, Kim. 1988. "Crossover PDs: We'll Keep On Dancin'." *Billboard*, February 13, 1988.

Goodman, Fred, and Nelson George. 1986. "Majors See Black Music Boom." *Billboard*, January 25, 1986.

Grein, Paul. 1988. "Mass-Appeal Dance Music Still Calling the Tune: But Some Record Producers Are Hoping for a New Voice to Break Through." *Los Angeles Times*, January 6, 1988. http://articles.latimes.com/1988-01-06/entertainment/ca-22857_1_dance-music.

Grenier, Guillermo J., and Aliex Stepick III, eds. 1992. *Miami Now!: Immigration, Ethnicity, and Social Change*. Gainesville: University Press of Florida.

Hammou, Karim. 2023. "La racialisation musicale comme action conjointe. La carrière de la catégorie d'« Urban Contemporary » dans l'industrie musicale états-unienne (1979–1986)." In *L'épreuve des frontières sociales*, edited by Marion Fontaine and Emmanuel Pedler, 6–88. Ed. de l'EHESS, coll. Enquêtes.

Harrison, Anthony Kwame. 2009. *Hip Hop Underground: The Integrity and Ethics of Racial Identification*. Philadelphia: Temple University Press.

Harrison, Anthony Kwame, and Craig E. Arthur. 2011. "Reading Billboard 1979–89: Exploring Rap Music's Emergence through the Music Industry's Most Influential Trade Publication." *Popular Music and Society* 34 (3): 309–27. https://doi.org/10.1080/03007766.2010.522806.

Johnson, Phylis. 2009. *KJLH-FM and the Los Angeles Riots of 1992: Compton's Neighborhood Station in the Aftermath of the Rodney King Verdict*. Jefferson, NC: McFarland & Company.

Keith, Michael C. 1987. *Radio Programming: Consultancy and Formatics*. Boston: Focal Press.

Klaess, John. 2022. *Breaks in the Air: The Birth of Rap Radio in New York City*. Durham, NC: Duke University Press.

Lopez, Ed. 1988. "South Florida Radio a Sound Business the Market's Booming." *Miami Herald*, September 5, 1988.

Love, Walt. 1985. "Miami's Hot 105: Dance Rock Fever." *Radio & Records*, June 21, 1985.

Love, Walt. 1987. "WEDR Holds On... And Proves the Point." *Radio & Records*, May 22, 1987.

Love, Walt. 1989. "Urban vs. Churban." *Radio & Records*, September 29, 1989.

Love, Walt, and Sean Ross. 1987. "The Return of the Zebra." *Radio & Records*, January 2, 1987.

Martin, Willie. 1988. "Willie M. Tells It Like T-I-S Is." *Jack the Rapper*, July 6, 1988.

McDougal, Dennis. 1987. "L.A. Turn-On Is a Top 40 Turnoff: Power 106 Top Local Radio Station, but Dispute Over Trade Publications' Hit List Is Proving a 'Black' and 'White' Issue." *Los Angeles Times*, January 8, 1987. http://articles.latimes.com/1987-01-08/entertainment/ca-3078_1_radio-station.

Nathan, David. 1988. "The World of Black Music." *Billboard*, June 18, 1988.

Nijman, Jan. 2010. *Miami: Mistress of the Americas*. Philadelphia: University of Pennsylvania Press.

Ofori, Kofi Asiedu, and Civil Rights Forum on Communications Policy. 1999. "When Being No. 1 Is Not Enough: The Impact of Advertising Practices on Minority-Owned & Minority-Formatted Broadcast Stations." Washington, DC: Office of Communications Business Opportunities, Federal Communications Commission.

Perry, Imani. 2004. *Prophets of the Hood: Politics and Poetics in Hip Hop*. Durham, NC: Duke University Press.

Radio & Records. 1985a. "Tanner Takes WEZI To Dance Rock Format," January 11, 1985.

Radio & Records. 1985b. "Black/Urban Adds & Hots," September 13, 1985.

Radio & Records. 1988. "Do Wah Diddy from the 2 Live Crew," November 11, 1988.

Rivera, Raquel Z. 2003. *New York Ricans From the Hip Hop Zone*. New York: Palgrave Macmillan. https://doi.org/10.1057/9781403981677.

Rose, Tricia. 1994. *Black Noise: Rap Music and Black Culture in Contemporary America*. Middletown, CT: Wesleyan University Press.

Ross, Sean. 1985. "The Fall '85 Ratings Wars." *Radio & Records*, November 15, 1985.

Ross, Sean. 1988a. "'Why' Questions Rule Radio Panels." *Billboard*, July 30, 1988.

Ross, Sean. 1988b. "PD of the Week." *Billboard*, August 20, 1988.

Ross, Sean. 1989a. "PD of the Week." *Billboard*, January 7, 1989.

Ross, Sean. 1989b. "10 Years After the Disco Boom, Some Rock, Some Dance." *Billboard*, April 22, 1989.

Ross, Sean. 1990a. "The '80s; Broadcasters Remember 'Money Decade.'" *Billboard*, January 6, 1990.

Ross, Sean. 1990b. "Teens, Adults Split on Top 40 Hits." *Billboard*, February 3, 1990.

Ross, Sean. 1990c. "More Dance Stations Are Now Stepping to an Urban Beat." *Billboard*, October 6, 1990.

Ross, Sean. 1990d. "Why Mom Hates Rap, Why It Doesn't Matter (and Other Notes on the Top 40 Crisis)." *Billboard*, November 3, 1990.

Ross, Sean, and Yvonne Olson. 1988. "Vox Jox." *Billboard*, October 8, 1988.

Schmalz, Jeffrey. 1989. "Miami Officer Guilty in 2 Killings That Prompted Rioting by Blacks." *New York Times*, December 8, 1989.

Simmons, Russell. 1985. "Rap Visionary Russell Simmons 'It's More Than Making Records, It's Building Careers.'" *Billboard*, April 20, 1985.

Stark, Phyllis. 1994. "Top 40 Swinging Mainstream?" *Billboard*, February 12, 1994.

Steinback, Robert L. 1990. "Adults Can Learn from Hammer's Rap." *Miami Herald*, November 9, 1990.

Terry, Ken. 1988. "Crossover Pioneers Leaning Top 40." *Billboard*, May 21, 1988.

Thornton, Linda. 1985a. "Tanner Returns in $1 Million Deal." *Miami Herald*, January 4, 1985.

Thornton, Linda. 1985b. "Mr. Wake-Up's New Shake-Up." *Miami Herald*, January 10, 1985.

Thornton, Linda. 1985c. "Follow-Up Stresses 'Life's' Strength." *Miami Herald*, April 27, 1985.

Thornton, Linda. 1985d. "Rivals Put Heat on Hot 105." *Miami Herald*, July 19, 1985.

Thornton, Linda. 1986a. "Radio Hot 105 Ousts Tanner, Three Others." *Miami Herald*, June 4, 1986.

Thornton, Linda. 1986b. "Will New Power 96 Pack a Punch? Time Will Tell." *Miami Herald*, August 6, 1986.

Thornton, Linda. 1986c. "Miami Outlets Go for Pieces of Pie." *Billboard*, September 20, 1986.

Turow, Joseph. 1997. *Breaking Up America: Advertisers and the New Media World*. Chicago: University of Chicago Press. https://doi.org/10.7208/chicago/9780226817514.001.0001.

Viglucci, Andres. 1989. "Radio War Hits Nerve in Black Miami." *Miami Herald*, August 7, 1989.

Washington, Kevin. 1985. "In Tune with the Listeners." *Miami Herald*, October 13, 1985.

Weisbard, Eric. 2014. *Top 40 Democracy: The Rival Mainstreams of American Music*. Chicago: University of Chicago Press. https://doi.org/10.7208/chicago/9780226194370.001.0001.

White, John Wallace. 1997. "Radio Formats and the Transformation of Musical Style: Codes and Cultural Values in the Remaking of Tunes." *College Music Symposium* 37: 1–12.

"Double the Struggle"
Chicano/Latino Hip Hop in *The Source* Magazine

Dianne Violeta Mausfeld

Abstract *The contributions of Latinos and Chicanos to hip hop have not been studied nearly as much as those of African American hip-hop artists. While it is largely acknowledged that Latinos played an active part in the creation of hip hop in New York, their contributions in Los Angeles are rarely included in West Coast hip-hop history. At the same time, Chicano/Latino actors are not represented in the popular narrative of the East Coast/West Coast conflict. Aiming to address this research gap, this chapter locates LA Latino and Chicano artists within the East Coast/West Coast dialectic and explores how it affected their careers. Drawing on discourse analysis of the East Coast-based hip-hop publication* The Source, *as well as ethnographic interviews with Chicano and Latino artists on the West Coast, this chapter offers a fresh perspective on hip hop's most infamous conflict. Media coverage of Chicano/Latino artists in* The Source *was scarce during the 1990s and clearly written from an East Coast perspective. My ethnography shows that Latino and Chicano artists faced "double the struggle" to build their careers in hip hop during the 1990s, as they were not only affected by the place-based east/west antagonism, but also by their ethno-cultural classification within music industry discourse. Despite this separation, my findings show that artists' alliances and collaborations do not necessarily run along the lines of an assumed sense of belonging to an ethnic group ("Pan-Latinidad", Rivera 2003) or coast.*

In the Fall of 2022, Bronx-born MC Fat Joe presented the annual BET Awards—proving that a Latino in hip hop can hold his own with African

American artists on a network that, according to its name, "Black Entertainment Television," originally focused on Black culture and music. Fat Joe's involvement was promoted by the network, who hailed him as "hip-hop royalty... [who] has represented the art form and the Bronx, the birthplace of hip-hop" (Lamarre 2022). On social media, however, this announcement was not always celebrated, with Fat Joe's engagement for this award show being called into question because of the artist's ethnicity. Born Joseph Cartagena to a Cuban father and a Puerto Rican mother in The Bronx (Rivera 2003: 222; Fat Joe 2022), Fat Joe was criticized for not representing hip hop because of his Latino and Caribbean heritage, while some even viewed him as "white" (Ocho 2022). Earlier that year, Fat Joe had already faced a similar wave of outrage after posting a video on Instagram that celebrated Latino/a participation in the beginnings of hip hop (@fatjoe, August 25, 2022), whereafter users had accused him of "stealing the culture from blacks" (Eustice 2022). In an interview with Jay Williams at National Public Radio (NPR), Fat Joe explained that he grew up in an overwhelmingly Black section of the South Bronx, "blond hair, green eyes—knowing I'm Latino but thinking I'm Black" (Williams and Fat Joe 2022). He confidently argued against the social media backlash, stating that he witnessed the birth of hip hop as a multi-ethnic culture and that he never experienced racism because of his ethnicity (ibid.). Still, the above debate exemplifies that in hip hop, ethnicity can still trump local origin: Fat Joe may be from The Bronx, the birthplace of hip hop, but his Latin ethnicity does not appear to give him the full ownership of hip hop in the eyes of fans and critics who consider hip hop a Black culture.

In hip-hop scholarship, likewise differing points of views are expressed on the ethno-cultural ownership of hip-hop culture, but it is largely acknowledged that Latinos took part in the creation of hip hop in New York, first and foremost Puerto Ricans (Flores 2000; Rivera 2003; Chang 2005; McFarland 2008). Latino/a and Mexican American contributions in Los Angeles, in contrast, are rarely included in West Coast hip-hop history or in the overall narrative of gangster rap that influenced hip-hop styles in the US and abroad. Fat Joe started his musical career in the early 1990s with the overwhelmingly Black rap crew D.I.T.C. and released his solo album *Representin'* in 1993. Though never concealing his ethnic background and always including nods to his culture in his music, he did not necessarily highlight this as much as Latino rappers from the West Coast such as Mellow Man Ace and Kid Frost: two artists who emerged a few years earlier that Fat Joe cites as a big influence on his artistry (Donohue 2018).

Back in the 1990s, social media was yet to be born, and hip-hop journalism largely featured in music publications, at times newspapers, and mostly in magazines dedicated to hip-hop culture that were almost exclusively East Coast-based—the most influential of these being *The Source*. Fat Joe, as well as the late Big Pun (Christopher Rios), who was signed to the former's Terror Squad label, went on to have far greater success and enjoy(ed) far more media attention than Latino rappers from the West Coast. On the surface, this inequality between the coasts bears resemblance to the highly mediatized "East Coast/West Coast beef." Quinn (2005: 84) states that "there was a simmering hostility based on market neglect and lack of exposure." New York hip-hop artists claimed the culture for themselves, overshadowing Los Angeles artists who developed an "inferiority complex" due to the neglect of labels and media outlets that were primarily based on the East Coast (ibid.). However, Latinos in hip hop did not partake in the conflict. The East Coast/West Coast-rivalry centered around African American rappers Tupac Shakur and Biggie Smalls and their respective labels Death Row Records and Bad Boy and culminated in the deaths of both rappers in 1996 and 1997, respectively (Keyes 2002: 167–71). Latinos/as and Chicanos/as are not represented at all in the popular narrative of the East Coast/West Coast division, despite the fact that they were affected by these animosities all the same. On the contrary, the myth of "pan-*latinidad*" (Rivera 2003) promotes Latino unity in hip hop across coasts and countries of origin.

Latinidad, "Latino-ness," describes "a unified U.S. Latina/o identity straightforwardly linked to a Latin American heritage that in some fundamental way binds together various disparate groups, such as… Chicanos/as, Puerto Ricans, Cuban Americans, [and] Mexican Americans" (Kirschner 2019: 340). Within hip hop, Latino artists are considered "the minority" (Weisberg 1998). Many Latino hip-hop artists, alongside some hip-hop journalists, proclaim a Latino unity that grows out of this marginalized position, and not only cuts across countries of origin in the Caribbean or Latin America, but across coastal affiliations as well. Rivera (2003: 106) refers here to "pan-*latinidad*," a highly essentializing concept that presupposes that Latinos, Afro-Latinos, and Caribbean Latinos "have experiences, histories, identities, and solidarities that 'naturally' place them within the pan-Latino aggregate." This assumption not only blurred the heterogeneity of Latinos in the US, it also forced Puerto Ricans in hip hop to pick sides, although "Latino and Afro-diasporic identities… are not mutually exclusive identities" (ibid.: 107).

"Racial identities are not categorically fixed," Suzanne Oboler and Anani Dzidzienyo (2005: 12) remind us, "they are subject to constant fluctuations in terms of both their meanings and social value." In hip hop, these identities operate at the intersection of *perceived* race/ethnicity and publicly *acknowledged* race/ethnicity, as the above debates around Fat Joe exemplify. Afro-Latinos and -Caribbeans in particular, have occupied an invisible threshold in the Black and Latino binary since hip hop's early days in the 1970s and 1980s. Many Puerto Ricans in early New York hip hop were assumed to be African American because of their dark complexion and slang (Rivera 2003: 75). Furthermore, many artists did not challenge this representation, as in the example of Ruby Dee of the Fantastic Five MCs, who in Charlie Ahearn's classic hip-hop film *Wild Style* (1983) raps: "Well, Ruby Dee is my name, and I'm a Puerto Rican/ You might think I'm Black by the way I'm speakin.'" Afrika Bambaataa, in turn, considered "Black" and "Caribbean" one and the same, as he stated in an interview with Nelson George (1993: 48) in *The Source*: "Now one thing people must know, that when we say black we mean all our Puerto Rican or Dominican brothers. Wherever hip-hop was and the blacks was, the Latinos and the Puerto Ricans was too." It is worth pointing out that all three "founding fathers" of hip hop—Afrika Bambaataa, DJ Kool Herc, and Grandmaster Flash—are of West Indian descent (Chang 2005; Keyes 2002: 54). Again, this was not a well-known fact during the early days of hip hop and is only alluded to in the above interview by George. In the case of Fat Joe, his very light-skinned phenotype allows for him to be perceived as "White" and thus his authority in hip hop to be called into question—despite his publicly embraced Cuban and Puerto Rican ancestry. Shortly after he had hosted the BET awards, in an interview on *The Breakfast Club* at the New York radio station Power 105.1, Fat Joe called out "colorism" in hip hop, stating that there would always be critics who did not accept him as a spokesperson for the culture simply because "he does not have the right look" (Breakfast Club 2022).[1]

On the West Coast, I encountered similar debates on "perceived ethnicity" in my ethnography of the Latino and Chicano hip-hop scene. Afro-Cuban rapper Mellow Man Ace remembers that, growing up, "Mexican kids didn't understand how come we [he and his brother, Sen Dog of Cypress Hill] were Black and spoke fluent Spanish. And Blacks didn't understand how we were Black and didn't speak English."[2] On the other hand, African American rapper Hi-C who was produced by Mexican American DJ Tony A. was frequently assumed to be half-Mexican because of his sound and use of "Spanglish" slang.[3] Cypress Hill, hailed "the biggest Latinos in the game" by Fat Joe (Donohue 2018), and arguably the most famous "Latin rap group on the planet" (McFarland 2008: 41), did not even want to be promoted as such and successfully built a fan base that far exceeded Latino and even hip-hop audiences on both coasts.

In this chapter, I aim to locate LA Latino and Chicano artists in the East Coast/West Coast dialectic during the 1990s, examining their relationship and media representation within the Latino hip-hop community, and the wider overwhelmingly African American hip-hop scene.[4]

---

1 What adds to the complexity of these issues is the use of the n-word by Latino artists. Fat Joe, who prominently used it on his 1993-track "Another Wild N***** From The Bronx," explains that he has been subjected to the term (used with a positive connotation) ever since his childhood despite his light-skinned phenotype and started to identify with it (Breakfast Club 2022).
2 Mellow Man Ace, interview by author, May 13, 2019, Alhambra, CA.
3 Tony A., interview by author, May 9, 2019, Los Angeles, CA.
4 The artists covered in this article are all male, which is why I mostly use the terms "Latino" and "Chicano." "Chicano/a" and "Latino/a" imply that the addressed group includes females. Occasionally, "Latino" is used as an umbrella

In the first part, I briefly sketch out the creative connections and influences between Latinos on the East and West Coasts. Drawing on Raquel Rivera's (2003) notion of "pan-*latinidad*" in hip hop, I will then examine the dialectical relation between East Coast and West Coast Latinos/as that suggests Latino unity is more fiction than fact. The main portion of the chapter concentrates on close readings of examples of how Latinos in hip hop were represented in the East Coast-based hip-hop publication *The Source* and explore if pan-*latinidad* applies.

The methodology brings together ethnographic interviews with Chicano and Latino artists conducted in 2019, 2022, and 2023, and discourse analysis of *The Source* magazine. While a complete physical archive of *The Source* does not appear to exist, the very well-organized Houston Hip Hop Archives Network at Rice University in Houston, Texas, holds a large collection of issues. There, I viewed 84 issues from 1990 to 2001, including numerous consecutive issues, which enabled me to examine discourse spanning over various issues and even years.[5] I also found several issues of *The Source* online, where fans had scanned and posted them for the community.[6] So, while I am drawing on a relatively large body of sources, I nonetheless highlight examples surrounding the discourse of pan-*latinidad*. Today, the magazine has a "Source Latino" section dedicated to Latino artists in hip hop and related genres such

---

term for people of Latin descent that is not meant to exclude persons who do not identify with it for reasons of gender or ethnicity. I do not use "Latinx" or "Chicanx" because these terms are not widely accepted in the community and are particularly rejected by some Chicano artists. "Latino hip hop" and "Chicano hip hop" are established genre terms, although there are debates about their validity as well (Rivera 2003; McFarland 2008; 2013; Castillo-Garsow and Nichols 2016).

[5] I visited the Houston Hip Hop Archives Network at the Fondren Library at Rice University in Houston, Texas, in 2019, 2022, and 2023. The issues of *The Source* can be requested under the call number ML3531 .S68 and viewed in the reading room. Many thanks to the staff for their assistance and support.

[6] Two gems of *The Source*, issues 28 and 40, are available at Internet Archive (archive.org), partial scans of further issues are available at *THMK*, a blog published by Vincent Lopez (http://thimkingman.blogspot.com).

as R&B, reggaetón etc.—but in the early-to-mid-1990s, coverage was scarce and clearly written from an East Coast perspective, often one-sided and even condescending.

My ethnography shows that Latinos and Chicanos had "double the struggle" to build their careers in hip hop during the 1990s, as they were not only affected by the place-based east/west antagonism, but also by ethno-cultural classification in the music industry. Focusing on media coverage of Chicano and Latino artists, as well as personal and musical influences that occurred between the coasts, this chapter offers a fresh perspective on the most famous divide in hip hop.

The Latino Hip-Hop Diaspora and Pan-*Latinidad*

The beginnings of Latino and Chicano hip hop on the West Coast can be traced back to Cuban American Mellow Man Ace (Ulpiano Sergio Reyes) and Mexican American Kid Frost (Arturo Molina Jr., commonly referred to as 'Frost'). Mellow Man Ace's hit single "Mentirosa" (1990) and Frost's "La Raza" (1990) are largely considered to be the corner stones of both genres because of the Spanglish lyrics and the Latin-tinged music samples. Both artists' sound is indebted to Cuban American DJ-producer Tony G. (Tony Gonzalez), who grew up between New York and Miami and moved to Los Angeles as a teenager. "Mentirosa" was "the first Latino rap record to go gold," as Juan Flores points out (2000: 115), and both Mellow Man Ace and Frost are frequently referred to as the "Godfather of Latin Rap," although the latter is better known as the "Godfather of Chicano Rap." While neither one of them particularly minds these titles, both artists shared with me that Puerto Ricans from the East Coast were instrumental to them: Mr. Schick (Daniel Rivera Jr.) of the New York group Mean Machine was the main influence for Mellow Man Ace to start rapping in Spanglish; and Frost proudly recalls how important it was for him to have Prince Whipper Whip (James Whipper II) of the Fantastic Five MCs endorse his music, as he assured him that "La Raza" was going to be a hit, when he played it for him before it was released.[7] Before he went solo in the late 1980s, Mellow Man Ace was part of the group Cypress Hill. He recalls that producer DJ Muggs (Lawrence Muggerud), an Italian American from Queens, made sure the group members listened to a lot of East Coast music. Because of their sound, the group was frequently assumed to be from New York, not Los Angeles.[8]

Frost and Tony G. initiated the first bicoastal Latin hip-hop supergroup Latin Alliance, which Mellow Man Ace was also a part of. The short-lived project included artists from various Latino backgrounds and released their sole self-titled album on Virgin Records in 1991. Group member Zulu Gremlin (Steve Roybal) views the importance of the group as not only bicoastal but also pan-Latino: "So, the Latin Alliance was the first assembled crew that had… Mexicans, Spanish, Puerto Ricans, Cubans, and Nicaraguans all in one crew."[9] Zulu Gremlin stresses, however, that the foundation of the Latino movement in hip hop came into existence in New York with Latino crews and artists like the "legendary Charlie Chase and Whipper Whip from Fantastic Five. But they weren't known as Latinos, they were known as members of legendary old school crews. … So, we were like the ones that followed [in] their footsteps, the next generation." Zulu Gremlin was very specific on chronology, pointing out that the creative flows started on the East Coast before they went west. His notion that not every Latino artist in hip hop *was known to be Latino* is very important when we consider the evolutions of the genres Latino and Chicano hip hop—and the fact that artists who did not advertise as Latinos in part had more success on a nationwide level. In his piece "How Ya Like Nosotros Now?" in the *Village Voice*, Ed Morales (1991: 91) announced that Latin Alliance was "a defining moment in the creation of a nationwide Latino/Americano hip hop aesthetic," claiming: "Where once the folks on opposite coasts were strangers, they've become one nation kicking Latin lingo on top of a scratch', sampling' substrate" (quoted in Flores 2000). Yet, even the members of Latin Alliance stated that their project

---

7   Frost, interview by author, Pasadena, CA, May 13, 2019.
8   Mellow Man Ace, interview by author, Monterey Park, CA, May 13, 2019.
9   Zulu Gremlin, phone interview by author, April 16, 2019.

was more of a vision, than a mirror of the actual disposition within the Latino communities themselves. As Mellow Man Ace put it: "There was no alliance in the communities, but we tried to lead by example with the project. And I think that was a beautiful thing that Kid Frost spearheaded, because eventually that started to happen."[10]

The Latin Alliance project promoted Latino unity along the lines of shared struggles of colonization, for example on their track "Latinos Unidos (United Latins)," but at the same time stressed the diverse origins of the contributing artists. Each verse is addressing a different aspect of the colonization of the Americas, sometimes related to the artists' ancestry and locality. Markski (Mark Santiago), for example, recalls the history of Puerto Rico and proudly self-identifies as a "Bronx-Rican." Frost, on the other hand, is addressing Chicanos in the state of California in his verse and implores rivaling Mexican American gangs (*Sureños* and *Norteños*) to make peace. So, within efforts to unite Latinos across the US, there is the aim to unite on a much smaller scale just within the Chicano community in California. Given these local conflicts, it is not surprising that unification on a national scale was an uphill battle.

Elaborating on the variety of Latino backgrounds of hip-hop artists was not always the case, as Raquel Rivera (2003) and Juan Flores (2000) point out. In their respective works on the agency of Puerto Ricans in East Coast hip hop, both criticize the idea of "pan-Latin unity" or "pan-*latinidad*" that supposedly unites Latinos/as in hip hop no matter where they are from and hereby blurs the heterogeneity of the Latino community. Flores (2000: 116) notes that "the 'Latinization' of hip-hop has meant its distancing from the specific national and ethnic traditions to which it had most directly pertained." Similarly, Rivera (2003: 103) suggests:

> In the haste to rescue Latinos from historical invisibility and to acknowledge their current role within hip hop, essentialized connections... are drawn, and crucial differences among groups within the Nation pan-ethnic conglomerate are slighted. The role played by New

---

10   Mellow Man Ace, interview by author, Monterey Park, CA, May 13, 2019.

York Puerto Ricans in hip-hop culture has been different from that of other Caribbean Latin groups in New York; the differences are even greater when Puerto Ricans are compared to Chicanos and other Latinos on the West Coast. But these specificities have become obscured by the growing force of *la gran familia latina* (the great Latino family) discourse within hip hop. The historical and current connections between Afro-diasporic Latinos and African Americans in New York are at times muted or even drowned out by the naturalizing call of pan-*latinidad*.

Rivera (ibid.: 10) critiques the "contradictory effects of the *latinidad* pan-ethnic discourse" that lie at the core of the self-understanding of Latino artists in hip hop as well as journalistic and academic scholarship on the topic, which in turn leads to misconceptions and oversimplifications of the diverse Latino demographic involved. Besides the conflation of the heterogenous Latino community in hip hop, Rivera (ibid.: 105) considers the rallying behind the collective term "Latino" problematic as it does not do justice to the specificity of Puerto Rican agency in New York, and permits other Latino groups to free ride on their accomplishments:

> Although the Latinos who participated in hip hop's earliest history were specifically Caribbean Latinos and overwhelmingly New York Puerto Ricans, the Latino aggregate as a whole reaps the claim to hip hop historical presence and authenticity. A transcoastal, transnational Latino 'us' enables this collectivization of the experience of a sector within the Latino population.

This sense of belonging to the "Latino hip-hop diaspora" was confirmed in the interviews I conducted in the scene as well. Numerous artists proudly reiterated that Latinos were involved in the creation of hip hop on both coasts, such as Frost who said: "*we've been a part of the movement of rap and hip hop as a whole since the origin. With Latinos in [the movie] Breakin', with the Rock Steady Crew and all that* [my emphasis]."[11] By mentioning *Breakin'*, Frost stresses the importance of

---

11 Frost, interview by author, May 13, 2019, Pasadena, CA.

Latinos in the creation of breakdance not only on the East Coast but especially on the West Coast, which was echoed in numerous interviews. The opinion that Latinos were instrumental in hip hop "since day one" was also expressed by Latino artists in Chang Weisberg's (1998) feature article "Hip Hop's Minority?" in *Industry Insider Magazine*. The magazine had brought together several Latino artists from both coasts for a Latino "summit" in New York that was covered by Weisberg for his article. A group shot of the artists involved—including Fat Joe, Big Pun, Kid Frost, Psycho Realm, Delinquent Habits, and Cypress Hill—graced the cover of the magazine. The image was shot by Estevan Oriol, a photographer and director of Mexican and Italian descent from Los Angeles, who was Cypress Hill's tour manager during the 1990s and is responsible for many iconic pictures of the group. This cover of *Industry Insider Magazine* is famous in the community and was mentioned to me frequently, also by artists who were not included.[12] ODM (Robert Gutierrez) from the Chicano rap group Lighter Shade of Brown from Riverside, California, for example, still regrets not having been there for this rare reunion.[13] Interestingly, most artists confuse *Industry Insider Magazine* with *The Source* or *XXL*—more prestigious hip-hop magazines that hardly ever put Latino artists on their front cover at that time.[14]

---

12 The cover and article have been posted on social media by several of the involved artists, for instance by Eric Bobo of Cypress Hill (2020) and Kemo the Blaxican of Delinquent Habits (2022).

13 ODM, interview by author, April 27, 2023, Corona, CA.

14 This confusion might be related to an even more iconic cover by *XXL*, entitled "The Greatest Day in Hip-Hop History," that brought together almost 200 hip-hop artists (mostly African American, but Fat Joe and DJ Muggs were also there) in September 1998 in front of a brownstone in Harlem, New York. And while Oriol's cover appears to be very much informed by this photograph—although the artists are lined up at the harbor, not in front of a brownstone—it actually came out a few months later. Therefore, it is more likely that Oriol's source of inspiration was the same as *XXL*'s, who drew their idea for the cover from Art Kane's "A Great Day in Harlem" photograph from 1958 that captured Jazz-icons such as Count Basie and Thelonious Monk in the very same spot in Harlem (Gonzalez 2014).

Rivera (2003: 105) criticizes Weisberg for "construct[ing] a mythical, pan-ethnic bond between Latino artists" in his article, but points out that the "family"-centered narrative was also expressed by some of the artists. Sick Jacken of the LA group Psycho Realm is cited as saying "Since we're all Latinos it's like were [sic] all family" (Weisberg 1998: 50–51). New York-based artists also claim that being Latino was more important than East Coast/West Coast affiliations, as for example Big Pun: "It's Latino first. That's more important than East/West. That's familia. That's La Raza" (ibid.). Fat Joe agrees: "Since we're Latino, I feel that we're all spiritual in a way. It doesn't matter if you're Mexican, Puerto Rican, Cuban, Columbian [sic], or whatever. ... It doesn't matter if you're from the West Coast or the East Coast. We're Latino. ... We cut across all that shit" (ibid.).[15] Rivera (2003: 105) concludes that "the Latino unity that these artists are advocating is as much a commercial necessity and market strategy as a spiritual, familial or historical imperative" due to Latinos' marginalization in a business dominated by African Americans. Almost twenty-five years after this "Latino summit," these opinions still remain strong among the West Coast Latino artists I interviewed. Kid Frost also referred to Latinos as "hip hop's minority" in a predominantly Black industry.[16] ODM confirmed that Latinos in hip hop did not participate in the East Coast/West Coast beef: "You didn't hear Big Pun dissing West Coast. You didn't hear Fat Joe dissing West Coast. It was all love. In fact, when we would run into Fat Joe on tour, it was all love. ... 'Cause there weren't many of us doing it, mainstream. So, for the most part, the artists stuck together."[17]

But paradoxically, transcoastal collaborations between Latino artists were rare in the 1990s. Apart from Latin Alliance, there were not many collaborative efforts. Delinquent Habits from LA are an exception as they featured the late New York Latina rapper Hurricane G. (Gloria

---

15   These quotes can also be retrieved in rare footage of the meeting in New York that was posted on Instagram by Kemo the Blaxican of Delinquent Habits (2023).
16   Frost, interview by author, May 13, 2019, Pasadena, CA.
17   ODM, interview by author, April 27, 2023, Corona, CA.

Rodríguez) on the track "Underground Connection" on their debut album *Delinquent Habits* in 1996. According to Rivera (2003: 104), "[t]he virtual lack of collaboration—particularly cross-coastal—among these artists… exposes this celebrated Latino unity as either still forthcoming or wishful thinking." ODM confirmed in our interview, that his group Lighter Shade of Brown "never really collab'ed with anybody on the East Coast, just producers."[18] What came up repeatedly in my interviews was the soundtrack of *I Like It Like That*, Darnell Martin's 1994 motion picture, which is set in The Bronx but features East- and West Coast Latino artists on its soundtrack. As Henry Puente (2012) points out, however, the promotional strategy of *I Like It Like That* focused on the African American director, not the Latino/a cast or soundtrack and despite massive publicity on the West Coast, the movie was not a success at the box office. According to Puente (ibid.: 65), this was largely due to the excessive marketing around the African American director Darnell Martin in Black media and the lack of promotion of the Latino/a cast, while the Latina PR director on the West Coast argued that "Mexican Americans did not relate to this Puerto Rican story" (ibid.). So, one of the rare occasions in the 1990s to find Latino/a artists from both coasts on the same record was due to marketing strategies of studio executives—not as a result of personal artist connections or an expression of pan-*latinidad*. In addition, the success of the movie was diminished by marketing strategies that built on false commonalities between Latinos in the US.

Hip-hop publication *The Source* criticized the "Cinderella story" Columbia Studios used to market Martin as the first African American woman to direct a feature length film in their only article on the subject—which ironically also focused on her and failed to mention the Latino/a cast or the Latino hip-hop soundtrack. The piece explains that even though the protagonist Lisette (played by actress Lauren Vélez) is "Black and Puerto Rican," the director herself was not, but that "she based the characters on Latin relatives, neighbors and friends" (*Source* 1994a: 32). Oddly enough, *The Source* as a magazine for "music, culture

---

18   ODM, phone interview by author, May 9, 2019.

and politics" does not mention the soundtrack at all—it only appeared in an advertisement one month later (*Source* 1994b: n.pag.). This omission of Latino/a artists fits into the overall lack of Latino representation in *The Source*, as we will see now.

Chicano/Latino Representation in *The Source* Magazine

Often referred to as "The Bible of Hip Hop," *The Source* magazine was founded in 1988 as a concert newsletter by two Jewish Harvard University students David Mays und Jonathan "Jon" Shector in Cambridge, Massachusetts, and moved its headquarters to New York City in 1990. The magazine represented a clear East Coast stance and focused on African American issues, considering hip hop as a primarily Black art form. This helps to explain why Latinos/as and Chicanos/as in hip hop from both coasts were not portrayed nearly as much as African American rappers and producers. New York Latinos such as Fat Joe and Big Pun, as well as Cypress Hill from LA received some coverage. In my study of Latino representation in *The Source* and the analysis of pan-*latinidad* I include hip-hop artists, journalists and fans/readers, whose opinions were voiced in the form of letters to the editor.

For the analysis of pan-*latinidad* in this medium, staff writer Ronin Ro, a Puerto Rican from the South Bronx, is an important figure. The magazine itself introduced him as an "eccentric character [that] has churned out some of the most controversial and exciting pieces in The Source" who "describes himself as a 'fast livin', shit talkin', freelancin', rhymin' hip-hop maniac from the South Bronx'" (*Source* 1993a: 14). Ro made a name for himself in *The Source* but also wrote for other hip-hop publications and authored several books. His debut, *Gangsta: Merchandising the Rhymes of Violence* (1996), a collection of essays about gangster rap on the West Coast, included journalistic work published in *The Source*, *Rap Pages*, and *Spin*. In contrast to Rivera's (2003) examples for pan-*latinidad* in hip-hop journalism, Ro did not seem to feel this kinship and thus did not portray Latino artists on the West Coast in a particularly good light. In *The Source*'s June issue of 1992, Ro (1992a: 56) authored a review of Frost's second studio album *East Side Story* (1992), stating:

> Frost understands his people on the West Coast and speaks to them about things they can understand: police harassment, drive-by's [sic], dying young, jail and trigger happy gangbangers. But musically the album suffers from too many melodies, sung choruses, familiar samples and old sounds. ... Maybe it's a West Coast thang and I'll never understand but methinks [sic] Frost could use some new breakbeats and a more exciting lyrical delivery 'cause as it stands now, not many outside of East LA will catch the vibe of this record.

The album received two and a half microphones out of five. Musical reviews are subjective and while Ro is acknowledging that "maybe it's a West Coast thang" [that he]'ll never understand," he also assumes that Frost's music could only be successful in East LA, an unincorporated part of LA County with a Mexican American demographic of 95 percent in 1990 (*Los Angeles Times* 1991). While it is a common misbelief that East LA is the only part of Greater LA to produce Mexican American art and music, it demonstrates Ro's East Coast stance and just how little he understands of the rising Chicano rap scene on the West Coast that included Chicano and Latino artists from all over LA County, San Diego, and the Bay Area. Ro also clearly differentiates between himself and Frost ("*his people* on the West Coast," my emphasis) and does not seem to register any "pan-Latin" commonality between them.

Shortly after this review, Ro was assigned a think piece on Frost and flew out to LA. The feature article entitled "Riding Shotgun" was published in the September issue of 1992 and is a Gonzoesque account of an interview trip to Los Angeles in the aftermath of the LA riots. The piece chronicles a day with Frost and some of his fellow artists, with stops at Frost's home in Van Nuys and a lowrider car show and concert in Pomona, California, including gang violence at the scene. In his book *Gangsta*, Ro (1996: 14) voiced his concerns about what Frost might have to say about his critical review in more detail than in *The Source*, and even included a backstory of why he did not want to cover the story in the first place, wondering "why, one month after dissing Frost's album in the *The Source* review section, I accepted this assignment." He goes on to describe a conversation with the then editor-in-chief Jon Shecter, urging him to cover Frost, even though Ro wanted to cover Public Enemy: "'Just do your Kid Frost story for "La Raza,"' he [Jon Shector] laughed. 'But no one wants to read about this guy!' I countered. 'Nobody likes his shit!' 'Frost has a large regional audience in parts of Texas,' I was told. What would I write about? I thought; Frost's whole 'Mexican Chuck D' schtick?" (ibid.) The editor seemed to assume that Ro as a New York Puerto Rican was a perfect fit to cover a Mexican American artist on the West Coast and that Ro shared the interest for "la raza." Clearly, he was mistaken. The mention of the "regional audience in parts of Texas" points to the fact that Chicano hip hop developed as a phenomenon in the Southwest throughout the 1990s (McFarland 2006; Mausfeld 2021) and that its audiences were not based in New York—which for Ro obviously made it less interesting for a feature article. This again demonstrates the New York-centeredness of Ro's perspective and that pan-*latinidad* was not a given among hip-hop artists and journalists. Ro mentions that the Samoan American group Boo-Ya Tribe also complained about record reviews published in *The Source*, establishing the impression that West Coast artists and *The Source* did not seem to have the best relationship at the time. Mellow Man Ace, however, who is covered only in passing in the "Riding Shotgun" article but has his own chapter in the book *Gangsta*, remembers Ro as a "really good dude [who] loved hip hop."[19] Interestingly, he has no recollection of Ro's ethnicity, only that he was from the East Coast.

Overall, violence and tensions are the main sentiments in the four-page article *Riding Shotgun*—a play on words of Ro's front-row seat to the events and actual use of arms—within the city of LA as well within the Latino hip-hop community. Announced on the cover of the magazine with the teaser "Kid Frost and Latino Gang Culture," the article focuses on Kid Frost's (alleged) link to gang culture, not his music. The pull quote on the third page of the article reads: "At the car show, I watch someone

---

19   Mellow Man Ace, interview by author, Hacienda Heights, CA, March 18, 2022.

get stabbed up five feet away from me. I watch him bleed as the victors run by me smiling" (Ro 1992b: 34). In the text, the stabbing is described more vividly, yet Ro trivializes it, noting: "I almost have to laugh at this senseless violence" (ibid.). Despite the raw violence that he experienced on his trip to LA, Ro (ibid.: 32) was not shy to broadcast what fellow Latino artists thought of Frost, quoting one group as saying: "It seems that Kid Frost is at war with other rappers. ... Particularly Latinos."

While I can corroborate the tensions within the Chicano hip-hop community, as I was confronted with them throughout my fieldwork, I am very careful with this information and would never print any names. I therefore find it highly troubling for Ro to publish these rumors in a nationwide magazine as he clearly did not reflect upon what might happen to the artists who now went on record speaking out against Frost. It also opposes the notion of pan-*latinidad*, while at the same time contributing to negative stereotypes about Latinos and Chicanos. While his article is certainly an interesting account of LA shortly after the riots and the heavy gang problem that LA was dealing with at the time, Ro is putting the tension in the city and in the music industry on the same stance as the unbridgeable gap between hip-hop culture in New York and LA.

In comparison to the extended version in *Gangsta*, Ro's piece in *The Source* was harmless, but it was still not well received by Latino/a readers. Several issues after the article, a letter by Luis from New Jersey was published in the "letters to the editor" section (*Source* 1993b: 11), entitled "Latino Love," criticizing Ro for not being "conscious" of Latino issues in the magazine:

> When are you going to hire a Brown conscious Latino(a) writer to do the knowledge from our perspective? I know you don't think Ronin Ro is it, because he's not. The brother is a good writer, don't get me wrong, but you need a Latino who is conscious about the state of his people, a Brown nationalist. ... Queremos Justicia! [We want justice]

Inspired by Luis' letter, Pequena (also from New Jersey), sent in a letter that was printed three issues later under the title "Latino Lessons"

(*Source* 1993c: 16). She views the lack of awareness for Latino issues in *The Source* as a mirror of overall society and particularly references the "Riding Shotgun" article:

> I also feel that Latinos are stereotyped, trivialized and in general ignored by not only our society but by your magazine as well. Barring the shameful piece on Kid Frost last year, which basically concluded that all Chicanos are *vatos locos* [gang members] out to kill each other, I have never seen a feature or interview with a Latino artist. How many people out there know that the lowriders that Dr. Dre and Ice Cube drive around in their videos were invented by the Chicano members of La Raza?

It is interesting that these letters were written by East Coast Latinos/as, but in the case of Pequena, advocated for the involvement of Chicanos on the West Coast. She is addressing an issue that came up repeatedly in my ethnographic interviews as well: that lowrider culture was in fact created by Chicanos but is often wrongfully attributed to African Americans because of its popularization in Black gangster rap. In the August issue of 1997, Roberto "Cuba" Jimenez II, from Hawaiian Gardens, California, complained that: "THE SOURCE doesn't cover any Latino artists. I also wanted to add that LA isn't only filled with Crips and Bloods. The majority of LA is Latin or cholos—'Ese's' [Mexican American gang members]. All I'm saying is recognize the majority from the minority" (*Source* 1997: 22). Similar to Pequena, Roberto felt the need to educate other readers in his letter, since *The Source* did not. His clarification of the presence of Chicano gang culture shows that the misunderstanding of LA culture by *The Source* is two-tiered: not only does the East Coast not understand the West Coast, but it also fails to comprehend the ethnic diversity of hip hop and gang culture in LA—which is highly intertwined. In *Gangsta*, Ro dedicates a section to Chicano gang culture and its impact on gangster rap, yet only African American artists can be seen on the cover of the book. *The Source* readership seemed to band together in lamenting the lack of coverage of Latino issues, and in this sense are somewhat expressing pan-*latinidad*.

To be fair, one issue prior to Pequena's letter, in July 1993, *The Source* had put Cypress Hill on the cover (maybe her letter had not yet arrived at the magazine). Cypress Hill had been regularly mentioned in *The Source* even before their cover and feature story in this issue. It is important to remember, however, that Cypress Hill were not primarily promoting themselves as Latinos and rather performed at cross-genre festivals like Lollapalooza and Woodstock than lowrider car shows. The title of the story, "The Cypress Hill Experience," alludes to "The Jimi Hendrix Experience" and puts the group closer to psychedelic music from the 1970s than to hip hop (Gonzales 1993: 54). Author Michael A. Gonzales, focuses on the group's DJ-producer Muggs' New York roots, but does not mention the other group members B-Real's and Sen Dog's Latino ethnicity at all: B-Real (Louis Freese) is of Mexican and Cuban descent and Sen Dog (Senen Reyes) of Afro-Cuban descent.[20] This could be linked to the group's desire to be "mysterious" and not be judged based on their ethnicity alone, something which they have mentioned on several occasions.[21]

The late 1990s saw an increased Latinization of the hip-hop industry (Rivera 2003; Pacini Hernandez 2010). Rivera (2003: 116) notes that "[b]y 1998, not only had they been accepted and legitimized within hip hop, but Latino images and artists had become somewhat of a fad." This development was also reflected in hip-hop media and there is a noticeable change in the way Latinos are being portrayed in *The Source*, both in frequency and tone. In August 1997, an interview with Frost by

---

20 The literature is full of inaccurate ethnicities for the members of Cypress Hill, so I confirmed with B-Real and Sen Dog's brother, Mellow Man Ace, to verify this information. I was not able to meet Eric Bobo, son of Latin jazz legend Willie Bobo, who joined the group in 1994 and, according to several sources, is of Puerto Rican descent (Smithsonian n.d.).

21 See for example B-Real on American Latino TV (Pacheco 2012) and DJ Muggs on the footage of *Industry Insider Magazine's* Latino summit (Kemo the Blaxican 2023). In my personal interview with B-Real, however, he ascribed their strategy to stay mysterious to their heavy-metal influences, not their unwillingness to reveal their ethnicity (B-Real, interview by author, April 16, 2022, Los Angeles, CA).

Soren Baker showed Frost (who officially dropped the "Kid" in 1995), as a matured rapper and responsible family man and father, whose "place as one of hip-hop's West Coast legends is secure." Baker, a White journalist from Maryland who has written for several hip-hop publications and newspapers such as the *Los Angeles Times*, strikes a much more respectful tone than Ronin Ro did in the early 1990s. It is possible that Baker was more cautious, precisely because he is White and comes from neither LA nor New York, and therefore is a more neutral player than Ro.[22] In the same issue, two Chicano hip-hop albums are credited with three microphones in the Record Report section: Psycho Realm's debut *Psycho Realm* (1997), reviewed by Baker, and Frost's fourth studio album *When HelLA Freezes Over* (1997), addressed by Latino staff writer Rigoberto Morales.[23] Morales (1997: 156) starts his critique of Frost's album with a nod to the regional differences in Latin rap: "Depending on where you live, when you think of Latin rap acts that have made a name for themselves, Frost might not be the first name that pops out your mouth." Yet he acknowledges that Frost "has been on the forefront of West Coast and Latino hip-hop for a decade-plus" and that with this album he "attempts to expand his audience with a change in lyrics, beats and style," no longer exclusively catering to "the low rider section of hip-hop" (ibid.: 158). Morales closes his critique far more diplomatically compared to Ro's five years earlier: "Although Frost's musical style is surely not everyone's cup of tea, one cannot dismiss his significance in the rap world" (ibid.).

In 1998 and 1999, *The Source* published several issues with Latino topics. In March 1998, Carlito Rodriguez' article "Vamos a rapiar" (Let's rap) examined the Latino involvement in hip hop, even challenging the Afrocentricity of the culture, opening with the line: "They call hip-hop Black

---

22   In his epic *History of Gangster Rap* (2018) that focuses on gangster rap on the West Coast, however, Baker mentions hardly any Latino artists.
23   Rigoberto, better known as "Rigo" or "Riggs," Morales started his career as a music journalist for *The Source*, *XXL*, and *Vibe* among others before he became involved in music production and Artist & Repertoire. He is currently Executive Vice President of A&R at Def Jam Records (Morales 2023).

music. But is it?" (Rodriguez 1998: 152). Rodriguez is of Cuban and Dominican descent and, like Ro, grew up in the South Bronx. He joined the staff of *The Source* in 1996, had his own column "Carlito's Ways," in which he "wrote about upcoming music but also dropped in some cultural commentary" (King 2021), and even became editor in chief, before he left the magazine in 2002. Given the positive tone towards Latinos in this article, I assume he played a vital role in pushing Latino issues at *The Source*, besides pressures from readers and the overall Latinization of the music industry in the late 1990s. Big Pun received four microphones for his debut album *Capital Punishment* (1998) in the June issue of 1998, which was also the first album by a Latino rap artist to go Platinum.[24] In an article entitled "Spanish Fly" on Latino celebrities in sports, movies, and hip hop, author Kevin Baxter pondered: "If society hasn't changed, why has Latin culture suddenly become so hot? ... why are bicultural and bilingual acts such as Noreaga, Fat Joe, Big Punisher and Cypress Hill, los padrinos [the godfathers] of crossover hip-hop suddenly on top of rap's most-wanted list?" (1999: 138) The same issue entailed a feature article on Big Pun by Riggs (formerly Rigoberto) Morales (1999: 154–58).

The Source's readership showed appreciation for this turnaround and specifically rallied behind Big Pun. In the August issue of 1998, Jesus Rivera from Milwaukee wrote: "Much love goes out to THE SOURCE for finally giving props to Latino artists. It was a dream come true to see Big Pun receive four mics, and appear in the Best Buy section. Maybe one day we'll get a little piece of the front page" (Source 1998: n.pag.). The same issue entailed an article on Big Pun's album debut *Capital Punishment*. In April of 1999, Chris from Orlando, Florida, complimented the increased coverage on Big Pun, arguing that "Pun could be the next Biggie if people would stop limiting his abilities to the Latino community" (Source 1999a: 33). And Shorty, again from Milwaukee, expressed his happiness with Baxter's "Spanish Fly" article, especially because it entailed so much

---

[24] This issue of *The Source* is available on *THMK*, a blog published by Vincent Lopez (http://thimkingman.blogspot.com/2010/01/source-june-1998-issue-featuring-big.html).

Latino history. The letter concludes: "It's really refreshing to see Latinos make it in the industry. Viva la raza!" (*Source* 1999b: 33).

Regardless of the increased frequency of Latino issues in *The Source*, it is important to point out that New York Latino artists such as Fat Joe and Big Pun were featured more frequently than West Coast Latinos. This may not only be grounded in locale, but also in success as East Coast Latino/a artists were (and still are) far more successful than Latino/a and Chicano/a hip-hop artists from the West Coast. After the untimely passing of Big Pun in early 2000, the May issue of *The Source* did finally put him on the cover, a decision that was made shortly before his death, as Carlito Rodriguez explains in the editorial (2000: 32). The issue also featured a lengthy "Rest in peace" photo article focusing on the murals that were painted in his honor all over New York City. Rivera (2003: 174) writes about the big crowds that attended Big Pun's funeral and that he was posthumously covered in a wide range of media, from the *New York Post* to *New York Magazine* and *El Diario/La Prensa* (which had previously disregarded him completely). So, without diminishing Big Pun's talent or his presence in hip hop, this broad coverage also needs to be considered in the context of his passing.

Despite this regional focus on New York Puerto Ricans, most readers appreciated the acknowledgment and the newfound "Latino presence" as a success for Latinos in general. In some instances, however, internal group animosities were still quite apparent. A letter from Sergio, a "Cuban-American mc" from Miami, for example, thanks *The Source* for the recognition but also points out that "Cubans are overlooked by Dominicans and Puerto Ricans when it comes to hip-hop, but we appreciate it just as much" (*Source* 1998). In Roberto "Cuba" Jimenez's above-mentioned letter, "Vanishing Latino Acts," he enquires about Mellow Man Ace, Sen Dog, and Skatemaster Tate—all Angeleno rap artists of Cuban descent—and why they were not being covered in *The Source*. Judging by his precise interest in Cuban artists and his nickname, "Cuba," it is conceivable that this reader is himself of Cuban descent; regardless, he does not appear to dwell on it. Rather, his letter primarily aims to set the record straight on the Latino presence in LA, implying a critique of *The Source*'s East Coast stance that overlooks Latinos on the West Coast hip-hop spectrum (*Source* 1997).

Pan-*Latinidad*—Fact or Fiction?

Latino hip-hop artists were not a part of the East Coast/West Coast beef, but they were affected by it, nonetheless. ODM emphasized that it was twice as hard for Latino artists to overcome the differences between the coasts: "Even to this day, it's tough for the East Coast to understand and respect West Coast hip hop, because of the whole West Coast/ East Coast thing. And then being Latino—again, it was even double the struggle."[25] I argue that Latinos/as in hip hop can neither be considered a homogenous group nor be categorized in this binary opposition of east and west. Instead, Latino/a and Chicano/a hip-hop artists form a complex network of alliances, musical influences, and media representation that do not necessarily run along the lines of an assumed sense of belonging to an ethnic group. Pan-*latinidad* is a complex and contradictory concept: LA Latino artists strongly identified with Latinos in the east and their contribution to hip hop, and vice versa, yet bicoastal collaborations rarely occurred in the 1990s.

In addition, on the West Coast especially, the considerable tensions within the Chicano/Latino hip-hop scene undermine the notion of pan-*latinidad* on a smaller scale. The Latino readership of *The Source*, however, mostly rallied behind "Latino issues," felt the need to educate on the heterogeneity of the Latino community, and complained about the nature of the coverage of Latinos altogether, regardless of their origin in the US. The examples from *The Source* suggest that Latinos in hip hop were not considered crucial figures until the late 1990s, when rap "went Latin" (Flores 2000: 132). Putting Latino writers on assignments did not necessarily change that. To clarify: it is not my intention to disparage Ronin Ro—his book *Gangsta* is a great read and his position on gangster rap

---

25   ODM, phone interview by author, May 9, 2019.

very compelling. The point I want to make here is simply that pan-*latinidad* in hip hop during the 1990s was a myth—in music as well as in music journalism. The increased coverage of Latino issues in *The Source* toward the end of the millennium also needs to be considered in the context of the overall Latinization of the music industry. And while Fat Joe's involvement in the BET Awards 2022 proves that this trend is still ongoing twenty-five years later, the social media turmoil following his open acknowledgement of Latino/a hip-hop pioneers demonstrates that these issues are not a thing of the past and Latino/a artists are still fighting for acknowledgment of their rightful place in hip-hop history.

Discography/Videography

Ahearn, Charlie, dir. *Wild Style*. 1983; Merenberg: ZYX Music, 2009, DVD.

Delinquent Habits. "Underground Connection", featuring Hurricane G. and Sen Dog [uncredited]. *Delinquent Habits*. Loud/ RCA, 1996, compact disc.

Fat Joe Da Gangsta. "Another Wild N***** From The Bronx", featuring Gismo, Kieth Kieth, King Sun. *Represent*. Relativity/ Violator Records, 1993, compact disc.

Kid Frost. "La Raza." *Hispanic Causing Panic*. Virgin Records America, 1990, compact disc.

Latin Alliance. "Latinos Unidos (United Latins)." *Latin Alliance*. Virgin Records America, 1991, compact disc.

Martin, Darnell, dir. *I Like It Like That*. 1994; Culver City, CA: Columbia Pictures, 2000, VHS.

Mellow Man Ace. "Mentirosa." *Escape From Havana*. Capitol Records, 1989, compact disc.

Pacheco, Ruben. 2012. "BReal.mov." YouTube video, 6:41, March 15, 2012. https://www.youtube.com/watch?v=RJsHtalV52Y&list=PLOHBpeNPxEO_NvXldprCa-DpFsBl4_9a9&index=1.

The Breakfast Club. 2022. "Fat Joe On Getting Robbed By Accountants, Using The N-Word, BET Hip Hop Awards + More." Breakfast Club

Power 105.1 FM. Posted on October 5, 2022, YouTube video, 49:24. https://www.youtube.com/watch?v=xL3RV6SHY4E&t=1457s.

References

Baker, Soren. 1997a. "Frost. Family Matters." *The Source*, no. 95 (August).
Baker, Soren. 1997b. "Psycho Realm: Psycho Realm." *The Source*, no. 95 (August).
Baxter, Kevin. 1999. "Spanish Fly." The Source, no. 113 (February).
Byi, Chino, and David Yellen. 2000. "The Mural of the Story." *The Source*, no. 128 (May).
Castillo-Garsow, Melissa, and Jason Nichols, eds. 2016. *La Verdad: An International Dialogue on Hip Hop Latinidades*. Columbus: Ohio State University Press. https://doi.org/10.2307/j.ctvr7fbvd.
Chang, Jeff. 2005. *Can't Stop, Won't Stop: A History of the Hip-Hop Generation*. New York: St. Martin's Press.
Donohue, Caitlin. 2018. "Fat Joe on the Foundational Role Latinos Played in Hip-Hop History." *Remezcla*, September 26, 2018. https://remezcla.com/features/music/fat-joe-latinos-hip-hop-history/.
Dzidzienyo, Anani, and Suzanne Oboler. 2005. "Flows and Counterflows: Latinas/os, Blackness, and Racialization in Hemispheric Perspective." In *Neither Enemies, nor Friends. Latinos, Blacks, Afro-Latinos*, edited by Anani Dzidzienyo and Suzanne Oboler, 3–35. New York: Palgrave Macmillan. https://doi.org/10.1057/9781403982636_1.
Eric Bobo (@ericbobomusic). "In the '90s Estevan Oriol took this classic pic in New York representing Latinos in hip hop." Facebook photo, January 26, 2020. https://www.facebook.com/ericbobomusic/photos/in-the-90s-estevan-oriol-took-this-classic-pic-in-new-york-representing-latinos-/10157967530749100/.
Eustice, Kyle. 2022. "Fat Joe dragged on Twitter for saying both Latinos + Blacks created Hip-Hop." *HipHopDX*, August 28, 2022. https://hiphopdx.com/news/id.72946/title.fat-joe-dragged-twitter-latinos-blacks-created-hip-hop.

Fat Joe (@fatjoe). 2022. "Thank You Thank You Thank You for your contribution to HIP-HOP." Instagram video, August 25, 2022. https://www.instagram.com/reel/Chr_SrSF4Ii/?igshid=YmMyMTA2M2Y%3D.

Flores, Juan. 2000. *From Bomba to Hip-Hop: Puerto Rican Culture and Latino Identity*. New York: Columbia University Press.

George, Nelson. 1993. "Hip-Hop's Founding Fathers Speak the Truth." *The Source*, no. 50 (November).

Gonzales, Michael A. 1993. "The Cypress Hill Experience." *The Source*, no. 46 (July).

Gonzalez, Michael A. 2014. "XXL's A Great Day in Hip Hop: 16 Years Later." *Red Bull Music Academy*, September 29, 2014. https://daily.redbullmusicacademy.com/2014/09/xxls-greatest-day-in-hip-hop-feature.

Internet Archive. 2017. "Source 28 (1992 Jan) 1991 Hip-Hop Year in Review." Accessed February 15, 2024. https://archive.org/details/source_28.

Internet Archive. 2017. "Source 40 (1993 Jan) 1992 Hip-Hop Year in Review." Accessed February 15, 2024. https://archive.org/details/source_40.

Kemo the Blaxican (@kemotheblaxican). 2022. "New York City 1998 – Industry Insider did a feature on Hip Hop's Minority." Instagram photo, April 22, 2022. https://www.instagram.com/p/CcoXyxWvjXH/.

Kemo the Blaxican (@kemotheblaxican). 2023. "LATINO ARTISTS – Hip Hop's Minority." Instagram video, January 27, 2023. https://www.instagram.com/p/Cn7Sd7Xp78r/.

King, Aliya S. 2021. "How a Few Great Hip-Hop Journalists Won in Hollywood." *Medium.com*, February 9, 2021. https://level.medium.com/how-a-few-great-hip-hop-journalists-won-in-hollywood-fd4ddca723ec.

Kirschner, Luz Angélica. 2019. "Latinidad." In *The Routledge Handbook to the History and Society of the Americas*, edited by Olaf Kaltmeier, Josef Raab, Mike Foley, Alice Nash, Stefan Rinke, and Mario Rufer, 339–346. London/ New York: Routledge. https://doi.org/10.4324/9781351138703-34.

Lamarre, Carl. 2022. "Fat Joe to Host 2022 BET Hip Hop Awards." *Billboard*, September 6, 2022. https://www.billboard.com/music/awards/fat-joe-host-2022-bet-hip-hop-awards-1235134923/.

Los Angeles Times. 1991. "LOS ANGELES COUNTY: THE CENSUS STORY: Los Angeles County Population Figures." May 6, 1991. https://www.latimes.com/archives/la-xpm-1991-05-06-me-1068-story.html.

Mausfeld, Dianne Violeta. 2021. "'Brown and Proud!' Die Ästhetik von Chicano Rap im Südwesten der USA." In *Lied und populäre Kultur/Song and Popular Culture 66 (2021): Jahrbuch des Zentrums für Populäre Kultur und Musik. Musikalische Regionen und Regionalismen in den USA / Musical Regions and Regionalisms in the USA*, edited by Julius Greve and Knut Holtsträter, 89–106. Münster/New York: Waxmann.

McFarland, Pancho. 2006. "Chicano Rap Roots: Black-Brown Cultural Exchange and the Making of a Genre." *Callaloo* 29 (3): 939–955. https://doi.org/10.1353/cal.2006.0150.

McFarland, Pancho. 2008. *Chicano Rap: Gender and Violence in the Postindustrial Barrio*. Austin: University of Texas Press.

Morales, Rigoberto. 1997. "Frost: When HelL.A. Freezes Over." *The Source*, no. 95 (August).

Morales, Riggs. 1999. "Heavyweight Champion." *The Source*, no. 113 (February).

Ocho, Alex. 2022. "Why Are Some People Upset with Fat Joe Hosting the BET Hip-Hop Awards?" *Remezcla*, September 7, 2022. https://remezcla.com/music/why-are-some-people-upset-with-fat-joe-hosting-the-bet-hip-hop-awards/.

Pacini Hernandez, Deborah. 2010. *Oye como va! Hybridity and Identity in Latino Popular Music*. Philadelphia: Temple University Press.

Puente, Henry. 2012. "US Latino Films (1990–1995): A Three-Tiered Marketplace." *Bilingual Review / La Revista Bilingüe* 31 (1): 51–70. https://www.jstor.org/stable/24705994.

Quinn, Eithne. 2004. *Nuthin' but a 'G' Thang: The Culture and Commerce of Gangsta Rap*. New York: Columbia University Press.

Riggs Morales (@riggysmallz). 2023. "If you know me personally, then you know what this means." Instagram photo, November 28, 2023. https://www.instagram.com/p/CoN2tYgs-65/?img_index=1.

Rivera, Raquel Z. 2003. *New York Ricans from the Hip Hop Zone*. New York: Palgrave Macmillan. https://doi.org/10.1057/9781403981677.

Ro, Ronin. 1992a. "Kid Frost: Eastside Story." *The Source*, no. 33 (June).

Ro, Ronin. 1992b. "Riding Shotgun." *The Source*, no. 36 (September).

Ro, Ronin. 1996. *Gangsta: Merchandizing the Rhymes of Violence*. New York: St. Martin's Press.

Rodriguez, Carlito. 1998. "Vamos a rapiar." *The Source*, no. 102 (March).

Rodriguez, Carlito. 2000. "Dream Shatterer." *The Source*, no. 128 (May).

Smithsonian National Museum of African American History and Culture; n.d. "Cypress Hill." Accessed August 17, 2023. https://nmaahc.si.edu/latinx/cypress-hill.

The Source. 1993a. "The Source Mind Squat." *The Source*, no. 40 (January).

The Source. 1993b. "Latino Love." *The Source*, no. 44 (May).

The Source. 1993c. "Latino Lessons." *The Source*, no. 47 (August).

The Source. 1994a. "Herstory in the Making." *The Source*, no. 62 (November).

The Source. 1994b. "I Like It Like That." *The Source*, no. 63 (December).

The Source. 1997. "Vanishing Latino Acts." *The Source*, no. 95 (August).

The Source. 1998. "Hip-Hop Worldwide." *The Source*, no. 102 (March).

The Source. 1999a. "Big Gun." *The Source*, no. 115 (April).

The Source. 1999b. "Brown Power." *The Source*, no. 115 (April).

The Source; n.d. "The Source Latino: Latin Music News and Entertainment." Accessed August 17, 2023. https://thesource.com/category/culture/source-latino/.

Weisberg, Chang. 1998. "Hip Hop's Minority? Latino Artists Unite and Speak Out." *Industry Insider Magazine*, no.15.

Williams, Jay, and Fat Joe. 2022. "Fat Joe on witnessing the birth of hip hop, and how he stays in the game," Released October 18, 2022, in *The Limits with Jay Williams* (NPR), podcast, 39:00, https://www.npr.org/transcripts/1129630172?ft=nprml&f=510365.

"Where the Rhymes at?"
How Contemporary Artists are Transforming Notions of Liveness in Hip Hop

Kevin P. Green

Abstract *Artists in popular music who are media-constructed "stars," have historically been granted live performance opportunities where lip-syncing or the use of performance tracks is employed. Although hip-hop performance practices originally shunned this value system, the eventual mainstream acceptance of hip hop, plus the current state of gaining traction within the popular music industry, through the advent of social media and digital streaming platforms, has prompted a transformation. As a result, the widespread adoption of performance tracks or TV tracks, with audible lead and background vocals, has altered notions of liveness in hip hop for both younger and established artists. In this study, I explore the cultural shift that has taken place that led to the use of performance tracks during hip-hop performances. By explaining how artists construct themselves as consumable brands, which are mediated by fans through television, social media, and streaming audio interaction, I display how the practice of using performance tracks is a natural conclusion to hip hop transforming from a countercultural entity to a mainstream fixture. However, I also identify places of defiance to this phenomenon, through critical assertions of hip-hop authenticity. Concepts from popular music and media studies allow me to contextualize newer and older aspects of liveness for multiple generations.*

During a 2017 interview with New York's Power 106 Breakfast Club crew (18:47), New Jersey-bred MC Redman (Reginald Noble) described his pathway to a successful career. He cited his ability to deliver memorable live performances as being a primary reason for his longevity, with KRS-One's (Lawrence "Kris" Parker) mastery of breath control, lyrical clarity, and vocal stamina being his exemplar. He warned that a "hip-hop rule" dictates that you never perform after KRS-One, and that his real-time vocal delivery factors into him being "phenomenal" onstage (ibid.: 19:10).

Afterwards, a pivot point in the discussion occurred. Redman proceeded to juxtapose his historically rooted performance style with the current trend of hip-hop artists employing what's known in the music industry as performance, backing, or TV tracks.

> Where the f**k do all this lip-synching be coming from with these artists? That's the fad? You throw on a record [that] got the lyrics playin' and you [rhyme] on top of it? So when you rockin' they can see you pause while the lyric is still goin'? That's horrible. Y'all need to cut that s**t out... Stop lip-synching. Hip hop wasn't based [on that]... Go to the gym. Get your wind up. (ibid.: 19:37)

In theory, performance tracks/TV tracks are defined as a version of the song with the lead vocals removed, but background or ad-lib vocal material included. If lead vocals are incorporated, they are used to bolster, not replace, the voice of the artists and are brought down to a relatively low dynamic level in the mix. Presently, rappers perform over completed versions of songs without any dynamic adjustments to the vocal levels. The underlying perspective in Redman's assertion, even while using the term "lip-synching" erroneously in this context, addressed the alleged changing notions of liveness in hip hop.[1] His statement accomplished

---

1   "Lip-synching" is comparable to another term that will be introduced in the article: "pantomiming." This is when one moves their lips along with the vocal material of a track without any audible sound emanating from the individual's throat. Popular examples occur in drag performances or the 1980s television program *Puttin' On The Hits*.

multiple objectives: it created a fixed methodology in hip-hop vocal performance, based upon historical notions of liveness in the genre, and it contributed to the generational divide amongst hip-hop practitioners by suggesting that it is younger artists who are primarily guilty of engaging in this practice.

In this chapter, I detail the specific factors that have helped usher in new ways practitioners and aficionados think about performance practices in hip hop. The influence of commercial music and access to its trappings, which was once closed to hip hop, begs for a comparison between historical notions of liveness between hip hop and popular music. There is a marked difference in the acceptance of backing tracks, or lip-synching within pop music which was not always true of hip hop. Practitioners' eventual access to media outlets, like broadcast television programs or music video airplay, contributed to the overall mainstreaming of the genre and the acceptance of vocal practices employed in pop performance.

Presently, changes in all media consumption, creation, and contextualization that have transpired in the digital age are concurrent with an absorption of hip hop as part of the general entertainment business. Millennials and Gen Zers, who grew up with this depiction of the genre, have been influenced by reality or "self-help" television shows, and use audio streaming portals, social media, and other forms of participatory culture to rework all media content to either construct themselves as celebrities and influencers, or anoint others as so.[2] The live performance has become just one of many ways to interact with a "content creator," regardless of the use of real-time vocals or not.

Redman, and others that support his sentiment, present dichotomous arguments to an issue based on performance practices tied to historical constraints but fail to consider how societal influences both within and outside of hip hop have engendered a reality that is not simple to codify, but rather layered and complex. I contend that it is better to allow one's ears and eyes to assess the ways artists negotiate

---

[2] Generational distinctions can be defined as Gen X, born between 1960 and 1979, millennials (1980–1994), and Gen Z (1995–2010).

newer and older aspects of liveness, and more interesting to find out how and why this practice became an acceptable and typical mode of live hip-hop presentation.

Historical Notions of Liveness: A Comparison

What is or isn't deemed a live musical performance isn't a universally accepted idea. Early hip-hop acts had to deal with multiple audiences. Openly hostile crowds that correlated liveness with singers and bands who associated what they were witnessing with a maligned disco scene, differed from hip-hop insiders who demanded skillful displays of turntable and MC virtuosity (Toop 2000; Chang 2005). Although his definition for musical performance is derived from Western Art Music, Theodore Gracyk (1997: 139–140) provides one that is sufficient:

> A public situation in which an audience attends to the actions of one or more performers, during which specified sounds are intentionally generated for the express purpose of being attended to as music by the audience… It is also a necessary condition of a musical performance that the sounds to which the audience attends are sequenced and coordinated by human performers in real-time, in the presence of an audience, for that audience.

Liveness not only has different connotations between genres, but "[it] is [also] a fluid concept, contingent upon historical context, cultural tradition, implicated technologies, and various other factors for its exact articulation" (Sanden 2013: 3). By using this framework, we can compare aspects of liveness between hip hop and pop music to understand how it has been standardized in each genre.

Hip Hop as a Subculture

Regarding performance practice methodology and the centrality of real-time music making in the live space, the concept of liveness in hip hop is partially descended from Jamaican sound system culture. As Hess (2007: 20) says, "the precommercial culture of [hip hop] focused on musical skills in live performance rather than recordings." Similar to performance practices in Jamaican music making, non-vocal sounds from the DJ centered on making new musical statements by manipulating the once fixed recorded object in real-time. This occurred in conjunction with musical contributions from vocalists being made through reciting party-rocking rhymes and chants, or by making music using vocal percussion sounds, aka "beatboxing."[3] First generation hip-hop acts like Grandmaster Flash (Joseph Saddler) and the Furious Five and Doug E. Fresh relied on these musical devices to entertain patrons during notable performances (Toop 2000: 93–94).

Traditionally, rhyming in real-time was a necessary component of an MC's development. It implies a certain required vocal mastery before getting a chance to "bless the mic," and be heard over the sound system. One needed to be able to display lyrical prowess in the live space before the DJ would allow them to "rock" during their DJ set. MCs had to perfect their craft. This would sometimes occur in public settings by participating in cyphers (ciphers/ciphas), regardless of whether an audience is present or not.

These sessions take place on street corners, in school lunchrooms, in between acts at venues, or at any locale where MCs are in attendance. A cypher isn't an open mic, where you may have one person performing to an audience, but it is a collection of individuals, usually standing in a circle, trading pre-written or improvised rhymes over a beat. Observers usually listen standing outside of the circle. The MC Ras Kass (John Austin IV) emphasizes, "it ain't really fans in the [cypher]" (Alim 2006: 97). In his in-depth study of hip-hop linguistic and performance

---

[3] The song "La Di Da Di" (1985) by Doug E. Fresh (Douglas E. Davis) & The Get Fresh Crew, feat. Slick Rick (Richard Walters) being a prime example.

traditions, scholar H. Samy Alim (ibid.) paraphrases testimony from well-respected MCs, like Kurupt (Ricardo Brown), about the pedagogical and communal, but sometimes competitive nature of these sessions. "Several skillz are developed in the cipha. Rap delivery, reacting under pressure, verbal battling… The cipha is like Hip Hop's classroom, where one studies to learn the tricks of the trade" (ibid.: 98).

Beyond cyphers, open mics, house parties, or talent shows were seen as places to rhyme. Performances in these situations were considered stepping stones on the path from novice to professional (Harkness 2014: 139–66). The rapper Snoop Dogg (Calvin Broadus Jr.) has emphasized that an MC's skill was measured by their ability to rhyme in these performance situations. He implores that proving oneself in cyphers and battles were *mandatory* steps for an MC to take before getting on the mic in public, and he details what could happen if you had not done so. Snoop informs that "I started rappin' [in 1984], '85… I had to battle about a hundred ni**as before I even got to a microphone… And when I got to a microphone… if you ain't sayin' the right s**t, they [take the mic away]… I've seen ni**as get shut down at a house party" (Thompson et al. 2021: 00:31:01). Busta Rhymes (Trevor Smith Jr.), as one-third of the group Leaders of the New School, was asked to spit bars while running laps at a high school track to build stamina and gain breath control when training with Public Enemy's Chuck D (Carlton Ridenhour) and The Bomb Squad (Talib Kweli et al. 2020: 00:05:23).[4] Embracing liveness was part of the mentoring process that distinguished amateur versus professional practitioners.

Second generation pioneer Kurtis Blow (Kurtis Walker) speaks to the importance of this ethos at a time when hip hop was unproven as a mainstay and was considered a fad by the music industry, "We had to actually be good on stage. That was… important to the success of the culture… It was… important for us to rock the house. That was key to my experience in New York City… playing the clubs… the block parties and the park jams. … I just thank God I had that experience… before I made my first record" (Thompson et al. 2019: 00:35:05). Kurtis makes it clear that one's

---

4   The Bomb Squad was the production group of Public Enemy.

ability to perform live prepares an MC to make a recording and is clearly tied to professionalism in hip hop.

Pop Music/Popular Mainstream Culture

Mainstream musical practices in American traditional pop music come from minstrel shows, vaudeville, Broadway, MGM (Metro-Goldwyn-Mayer) musicals, and vocalists connected to swing bands. I agree with Andrew Goodwin's assertion, when he emphasizes that pop music has "always been a multi-discursive cultural form in which no one media site is privileged" (1992: 26). The musical activity of artists like Judy Garland and Frank Sinatra moved in between film roles, television appearances, club dates, and live radio broadcasts. While this type of performer/celebrity became more prominent in the American consciousness during the 1940s and 1950s, one's celebrity status did not excuse performers from having to prove their vocal mastery in live settings. In the 1950s, the maturation of pop and commercial music, and the emergence of rhythm and blues being rebranded as rock 'n' roll, coincided with a fermenting, symbiotic relationship between music and television at a time when the first generation of children who were weaned on television were becoming teenagers (Austen 2005: 5). Programs targeted at teens and young adults were used as visual vehicles for artists to promote their music. Singing in real-time with an instrumental TV track or lip-synching were both techniques exploited by artists at varying points of time.

Murray Forman in his text, *One Night on TV Is Worth Weeks at the Paramount*, offers fresh analysis when "addressing the conjoined histories of popular music and television during the earliest phase of TV broadcasting," (2012: 3) and sharing the processes of each industry in the "breaking" of new artists. He highlights the adjustment process of executives, musical artists, media critics, and the viewing public to the new medium in the 1950s and explains that it steered executives towards presentations that were tame, safe, and predictable (ibid.: 170). This led to "implementing pre-recorded vocal tracks as a means of ensuring vocal quality during live broadcasts" (ibid.: 214). Although established vocalists like Dinah Shore refused to comply, in general, television crews and network executives were not yielding to the wishes of the performer.

This type of power was wielded by executives of the teen and young adult dance programs *American Bandstand* and *Soul Train* (Bruenger 2016: 172). *American Bandstand*, which first started in 1953, with Bob Horn as host, was taken over by entertainment industry mainstay Dick Clark in 1957 (Austen 2005: 28–29). Lip-synching was standard fare for reasons of production, time, and costs. At first, the practice was unfamiliar to the young dancers, but Clark sold it to his audience by saying it was a technique often used in motion pictures. He insisted that "we used the [lip-synch] primarily because it was cheaper, but also because it was impossible to duplicate the sound of the record—and it was the record that kids wanted to hear. That was what they bought" (Clark and Robinson 1976: 72). Notable artists who refused to lip-synch on the program were blues musician B.B. King, who played in real time, and Syd Barrett of Pink Floyd, who declined to move his lips while the rest of the band pantomimed playing to the track (Shore and Clark 1985: 16, 110).

Soul Train, which started as a local Chicago broadcast in 1970, was soon syndicated to six other cities in 1971 (Questlove 2013: 15, 29). This program was conceived for African Americans, by its creator Don Cornelius, and was meant to portray a positive African American media presence. It was a prominent showcase for Black musical styles throughout its run, with artists, and sometimes political figures, working towards the goal of "racism, poverty, and social justice issues being addressed through both words and song" (Lehman 2008: 31, 33). Both textual analysis of *Soul Train* videos and archival research reveal that lip-synching was the preferred method of presentation for the program. Cornelius insisted on lip-synching, or at least a song rendering that mirrored the recording, because of an incident in January of 1972. Guitarist Dennis Coffey performed his hit instrumental "Scorpio" (1971) for the enthusiastic dancers, but his lengthy improvisation altered the production schedule (Danois 2013: 58). Perhaps due to feelings of resistance from artists, a flexible and fluid approach to liveness, with artists singing live to instrumental backing tracks or instrumental accompaniment, or by choosing to lip-synch, became standard. However, as the show transitioned from the 1970s to the 1980s, live presentation was blatantly phased out. Video evidence shows Bill Withers performing in real time with a full band in the 70s but visibly disengaged while lip-synching to a track in 1980.

The emergence of Music Television (MTV) in the 1980s provided record companies further opportunity to promote artists without them having to perform in real-time. With the expectation of videos being part of the music consumption process, a marked shift to the visual and away from the aural had occurred. The new state of things was solidified on March 25, 1983, with Michael Jackson's performance of "Billie Jean" during the *Motown 25* anniversary television broadcast. Despite Jackson choosing to reenact his music video through movement and dance while lip-syncing, it was still described glowingly by critics from *Rolling Stone* and *Black Beat* magazines (Kooijman 2006: 119, 122). It was this performance, and the airing of his "Thriller" music video on MTV that ushered in his "King of Pop" status. Jackson embraced an aesthetic that was focused more on the visual image, rather than the music itself.

A Period of Adjustments for Commercial Music

As hip hop began to infiltrate mainstream media spaces in the 1980s, practitioners were reluctant to incorporate popular music performance practices. Hip-hop artists on *Soul Train* were encouraged to lip-synch. Kurtis Blow was the first hip-hop act booked on the show and was shocked when he found out artists had lip-synched during broadcasts. Correctly, he knew hip hop did not hold a position of esteem to consumers and felt lip-synching would feed into assumptions of practitioners lacking talent. "I am not gonna lip-synch. That is not what I do. This is hip hop. This is live... I didn't want to have that reputation [of lip-synching]" (Thompson et al. 2019: 00:40:47). Eventually, hip-hop performers on *Soul Train* had to compromise. Big Daddy Kane (Antonio Hardy) re-recorded his verses and crowd participatory ad-libs without reverb, and at a higher volume, to make his TV track for his lip-synched performance (Danois 2013: 142).

Touring musicians and sound technicians estimated that, by the 1990s, 25 percent or more of what the audience hears in a pop, rock, or R&B arena show is prerecorded, with audience members being aware of the process (Handelman 1990: 15). However, expectations of vocal liveness for hip hop were still aligned with its own cultural mandates, as Eminem (Marshall Mathers III) found out. After being informed of the visceral reaction to the disclosure of him rapping over his lead vocal tracks during a 2013 appearance on *Saturday Night Live*, it remained clear that even the most accomplished rapper still had to contend with rhyming in real time being the only acceptable vocal practice in hip hop, until it wasn't (Gracyk 2020: 151). Other factors coalesced that shifted the landscape in general, which affected all commercial music making.

Music, Media, and Attention Capital

In 2001, educational consultant Marc Prensky (2001) coined the terms "digital immigrants" and "digital natives" to describe the differences in learning styles between individuals who were born in a pre-, versus post-digital age. These distinctions fall across generational lines, with natives born at a time where the creation and access to content via the internet and mobile devices, and engagement with social media is ubiquitous in their daily interactions. Children as young as two demonstrate the means to take a mobile device and access desired content. It doesn't take them much longer to figure out how to create media, even if it's as simple as a selfie, regardless of whether they choose to distribute it or not.

My use of the media term "content" is deliberate here. Keith Negus (2019) elaborated on the act of musicians making, posting, and consuming content. Distinctions between amateur and professional level material is unclear, as is the criteria that people use to define these boundaries, mainly because the perceived value of recorded music is nebulous. The concepts of prosumerism, participatory culture, or producerism are ideas formed by media scholars that all encompass the notion that fan engagement with content is interactive, and the need for quality control is antiquated. As William Deresiewicz illuminates in *The Atlantic*, "[w]hat we're now persuaded to consume, most conspicuously, are the means to create... and the democratization of taste ensures that no one has the right (or inclination) to tell us when our work is bad" (2015). Content makers can move from social media platforms like SoundCloud, which can be classified as an amateur site of participatory culture, to revenue generating, streaming services like Spotify in an instant, regardless of the supposed quality of the music.

Generation-X aficionados didn't anticipate changes in the media scape, and mistakenly felt hip hop would be immune to these developments when they started to occur. Roy Shuker in *Understanding Popular Music Culture* (2008: 129), lists three key pieces of evidence addressing hip hop's transformation from underground status to the American mainstream: the 1999 *Time* Magazine cover story with Lauryn Hill; hip hop becoming the highest selling genre in America, with its growth in sales starting in the 1990s; and the marriage of hip hop to corporate culture by rappers and entrepreneurs, like Sean "Diddy" Combs and 50 Cent (Curtis Jackson III), which eventually led to *Forbes* magazine publishing a yearly top-ten earners in hip hop.[5] Now, the Millennial and Generation-Z hip-hop participant prefers to be called an artist, or even a rock star, and is seemingly more concerned with their brand than their ability to write and spit rhymes effectively. The use of vocal-laden performance tracks should not be perceived as a shock, but more as a foregone conclusion as part of a modern-day hip-hop persona. This negotiation between aesthetics is ongoing because the larger idea of celebrity and attention capital has altered the importance of liveness for artists and patrons who consume and make content through the digital space.

---

5   It doesn't get more mainstream than a toy doll, and a children's animated program with (MC) Hammer (Stanley Burrell); The *Forbes* list displays hip-hop associated individuals earning in the millions and billions.

SoundCloud and Spotify

Simon Frith, as early as 2000, forewarned about the transformational state of affairs brought about by the nexus of technology and media use when stating, "[t]hrough 'upload ability' music, people who have never performed in a live setting have means to global distribution... Posting things online is akin to a kind of electronic cottage industry. [Hip hop] no longer relies on the live event as it did in its pre-recorded or post-recorded era" (391–392).

The combination of digitally downloaded or streamed audio has become the primary source for US consumer audio consumption according to year-end-2020 revenue statistics published by the Recording Industry Association of America (Friedlander 2020). Although downloading is different from streaming, and statistics are accumulated differently, many platforms, such as Amazon Music, YouTube Music, and Apple Music, combine the two services. Two platforms in particular, SoundCloud and Spotify, have been used in a manner that has resulted in a decrease in the demand for real-time rhyming in hip hop. An exposé written by Craig Marks encapsulates how Lil Uzi Vert (Symere Woods) gained prominence in the music industry through SoundCloud and Spotify.

> In the three years since he uploaded his first song on to the DIY streaming platform SoundCloud, he collaborated with everyone from Gucci Mane [Radric Davis] to Pharrell [Williams], built a 4 million + Instagram following, and racked up a *Billboard* Hot 100 number one record with his featured verse on Migos's viral smash 'Bad and Boujee'... [His song] 'XO Tour Llif3' became a sensation on SoundCloud first, and then a success on [streaming services] Apple Music and Spotify.[6] (2017)

---

[6] The Migos were a rap trio from Lawrenceville, Georgia consisting of Quavo (Quavious Marshall), Offset (Kiari Cephus), and Takeoff (Kirshnik Ball). At the time of writing, Ball is deceased, and the remaining two members are not working together.

SoundCloud, a site created in 2008, became a huge part of the DIY rapper ecosystem because it enables anyone to upload and share audio with friends. The price model allowed users to load up to two hours of content for free and features embeddable players that integrate with social media sites like Facebook and Twitter (X) (Giannetti 2014: 499). The portal became so omnipresent as a medium for Gen-Z rappers to share music with each other, that a somewhat pejorative term, "SoundCloud Rap," became part of the cultural lexicon, but in essence, many rappers with various styles and aesthetics were using the site.[7] An MC named Russ (Russell Vitale) was releasing physical copies of music independently and doing shows in Europe before using SoundCloud, but he decided to use the site to amplify his presence by switching from an album-based distribution approach, to focusing on singles (Miller et al. 2016: 00:02:38). Russ's attorney Josua Binder detailed the results of this strategy: "The kid was dropping a song on SoundCloud every week and was able to get over 100,000 plays within a 24-hour period... At first, he was touring 500-person rooms, then 1,000, then 2,000. By that time there was a five-label bidding war over Russ. We ended up signing a *ridiculous* [original emphasis] deal with Columbia Records" (2017).

$not (Edy Edouard) is a rapper who is the aesthetic opposite of Russ. He has described himself as "just having fun" when starting to rhyme, without having any allusions to a career (Kennedy 2019; Inman 2020). He found himself in demand for live shows in 2019, after only two years of actively loading music onto SoundCloud. His breakout record "Gosha" (2020) had accumulated over 45 million streams between SoundCloud and Spotify, and his music gained placements on the cable television program *Euphoria* (ibid.). As an indicator of Friths' point, none of his success was tied to live performance. An analysis of a show during the 2019 Rolling Loud Music Festival, reveals that $not was using finished versions of his songs as performance tracks. It is noticeable that the voice for one of his hype men was clearly audible, but his own voice was not

---

[7] "SoundCloud Rap" or "mumble rap" became shorthand for a sound and style where lyricism has been diminished and auto-tuned vocals are prominent. Sounds and content take cues from emo rock and recreational drug use.

cutting through the mix. In an interview, $not described his relationship with performance by "admitting that he had only performed once prior to Rolling Loud, that he was essentially a novice and was routinely forgetting the lyrics to his songs" (Gengo 2019: 42, 40).

Edouard was the recipient of his song graduating from SoundCloud to Spotify, which is characterized in the industry as a step forward for artists. Spotify, which launched in the US in 2011, is not a DIY portal and represents a type of curated professional distinction that rappers want their music associated with, along with potential earnings from streams. Status and revenue that artists seek are generated through company-compiled playlists (Eriksson et al. 2019: 120).

Reports indicate that "values and identities are contextualized through the crafting of playlists, which constitutes a politics of content where the delivery of music implicates prescriptive notions of the streaming user" (ibid.: 115). In other words, there is an exchange of cultural cache, or a certain type of "coolness" reinforced between the artist, who is included on the playlists, and the user, who is an official follower of said list. As Money Bagg Yo (DeMario White Jr.) insisted, "Spotify is the new street" (Marks 2017).[8] No playlist offers this more so than the portals' 50-song, hip-hop juggernaut, RapCaviar.

Created in 2017, and with over 10 million followers, RapCaviar siphons songs from feeder lists and assembles them under one umbrella. The formula was so successful, it was decided by the company to transform and extend RapCaviar from a playlist to a cultural sub-brand. The concept was created and curated by executive Tuma Basa, with the visual branding designed by Tal Midyan.[9] Rappers whose songs have performed well metrically on the RapCaviar playlist become featured in print ads, other forms of media, and in branded live performances.

---

8   The "street" represents authenticity in hip hop. If one is popular, or "hot in the streets," that means your music is acceptable and notable with hip hop's supposed African American and Latino core audience.

9   Basa is no longer employed by Spotify. His current position is director of Black music and culture for YouTube.

Vibe magazine reporter Stacy-Ann Ellis wrote a concert review of a 2017 RapCaviar Live event in Toronto. This provided an opportunity to examine modern day liveness. She described the event as "lit" and that rappers like Playboi Carti (Jordan Carter) and Baka Not Nice (Travis Savoury) "delivered the goods" to adoring fans. After viewing an Instagram video linked to the story, it is clear that the DJs injected vocal exclamations to excite the crowd, but the rappers themselves didn't need to rhyme in real-time to elicit such reactions. The crowd was fully engaged and rhyming along with Playboi Carti's lyrics-laden version of "Magnolia" (2017), while he jumped, danced, and peppered them with occasional sounds of his voice. Huge streaming metrics have given concert promoters reason to book millennial or Gen-Z rappers to large stages based on user engagement with the recorded object. Company-curated playlists notwithstanding, platforms such as SoundCloud and Spotify are considered part of the shareable and embeddable social media matrix that has emerged as part of identity, or perhaps celebrity construction for artists.

The Lox on Verzuz and Megan's Multi-Styled Performances

Comparative examples of performance style, and the aforementioned generational shift, can be found through media analysis of two cases: The Lox and Dipset in-person/virtual *Verzuz* battle, and post-event reflections, and iterations of Megan Thee Stallion (Megan Peete) embracing various methods of performance.[10] In fact, material from Megan supports a strong case for employing newer and older methods of liveness.

Succinctly, the *Verzuz* platform is a live streamed, music showcase first consumed by millions of music aficionados on Instagram Live (IG)

---

10   The Lox are Jada Kiss (Jason Phillips), Styles P (David Styles), and Sheek Louch (Sean Jacobs). Dipset, or The Diplomats, consists of Cam'ron (Cameron Giles), Jim Jones (Joseph Jones II), Freekey Zekey (Ezekeil Giles), and Juelz Santana (LaRon James).

and Apple TV, starting in March 2020 (Cochrane 2021; Kennedy 2021). Producers Timbaland (Timothy Mosley) and Swizz Beatz (Kasseem Dean) began *Verzuz* not as an event, but as an impromptu, song-for-song playback challenge while they were each isolating at their residences during the unprecedented shutdown of live music events due to the COVID-19 pandemic. Eventually, vocalists were included in the forum, with some electing to just play their songs. Others chose to sing or rhyme over their pre-recorded vocals on the track. As pandemic-related restrictions began to be eased, and the platform was sold to Thriller Network, individuals were able to experience *Verzuz* as both a virtual and in-person concert (Yoo 2021).

This new format set the stage for a battle between The Lox and Dipset, where the former rhymed in real time, and the latter group used performance tracks. Arguably, the highlight of the night transpired during a Jadakiss (Jason Terrance Phillips) freestyle he performed over a Trackmasters produced, Notorious B.I.G. (Christopher Wallace) affiliated, "Who Shot Ya" (1994) beat.[11] He used several tropes to assert hip-hop authenticity: his status as a native New Yorker still accessible to residents in his neighborhood; acknowledging the importance of mixtape culture; a full integration of the DJ into the performance; and, most importantly, embracing historical notions of liveness by rhyming in real time. Before he began, Jadakiss discredited Dipset by implying that using performance tracks in New York was inappropriate. "Why these n***as keep rhymin' over the words? Y'all could've stayed in the car and listened to Apple Music. These n***as is cheatin'... This is hip-hop. We in the Mecca of New York" (YungWillieWill 2021: 00:29:59).[12]

A few bars into the freestyle, and after receiving an explosion of adulation that erupted from the audience and Instagram commenters, Jada stops at a significant punchline. Again he displays a high working knowledge of hip hop, when cuing Technician, the DJ, to stop and rewind at

---

[11] The Trackmasters are the production duo of Poke (Jean-Claude Oliver) and Tone (Samuel Barnes), who made beats for Bad Boy Records, among others.

[12] There are several ways to access this media. I chose this posting because of the visible Instagram comments.

an impactful place in the song—a classic performance practice imported from Jamaican sound system culture. He then reasserts his authority by specifically targeting social media and Dipset's reliance on that medium. "We ain't playin'! This is New York. This what these n***as want, right? I don't do Instagram! I don't do Twitter! I don't do none of that s**t" (ibid.: 00:31:20). Throughout the night, The Lox continued with barbs, with Jada saying, "Them n***as is lip-syncing," Sheek insisting that, "They don't got no freestyles," and Styles P insisting that Dipset is unable to meet his challenge after he rhymed acapella. The rapper Russ expressed the general opinion of practitioners in the Instagram comments when stating, "Lox not rappin' over the vocals so the performance cuttin' thru way cleaner" (ibid.: 00:19:27).

Reactions at the event's conclusion were extensive and drove a large amount of discussion. Again, individuals are not making clear distinctions between lip-syncing and rhyming over vocals, but both are openly disparaged. The overwhelmingly positive reaction to the Lox is seen as reaffirming an unadulterated, unfiltered brand of hip hop, especially for an older audience, who feel the younger audience hasn't widely experienced this style of performance.

During their podcast, rappers and hosts Lord Jamar (Lorenzo Dechalus) and Rah Digga (Rashia Fisher) discussed how they should digest and merit what they witnessed.

> Rah Digga: "Did they do such a phenomenal job for a stage show, or have we just seen the quality of performance deteriorate? I feel like... you not rhyming over the vocals, knowing your words, breath control... Aren't these things normal? At least all the shows that I go to. I'm like, 'Have you been to a Black Thought show?' This is normal s**t."
> Lord Jamar: "This is not normal anymore. These kids are rhyming off the words. People like Lil' Wayne have made them feel like you can be a superstar. It's ok to rhyme off the words. I've seen some of the biggest rappers out here get on stage, get paid $100,000, and then go out there and... rhyme over the words. And then let the crowd say most of the s**t for them... That's the kind of s**t that it's deteriorated into with this new generation. So yes, I think it's a little bit of both of what you're talkin' about." (2021: 00:23:00)

In a post-event interview on The Breakfast Club (2021) the Lox explained their performance mind-set to host DJ Envy:

> Jadakiss: "We planned on goin' live. Goin' off the instrumentals. Given em' live things, and doin' the freestyles. You gotta rock for the camera and you gotta rock the crowd... We can go live, [but Dipset] wasn't gonna do that."
> DJ Envy: "How did y'all know that [they would rap over performance tracks/TV tracks]?"
> Jadakiss: "People is doin' that at iHeart shows, the biggest platform of shows. Unless it's a certain caliber of artist, TV tracks is what they giving you. It just became a thing. But we came from, that's no [good]."
> Styles P.: "And actually, they switched that around, [because] the TV track used to just kinda have the [background or adlib vocals] here and there. Now they say 'TV track' and it's the whole verse." (09:05)

The difference between performance concepts is explained in detail here, with The Lox indicating the type of show they prefer to give. In actuality however, when looking closely into the history and performance practices of Megan Thee Stallion, it would be hard for The Lox to compare her level of performance with Dipset, even though she does use performance tracks at times, and engages with social media for performative purposes.

She has built her brand by combining newer and older ideals of manifesting hip-hop performance in the popular space. This duality is in reference to an ethos she formed as a teenager, citing her own (now deceased) mother, Holly "Holly-Wood" Thomas, as her primary writing and rhyming influence, which operates in tandem with social media engagement that was originally independent of her music-making activities. While in college, she became known for posting twerk videos featuring herself and friends, but also received attention after a video of her verse over a Drake (Aubrey Graham) instrumental went viral (Gracie 2019; Holmes 2020). Perhaps it is easy for Jadakiss, a Gen-X digital immigrant to insist he doesn't use social media, but for Megan it is a manifestation of how she expresses herself in the wider world, both within and outside hip hop.

There are several examples of her employing various modes of performance onstage. When conducting a close reading of a show during a 2019 North Carolina Central University homecoming celebration, she uses finished versions of her songs as performance tracks (Megan Thee Stallion 2019a: 00:00:42). Megan rapped and rocked the crowd in the arena-sized venue, in the style of The Lox.[13] However, her live vocals were not easily distinguishable from the lead vocals on the track. She chose to voice the words in some, but not all instances, because she chose to initiate performative gestures that gave new layers to liveness. Twerking in lieu of rapping, inviting patrons onstage to twerk, or grabbing a concert-goer's phone to take a selfie or video of herself rapping into the device all added value to the concert experience for the students. She understood her college-aged audience and provided a memorable show tailored to them.

Understanding the ways her fans engage in media has been as important to building her brand. Scholar Keshia Jennings argues this realization has spawned a "re-imaging of black women in hip hop in digital spaces," where similar to Taylor Swift or Beyoncé, "rappers like [Megan], Cardi B [Belcalis Almánzar], and The City Girls have deemed it appropriate to *adopt* [original emphasis] their fans" (2020: 51–52).[14] This symbiotic relationship, forged via social media, between Megan's "Hottie's" and the artist helped contribute to the success of her single "Savage" (2020).

In early 2020, Megan's management team contacted executives at TikTok, which is now universally recognized in the entertainment industry as a primary means for promoting music. The short-video, mobile device, social media platform, has been embraced by marketing executives and fans since the "Old Town Road" (2019) success of Lil Nas X

---

13 The "Golden Era" is a time marked in hip hop from roughly 1988 to 2000, when the balance between a high standard of music making, and access to wealth via a career in hip-hop music was at its pinnacle.
14 The City Girls are a duo composed of Yung Miami (Caresha Brownlee) and JT (Jatavia Johnson).

(Montero Hill) and is used alongside SoundCloud and Spotify (Millman 2020: 24–25; Beau 2022). Although the campaign for her song "Captain Hook" (2020) was effective, the song "Savage" (2020), became a social media phenomenon, due to the creativity of a fan named Keara Wilson. Wilson used TikTok when ushering the #SavageChallenge after creating choreography to the song and "challenging" others to learn it. Participants included Justin Bieber and Janet Jackson, and despite using Instagram, Megan herself, helped furnish a viral moment (Hill 2020). It was reported in *Rolling Stone* that "the song has now appeared in more than 31 million clips on the app [and] it garnered in excess of 4 billion views" (Millman 2020). Megan repaid Wilson by using her image, likeness, and choreography in an animated lyric video posted on YouTube in April 2020, which to date, has over 113 million views.

While YouTube and TikTok engagement metrics don't assess the quality of the content, or gauge an MC's performance prowess, a National Public Radio (NPR) *Tiny Desk Concert Series* performance by Megan does complicate criticism one may have of her approach. Historical notions of liveness were pre-built into the manner of presentation: it is meant to be an intimate affair, with performances from the office space livestreamed on Facebook and YouTube. And the iconic stereo-shotgun condenser mic is not handheld, which dictates that vocal talents of artists are laid bare. Megan's use of breath control, and clear recitation of verses and ad-libs displays an understanding of classic methods of real-time vocal hip-hop delivery (Megan Thee Stallion 2019b: 00:00:25). In addition, her ability to gel with first-time live band collaborators, Phony Ppl, is a testament to her adaptability to perform in a manner appropriate for the situation. Evidence proves that newer and older aspects of liveness can coexist in a highly skilled individual.

Conclusion

Practitioners deemed worthy of praise in countercultural movements such as hip hop have always been defined by the participants, but the rule of who is and who isn't "relevant," is now subject to what is valued according to popular and social media metrics. SoundCloud, Spotify, Instagram, and TikTok are free and user friendly on home and mobile devices, and younger listeners tend to invest their attention capital based on an artist's presence on these platforms. It is naive to believe that hip-hop musical techniques would be unaffected by this era's marriage of music, media, and technology. The ability to perform real-time rap vocals at a high level has retained a shred of value for younger fans, but it is no longer a major determining factor for a rapper's said "relevance," when being a prominent presence in the mainstream media space is deemed equally or more important than live show performance prowess. Generation-X aficionados need to heed the wise words of Snoop Dogg when he reflects on the present state of the culture: "This ain't what it used to be... You can't expect them to be on the level of the game that ain't the same" (Thompson et al. 2021: 00:30:33).

Discography/Videography

Coffey, Dennis, and the Detroit Guitar Band. "Scorpio." *Evolution*. Sussex, 1971, vinyl.

Dechalus, Lorenzo "Lord Jamar," and Rashida "Rah Digga" Fisher. "Lord Jamar, Rah Digga, Lox vs Dipset recap 'What Are We Doing Here?'" Yanadameen Godcast. Posted on August 6, 2021. YouTube video, 23:00. https://www.youtube.com/watch?v=PorU7K1tszc.

Doug E. Fresh & M.C. Ricky D. "La-Di-Da-Di." *The Show / La-Di-Da-Di*. Reality, 1985, vinyl.

Gengo, Roger. "$not Interview-Masked Gorilla Podcast." Masked Gorilla. Posted on July 17, 2019. YouTube video, 42:40. https://www.youtube.com/watch?v=PZtioGaSrzw.

Hill, Tia. "Megan Thee Stallion's Savage Challenge Creator On Her Viral TikTok | Song Stories." Genius. Posted on April 2, 2020. YouTube video, 02:46. https://www.youtube.com/watch?v=5jYe1HleqDM.

Megan Thee Stallion. 2019a. "Megan Thee Stallion – Live Performance @ NCCU Homecoming (FULL VIDEO) 11/07/19." gSP1K. Posted on

November 24, 2019. YouTube video, 19:30. https://www.youtube.com/watch?v=5XFJin9egXY.

Megan Thee Stallion. 2019b. "Megan Thee Stallion: NPR Music Tiny Desk Concert." NPR Music. Posted on December 9, 2019, YouTube video, 25:58. https://www.youtube.com/watch?v=GYJo3MIPoIk&t=88s.

Miller, Brian "B. Dot," and Elliot Wilson. "Russ (Full)-Rap Radar." Radiodotcom. Posted on November 18, 2016. YouTube video, 1:07:42. https://www.youtube.com/watch?v=_uX9SFbqlc4.

Talib Kweli and Busta Rhymes. "Talib Kweli & Busta Rhymes Talk ELE: 2, J Dilla, Q-Tip, Kendrick, 5% & Chuck D | People's Party Full." Uproxx Video. Posted on December 14, 2020. YouTube video, 2:00:10. https://www.youtube.com/watch?v=no1N1DLKZmk&t=2159s.

The Breakfast Club. "Redman Talks His New VH1 Show, Inspiring Eminem, Wu-Tang + More." Breakfast Club Power 105.1 FM. Posted on October 23, 2017. YouTube video, 32:38. https://www.youtube.com/watch?v=bSA5MJ0vRsQ.

The Breakfast Club. "The Lox On Showmanship, Brotherhood, Dipset Verzuz + More." Breakfast Club Power 105.1 FM. Posted on August 11, 2021. YouTube video, 59:22. https://www.youtube.com/watch?v=a6E2TF8uHOc&t=719s.

The Lox and Dipset. "The Lox vs Dipset Verzuz Battle [08/03/2021]." YungWillieWill. Posted on August 3, 2021. YouTube video, 2:05:19. https://www.youtube.com/watch?v=IU5-h-wdqEM.

References

ABC News. 2014. "Why Artists Lip-Synch and How They Get Away With It." *ABC News*, June 11, 2014. https://abcnews.go.com/Entertainment/pop-stars-lip-sync/story?id=24086986.

Alim, H. Samy. 2006. *Roc the Mic Right: The Language of Hip Hop Culture*. New York: Routledge.

Austen, Jake. 2005. *TV a-go-go: Rock on TV from American Bandstand to American Idol*. Chicago: Chicago Press Review.

Beau, Paul. 2022. "A Rap About a Stylish Sweater Made the Spotify Viral 50 Thanks to TikTok." *We Got This Covered*, April 5, 2022. https://wegotthiscovered.com/videos/a-rap-about-a-stylish-sweater-made-the-spotify-viral-50-thanks-to-tiktok/.

Bruenger, David. 2016. *Making Money, Making Music: History and Core Concepts*. Berkeley: University of California Press. https://doi.org/10.1525/9780520966062.

Caramanica, John. 2019. "Want to Build A Rap Career in 2019? Learn To Love The Meme." *New York Times*, October 9, 2019. https://www.nytimes.com/2019/10/09/arts/music/teejayx6-rap-memes.html.

Chang, Jeff. 2005. *Can't Stop Won't Stop: A History of the Hip-Hop Generation*. New York: St. Martin Press.

Clark, Dick, and Richard Robinson. 1976. *Rock, Roll, and Remember*. New York: Thomas Y. Crowell Company.

Cochrane, Naima. 2020. "7 Unofficial Rules For the Verzuz IG Battle Series (i.e. How Not to F–k Verzuz Up)." *Billboard*, April 22, 2020. https://www.billboard.com/music/rb-hip-hop/verzuz-producer-battles-rules-teddy-riley-babyface-9363234/.

Danois, Ericka Blount. 2013. *Love, Peace, and Soul: Behind the Scenes of America's Favorite Dance Show Soul Train: Classic Moments*. Milwaukee: Backbeat Books.

Deresiewicz, William. 2015. "The Death of the Artist—and the Birth of the Creative Entrepreneur." *The Atlantic*, January/February 2015. https://www.theatlantic.com/magazine/archive/2015/01/the-death-of-the-artist-and-the-birth-of-the-creative-entrepreneur/383497/.

Ellis, Stacy-Ann. 2017. "Lil Uzi Vert, Playboi Carti, Baka Not Nice And More Brought The Party To RapCaviar Live Toronto." *Vibe*, October 2, 2017. https://www.vibe.com/photos/rapcaviar-toronto-lil-uzi-vert-playboi-carti-baka-not-nice.

Eriksson, Maria, Rasmus Fleischer, Anna Johansson, Pelle Snickars, and Patrick Vonderau, eds. 2019. *Spotify Teardown: Inside the Black Box of Streaming Music*. Cambridge: MIT Press. https://doi.org/10.7551/mitpress/10932.001.0001.

Forman, Murray. 2012. *One Night On TV Is Worth Weeks at the Paramount: Popular Music on Early Television*. Durham, NC: Duke University Press. https://doi.org/10.1215/9780822394181.

Friedlander, Joshua P. 2021. "Year-End 2020 RIAA Revenue Statistics." Recording Industry Association of America, February 26, 2021. https://www.riaa.com/wp-content/uploads/2021/02/2020-Year-End-Music-Industry-Revenue-Report.pdf.

Frith, Simon. 2000. "Music Industry Research: Where Now? Where Next? Notes from Britain." *Popular Music* 19 (3): 387–93. https://doi.org/10.1017/S0261143000000234.

Giannetti, Francesca. 2014. "SoundCloud (Review)." *Notes: Quarterly Journal of the Music Library Association* 70 (3): 499–503. https://doi.org/10.1353/not.2014.0039.

Goodwin, Andrew. 1992. *Dancing in the Distraction Factory: Music Television and Popular Culture*. Minneapolis: University of Minnesota Press.

Gracie, Bianca. 2019. "Chartbreaker: How Megan Thee Staillion's 'Big Ole Freak' Takes Ownership of Her Sexuality—and the Rap Game." *Billboard*, April 22, 2019. https://www.billboard.com/articles/columns/hip-hop/8507719/megan-thee-stallion-debut-album-fever-interview.

Gracyk, Theodore. 1997. "Listening to Music: Performances and Recordings." *Journal of Aesthetics & Art Criticism* 55 (2): 139–150. https://doi.org/10.2307/431260.

Gracyk, Theodore. 2020. "Liveness and Lip-Synching: Andy Kaufman and Eminem." In *Saturday Night Live and Philosophy: Deep Thoughts Through The Decades*, edited by Jason Southworth and Ruth Tallman, 151–168. New Jersey: Wiley Blackwell.

Handelman, David. 1990. "Is It Live Or..." *Rolling Stone* no. 568 (September 6, 1990): 15.

Harkness, Geoff. 2014. *Chicago Hustle and Flow: Gangs, Gangsta Rap, and Social Class*. Minneapolis: University of Minnesota Press. http://www.jstor.org/stable/10.5749/j.ctt9qh30j.9.

Hess, Mikey. 2007. *Is Hip Hop Dead? The Past, Present, and Future of America's Most Wanted Music*. Westport, CT: Praeger.

Holmes, Charles. 2020. "How Megan Thee Stallion Weathered the Hottest Summer." *Rolling Stone*, February 27, 2020. https://www.rollingstone.com/music/music-features/megan-thee-stallion-interview-hot-girl-summer-950292/.

Inman, Demicia. 2020. "$not's 'Pressure' Reveals a Changing Tide in Hip Hop." *Teen Vogue*, May 7, 2020. https://www.teenvogue.com/story/snot-rapper-tragedy.

Jennings, Kyesha. 2020. "City Girls, Hot Girls and the Re-Imagining of Black Women in Hip Hop and Digital Spaces." *Global Hip Hop Studies* 1 (1): 47–70.

Kennedy, Garrick. 2020. "Inside The Unstoppable Rise of Verzuz." *GQ*, November 19, 2020. www.gq.com/story/verzuz-oral-history.

Kooijman, Jaap. 2006. "Michael Jackson: Motown 25, Pasadena Civic Auditorium March 25, 1983." In *Performance and Popular Music: History, Place and Time*, edited by Ian Inglis, 119–127. Hampshire: Ashgate.

Lehman, Christopher P. 2008. *A Critical History of Soul Train on Television*. Jefferson: McFarland and Company.

Marks, Craig. 2017. "How a Hit Happens Now." *Vulture*, September 13, 2017. https://www.vulture.com/2017/09/spotify-rapcaviar-most-influential-playlist-in-music.html.

Millman, Ethan. 2020. "Inside TikTok's Hit Machine." *Rolling Stone* 9: 24–25.

Negus, Keith. 2019. "From Creator To Data: The Post-Record Music Industry and the Digital Conglomerates." *Media, Culture & Society* 41 (3): 367–84. https://doi.org/10.1177/0163443718799395.

Prensky, Marc. 2001. "Digital Natives, Digital Immigrants Part 1." *On the Horizon* 9 (5): 1–6. https://doi.org/10.1108/10748120110424816.

Questlove. 2013. *Soul Train: The Music, Dance, and Style of a Generation*. New York: Harper Design.

Sanden, Paul. 2013. *Liveness in Modern Music: Musicians, Technology, and the Perception of Performance*. New York/London: Routledge.

Shore, Michael, and Dick Clark. 1985. *The History of American Bandstand*. New York: Ballantine Books.

Shuker, Roy. 2008 [1994]. *Understanding Popular Music Culture*. London: Routledge.

Thompson, Amir "Questlove", Steven Mandel, Phonte Coleman, Laiya St. Clair, and Bill Sherman. 2019. "Kurtis Blow." Questlove Supreme. Released December 11, 2019. Podcast, 1:19:34. https://www.podchaser.com/podcasts/questlove-supreme-970390/episodes/kurtis-blow-49364338

Thompson, Amir "Questlove", Steven Mandel, Phonte Coleman, Laiya St. Clair, and Bill Sherman. 2021. "QLS Classic: Snoop Dogg." Questlove Supreme. Released October 20, 2021. Podcast, 2:00:14. https://www.podchaser.com/podcasts/questlove-supreme-970390/episodes/qls-classic-snoop-dogg-100180838.

Toop, David. 2000. "Hip Hop." In *Modulations–A History of Electronic Music: Throbbing Words On Sound*, edited by Peter Shapiro, 88–101. New York: Caipirinha Productions.

Yoo, Noah. 2021. "Swizz Beats and Timbaland Sell Verzuz to Triller, Share Equity With Performers." *Pitchfork*, March 9, 2021. https://pitchfork.com/news/swizz-beatz-and-timbaland-sell-verzuz-to-triller-share-equity-with-performers/.

YEEK!
Atlanta Hip-Hop Dance and the Subversion of Expressing "Your Energetic Explosive Klimax"

Kevin C. Holt

Abstract *This chapter focuses on Atlanta's yeek community in order to elucidate historical and social linkages between yeeking, Atlanta hip hop, and subversive embodiment as a means of expressing political resistance. Yeeking is a hip-hop dance format that emerged in Atlanta during the 1980s. By the 1990s, yeeking became one of the foundational tenets of Atlanta's hip-hop aesthetics. While it began in the roller rinks as a form of coordinated skate-dancing, eventually dancers began to form (un-skated) competitive troops that would move in perfect synchronicity as they battled for prestige and belonging. Dancers on the yeek scene began producing/performing music specifically to fit their movements, ultimately leading to the formation of several Atlanta hip-hop party formats. This happened during a time when the city of Atlanta increased policing surrounding Black youth, especially in limiting when and how they were allowed to occupy public space; Black youth were pressured to remain relatively unseen and unheard in public. In response, much of Atlanta's hip-hop party music brought focus back onto Black bodies expressing catharsis, which, this chapter argues, constituted a kind of performative resistance to aggressive policing tactics that were used specifically to restrict the recreational behavior of Black youth.*

Throughout the 1990s, as the political wit and funky flows of artists like OutKast and Goodie Mob began to establish the city of Atlanta as the center of hip hop's "third coast," Atlanta's local party music expressed political resistance by other means: by means not fully legible to the logocentric search for meaning often applied to hip-hop analysis. Atlanta bass, an offshoot of the more nationally recognized Miami bass, dominated Atlanta's party culture and the signature dance style that matched its high energy and fast pace was known as yeeking. Yeeking is arguably the corporeal catharsis that has electrified Atlanta hip-hop party aesthetics since the earliest days of the city's hip-hop scene. And yet, yeeking remains under-documented. Despite this, there is something viscerally familiar about the language and embodiment of yeeking. Yeeking is a high-energy hip-hop dance style that is performed in sync. Sometimes it's fully choreographed, and others a leader builds an emergent routine from a vocabulary of dance moves that are called out to ensure synchronicity is maintained.

Yeeking is a hip-hop dance format that formed in Atlanta during the 1980s and became one of the foundational tenets of Atlanta hip-hop aesthetics. It began in the roller rinks, as a form of coordinated skate-dancing, but eventually, dancers began to form (un-skated) competitive crews that would move in near-perfect synchronicity as they battled for prestige and belonging. This happened during a time when the city of Atlanta increased policing of Black youth, particularly to dictate the ways they were allowed to occupy public space. This chapter expands the discourse about meaning in hip-hop music and dance to encompass the subject of the identities that are overlaid onto bodies, and the meaning that is formed *between* performing bodies within shifting contexts. Yeeking became part of the embodied language of resistance as the first generation of Atlanta hip hoppers brought focus on the presence of their bodies as a means of claiming the right to congregate publicly. Dancers on the yeek scene laid the foundations for the core aesthetic elements of Atlanta's party scene, which had an impact on the sound of Atlanta hip hop overall. Consequently, much of Atlanta's hip-hop party music brought focus onto yeeking and its vocal and dynamic audience, which collectively constituted a kind of performative resistance to the confining respectability politics that sought specifically to restrict the recreational behavior of Black youth. The following offers an overview of yeeking and its sociopolitical subtext by outlining histories collected from members of Atlanta's active yeek community in order to explore the linkages between yeeking, Atlanta hip hop, and subversive embodiment as a means of expressing political resistance.

Yeek: An Etymology

The vocalization of the audience is an important part of the experience. The name of the dance style came from these vocalizations. As the dancers did their routines, audiences would yell words like "yeek" and "yued,"[1] which don't really have a specific meaning, but worked to mark skillfully performed cadential moves.

On several occasions, I asked my interlocutors to define "Yeek!" They always replied, in almost rehearsed fashion, "YEEK stands for your energetic explosive klimax" (klimax defiantly spelled with a "k"). I understood the packaged answer as a part of an effort to introduce yeeking to the world; a mnemonic device to convey to outsiders what this thing called yeek might be about. The people from the scene are constantly thinking about what it means to market the music, dance style, and the culture that it is connected to, and, for that reason, many of those with whom I spoke made sure they were on one accord with how they express their ideas, to be united as ambassadors of yeek. They have good reason to try to control the narrative surrounding yeek culture. As many of my conversations with these "yeek ambassadors" indicated, there's a sense that yeeking had already been mishandled, stolen from, or otherwise abused

---

1   I want to note that words like "yeek" and "yued" are, first and foremost, audible and, as such, resist being coded into written language. I have elected a spelling for "yued," though I could have spelled this word in many different ways: U-wed, you-ed, or U'ed. The centrality of orality in this scene means that the sound of the word surpasses its spelling. This is not to downplay the significance of the transcription process, especially for academic purposes, but to highlight that my choices here are less about asserting a specific spelling as definitive and more about capturing an imperfect semblance of the vocal gesture.

by outsiders who got a glimpse of it.[2] Even artists who were once steeped in yeek culture or stood at its fringes failed to introduce yeeking to the national hip-hop scene in a way that resulted in material social, cultural and economic benefits for participants.[3] And since being on one unified accord about the parameters of yeeking might literally yield material and social gains for participants, it's important for these dancers to maintain consistency in marketing.

As outlined above, the dance style known as yeeking did not have a name when it began and, according to people from the earliest era, it took years, some even say decades, before the dance style would be unified under the moniker "yeek." Even still, the term "yeek" was a defining part of the dance and its surrounding culture. The centering of this exclamation at once highlights the significance of the dynamic audience-performer engagement in defining the scene and its soundscape. Elsewhere I have argued that this vocal performance laid down the aesthetic foundations for subsequent hip-hop party music genres like Atlanta bass and crunk, both of which liberally incorporate chanted interjections (Holt 2018). And, just as those chants signify a kind of metacommunicative resistance defined more by the act of the performance than the meaning of the words, so too did the word "yeek" simultaneously resist reduction to

---

[2] Though currently unverified, one of the oft repeated stories I came across detailed how Bobby Brown and his dancers would hide in the back of roller rinks videotaping yeek crews in order to plagiarize the moves in concerts and music videos.

[3] T-Boz, a member of the 1990s girl group TLC known for her funk-adjacent contralto and pristine dance moves, was a part of the yeek scene before her musical career. The opening scene of the TLC biopic film *CrazySexyCool: The TLC Story* shows T-Boz, portrayed by Drew Sidora, yeeking at the Jellybean roller rink. The movie depicts T-Boz as an excellent dancer who is unable to find a yeek crew because of a general culture of sexism; moreover, the movie implies that this exclusion inspired T-Boz to investigate other creative outlets, eventually leading her to join TLC. Other Atlanta-based artists like Ciara, Usher, Lil Jon, and OutKast, hired yeek dancers in their music videos and, even occasionally, incorporated yeek dance moves into the lyrics of their songs. For instance the 1,2 Step, the A-Town stomp and the muscle from Ciara's "1, 2 Step" and Usher's "Yeah" all come from yeeking.

a strict definition and come to represent race, place, subcultural affiliation and, importantly, a specific syntactical and performative function. In short, to yell "YEEK!" meant something, but that meaning was more performative than semantic in nature.

It is possible that the word "yeek" has phased into the national lexicon for a younger generation without their direct knowledge of its origins in the word "yeet." In 2014, a YouTube user who went by the moniker Milik Fullilove released a video that featured Milik doing an impromptu dance, accompanied by his cameraman's syncopated utterances, among them "ooh" and "yeet" (Ritzen 2023); consistent with how Atlanta dancers used "yeek," "yeet" marks the last beat of an 8-count (GWA Liko 2014). Arguably, the word "yeet" really became anchored in youth speech when another video by user "Lil' Meatball" went viral on the platform Vine, amassing over 40 million views (Ritzen 2023). The video shows the young man dancing while walking forward on, what appears to be, a high school running track. His movements were punctuated with metered vocalizations, usually "ah"s, and on the rhythmic cadences of his improvised choreography, he made a gesture akin to throwing an invisible object and yells "YEET," or possibly "YEEK." It is difficult to parse out.

As anybody who has spent time basking in the lilting melodies of a Jawja[4] drawl, the last consonant phoneme of a word is sometimes more suggested than articulated. So, a viewer of this video hears an undeniable "Yee-" with an abrupt stop, implying a hard consonant ending, but the specifics of which consonant are somewhat elusive. Rather than associating the sound with punctuating the dance, the internet fixated on the throwing gesture. Additionally, given that social media necessitates encoding audible elements into a readable format, the spelling of "yeet" was established in the collective lexicon. There is no evidence that these dancers were part of the yeek scene. Despite the similarities in the vocables and their relationship to marked gestures in dance, the actual movements are distinct from yeeking. This does not, however, preclude the

---

4   A spelling of Georgia (US state) that evokes a sense of the accent with which many residents of the state pronounce its name.

possibility that yeeking and its related music indirectly seeded these viral performances. But beyond these parallels, it's possible that any definitive connection, if there is one at all, is lost to time, leaving at most the ephemeral signature of an underground pop cultural phenomenon that escaped in-depth documentation.

Since then, yeet has taken on the meaning "to discard an item at a high velocity"[5] which reflects the gesture in Lil' Meatball's viral Vine video, but its usage connoted more than that; it became a generational signifier. As is the case with most new slang, those who used the term "yeet" expressed a kind of insider knowledge that signaled to those around them their familiarity with internet culture. The term permeated internet memes and punctuated videos until eventually, it lost its novelty, as slang tends to do, but it remains part of the social media lexicon.

The popularity of the term "yeet" constituted a crisis of sorts for people on the yeeking scene. Despite there being evidence, circumstantial though it may be, that the two terms are the same, or, at the very least, that they are etymologically linked, yeek dancers worried that their decades-long tradition would be misinterpreted as an attempt to appropriate and capitalize off an internet trend. More importantly, given that the term yeet was symbolically affixed to younger millennials and Gen Zers, people on the yeek scene expressed concerns that their work in marketing yeeking to the national hip-hop scene would be derailed or dismissed by people confusing yeek for yeet. This generational distinction is important for the yeek community because yeeking represents Atlanta's hip-hop aesthetics during the 1980s-1990s, a cherished era in hip hop which offers a sense of prestige that might not be extended to more contemporary movements in hip hop, like trap and drill. During my fieldwork, these apprehensions were expressed during a yeek performance that included a short skit wherein a young actor, as a surrogate for younger hip hoppers, confidently announced that they knew all about yeet, to which an older actor/dancer responded "I'm not

---

5   This definition was pulled from the first result on the public web forum for slang (Urban Dictionary 2017).

talking about yeeT, I'm talking about yeeK" after which dancers took the stage to demonstrate Atlanta's hip-hop dance history beginning with yeeking and ending with more contemporary popular dances like the nae nae[6] (personal observation, 2016). The capitalization here represents an intentionally exaggerated emphasis on the closing consonant sound to highlight the velar plosive of the K, not to be confused with the alveolar plosive of the T, thereby symbolically heading off any potential misinterpretation. The message of the performance is clear: to confuse yeek with yeet is an affront to Atlanta hip-hop history.

Too Busy to Hate, but Not Too Busy to Regulate

The city of Atlanta holds a cherished symbolic space in African American history. It is one of few urban centers in the nation to consistently symbolize Black upward mobility and middle-classness, earning it the occasional moniker "Black Mecca" (Hobson 2017: 2; Hunter and Robinson 2018: 178).[7] There is good reason for Atlanta to be held in

---

[6] The nae nae is a dance whose invention is credited to the Atlanta hip-hop group We Are Toonz and their song "Drop That #Naenae" (2013), but it is most affiliated with Silentó's song "Watch Me (Whip/Nae Nae)" (2015). The dance move is performed by putting one hand in the air and rocking the body back and forth with feet planted.

[7] In the US, the term "Black Mecca" refers to a city that becomes an epicenter for migrating African Americans relocating specifically for opportunities related to socioeconomic ascension. It should be noted that this term has been used in reference to many cities, including Atlanta, Chicago, (the neighborhood of) Harlem, and others. The important assertion here is that a city referred to as a Black Mecca draws in and maintains a Black population that seeks to reproduce a middle-class experience regarding economic stability, education, property ownership, and professional opportunities. The evocation of Black Mecca here is not meant to flatten the city's complicated race and class history, but to indicate that for many, Atlanta, like all the other Black Meccas, became a symbol of African American wealth and cosmopolitanism in defiance of national trends of racial inequality.

such high esteem regarding its Black history. For over a century, Atlanta has had a stable and thriving Black middle class, bolstered in part by its unique bounty of collegiate institutions aimed at training and supporting Black professionals. Atlanta is the location of the Atlanta University Center Consortium (AUC),[8] which is the oldest and largest consortium of historically Black colleges and universities (HBCUs). This cluster of prestigious Black colleges drew in leading figures in radical Black philosophy, like W.E.B. DuBois (who taught at Atlanta University) and produced world-renowned figures in activism like Rev. Dr. Martin Luther King, Jr., who attended Morehouse College. Additionally, the city of Atlanta has a long history of Black engagement in politics, evidenced in part by Black representation in high offices as far back as the 1960s and its consistent election of Black mayors since 1973 (Hobson 2017: 66–67). All these facets of Atlanta's relatively progressive record for Black socioeconomics are doubly unique given Atlanta's location in the American south. While racism was never an issue confined by region, the US south was notorious for its political and legislative commitment to the subjugation of Black civilians throughout most of its history. That a southern city successfully established and maintained a Black middle class during the Jim Crow era stood as both a point of pride for Atlanta and a beacon of hope for a region grappling with the long-echoing influence of chattel slavery. And Atlanta's thriving economy was referenced as a testament to the pragmatic benefits of (at least professional) integration.

Mayor Ivan Allen Jr., who was in office from 1962 to 1970, announced that Atlanta was "a city too busy to hate" as a part of his initial mayoral campaign in 1961, and he later adopted the phrase as the city's unofficial slogan. This assertion was made during a time when White supremacist terrorism was rampant across the American south in response to Civil

---

[8] The AUC consortium currently includes Morehouse College, Spelman College, Clark Atlanta University, and Morehouse School of Medicine, but in the past has also included Morris Brown College and the Interdenominational Theological Center.

Rights organizing aimed at ensuring that equality, access, and protection would be made available to Black people. Atlanta had relatively few widely known incidents of anti-Black violence and when questioned about what the city had done differently to avoid the violence of its neighbors, Mayor Allen offered a simple reply: Atlanta is a city too busy to hate. On the surface, it was true. Atlanta was a racially diverse city with a growing economy. But the city was also cross-cut by a series of invisible barriers that could be freely permeated by White residents, but not Black ones. Black people crossing those invisible barriers could result in arrest, harassment, or worse.

Just one year after Mayor Allen first declared the city was too busy to hate, an incident reminded Atlantans of the prematurity and naïveté of the claim. In Peyton Forest, a White and at one time legally segregated neighborhood on the Westside of Atlanta, residents successfully lobbied the city to commission the building of a physical barricade, a wall, to clearly demarcate the edges of the neighborhood (Allen 1996: 137). In doing so, they hoped to create a marked boundary beyond which Black people would neither be welcome nor tolerated. Local Civil Rights activists understood the wall's erection as a hostile gesture and, one night, a group of unidentified people tore it down and threw its remnants into a nearby stream. The Peyton Forest residents responded by re-erecting the wall with trees and nearby debris. This pattern of tearing down and rebuilding persisted until the courts deemed the wall an illegal segregatory structure and ordered it be taken down in 1964, citing the passing of the Civil Rights Act as the guiding legal precedent. The incident was so profound for the city that it is sometimes referred to as "Atlanta's Berlin Wall" (Allen 1996: 137). In response to the wall's official destruction, within a year many of the homeowners in that neighborhood fled, some publicly lamenting that the court's support of the wall's destruction was an assault on their safety and their way of life, leaving the neighborhoods that they felt were most susceptible to integration (Allen 1996: 137–138). The fast drain of wealth from this community and others like it caused an abrupt shift in demographics; once wholly White middle-class suburbs were inhabited, dominated even, by poor and working-class Black residents within three decades, creating a unique topography of Black suburban poverty.

This instance, and undoubtedly countless undocumented and less dramatic scenes like it, demonstrates a lot about the spatial politics of race that germinated in Atlanta. In fact, it has been suggested that I-20, the interstate highway that runs through Atlanta, bifurcating it into two regions, was constructed strategically to strengthen the social and topographical barrier between the mostly White neighborhoods of the northern sector of the city and the mostly Black neighborhoods in its south (Rutheiser 1996: 84). While the Peyton Forest incident hinged on the presence (or absence) of a barrier, allowing courts to focus on a specific physical entity in upholding the Civil Rights Act, in most other cases the barriers were less tangible but were no less palpable. Segregatory tactics, like the use of aggressive policing, gerrymandering, and real estate redlining, fused with civic and regional authorities' hostility to Black Atlantans and effectively limited Black residents' and sojourners' ability to safely travel through and/or occupy public space in the city.

These social trends were exacerbated for those who were socioeconomically disadvantaged. As stated earlier, Atlanta has had a robust Black middle class for quite some time, but that doesn't negate the experiences of poor and working-class Black people. Those who did not have middle-class status or whose presentation of self did not align with middle-class respectability were further subjected to having their presence interrogated or policed. Paradoxically, the presence of a Black middle class can facilitate the further marginalization of poor and working-class Black people when policymakers and other officials conflate the desires and lived experiences of the Black middle class with those of less socioeconomically advantaged Black civilians (Hunter and Robinson 2018: 180).[9] This is not to suggest that intraracial solidarity did

---

9   For more on this discussion, see Michelle Alexander's book *The New Jim Crow: Mass Incarceration in the Age of Colorblindness*. This text dedicates considerable space to arguing that the discursive emphasis on middle-class and wealthy Black individuals and communities facilitates racial inequality on the macro level because of a related and false implication that anti-Black racism can-

not exist across class lines, but simply to highlight that the discussion of racial equality in Atlanta and elsewhere necessitates critical interrogations about intersecting identities and experiences that render equality conditional, rather than innate. In short, despite its reputation as the city too busy to hate, Atlanta was never a city too busy to regulate its delicate invisible barriers, its interracial peace revolving around Black citizens reproducing respectable selves and never crossing into *de facto* White areas.[10] This tension would bubble to the surface again decades after the Peyton Forest wall came down when one of the city's darkest chapters was exacerbated, if not fully enabled, by the city's propensity to restrict and ignore its poor and working-class Black residents.

White Flight, Black Space, and the Search for a Safe Place to Play

In the year 1981, Wayne Williams was arrested for murder. While he was charged and convicted of two murders, he was publicly declared the person solely responsible for dozens of missing and murdered Black children in the city of Atlanta over the previous few years. The case of Atlanta's missing and murdered children highlighted disconnects between the city's poor and working-class Black communities and its political leadership. Dozens of children went missing and theories abounded about why. Many in the local communities suggested that White supremacist terrorist groups were responsible. Others blamed

---

not coexist with Black socioeconomic stability, which then negates any discussions about systemic racism and ultimately impedes legislative and political attempts to combat racial inequality.

10   Segregation falls into two categories: *de jure*, or legally enforced segregation, and *de facto*, or socially enforced segregation. While *de jure* segregation was determined to be unconstitutional with the Supreme Court decision on *Brown v. Board of Education* in 1954, *de facto* segregation endured. In fact, despite the many decades since the official end of legally enforced segregation, many public institutions and neighborhoods/districts remain racially segregated.

sex trafficking rings. And still others argued that it was the police themselves, either working alone or in service to one of the other theories (Hobson 2017: 127–130). At the very least, many people in those communities felt that police forces and the media were apathetic and that their responses were too light and misguided.

The parents of these children were often derided as irresponsible or negligent or the children themselves were called "runaways and hustlers" (Hobson 2017: 100). The focus of the public responses to these cases brought attention to a failure of Black children to behave and Black parents to keep their children contained. A curfew was put in place for unaccompanied youth, though it should be noted that it was essentially enforced in the poor Black neighborhoods of the inner city. This is briefly referenced in CeeLo's verse in Goodie Mob's "Cell Therapy," where he laments "you know what else they trying to do? Make a curfew especially for me and you." Parents were encouraged to drop off and pick up their children directly to and from school. This, of course, was a problem for many of these parents whose working schedules and access to transportation lacked the malleability to accompany their children to and from school. If children or teens were found in violation of curfew or were unattended in public, they could be detained by police, and their parents could be arrested or fined, a potentially devastating penalty for poor and working-class people who worked diligently and strategically to cover their family's costs of living. For my interlocutors, this moment was a huge part of their relationship to public space. Their formative memories were haunted by a sense that when they were in public, they could expect to be watched by different kinds of threatening forces with the knowledge that if they went out to play or socialize, even in the best-case scenarios, they and their parents could be arrested. And in the worst case, they could disappear.

The framing of these murders as ultimately the result of cultural pathology placed life-or-death stakes onto Black youths' recreational behavior. Said another way, the implication was that these young people falling prey to violent crime was a result of an inability or unwillingness on *their* part to be inaudible, restrained. It still took nearly two decades into the 21st century for these victims to garner much sympathy or acknowledgment. In 2019, Mayor Keisha Bottoms announced that the case had been reopened (Dickson 2019) and at the time of writing this chapter, its reexamination is ongoing.

The impact this moment had on the Black youth who survived it remains underacknowledged; these young people who became Atlanta's first hip-hop generation were haunted by the looming shadow of a boogie man who could take them at any time. This moment is part of the reason why so many Black youth of this generation would cram into roller rinks. The rinks were one of the few semi-public spaces where Black youth had access to each other outside of school; the only place where they had a great deal of agency in defining the contours of their cultural experience. It was a literal safe space. But beyond that, it was the only place where Black youth felt free of the weaponized hyper-surveillance of the state and could react, unencumbered, to the multivalent pressure to be confined and unseen. And in that space, with time and effort, they developed the dancing and eventually the music of yeek culture.

By the 1980s, Atlanta, like many cities, had several roller rinks that catered to young people. They existed at a liminal crossroads between the playground and the nightclub. Roller rinks had DJs whose job it was to mix (and remix) dance music to keep the crowd satisfied; they also lacked an age minimum, so young people, even those younger than the legal age to attend other types of club spaces, were able to enter and enjoy, to actively evaluate and engage with new music in large gatherings. This positioned roller rinks as important nodes in Black youths' socialization in the metro-Atlanta area.[11] Roller rinks like Jellybean in Ben Hill, Cascade in the West End, and The Golden Glide in Decatur were flooded

---

11 Roller rinks were important for American youth culture at large and Black youth culture specifically in many places outside of Atlanta. The specificity with which the claim that roller rink culture is an important facet of Black youth experiences in 1980s Atlanta is not meant to negate the social role of the roller rink elsewhere; however, the interlocutors that helped construct this oral history spoke specifically of Atlanta roller-skating and the claims made here are bound by that.

with Black youth on weekends in the 1980s and 1990s. These were some of the few spaces in Atlanta that were defined exclusively by Black youth culture.

On weekends and over summers, school-aged Black youth would go to these rinks and stay there for hours; it was one of the few ways in which young Black people were able to create connections across school district barriers. While there were established school rivalries, particularly regarding sports and marching bands, roller rinks as a space provided a kind of interaction that was at once much broader, i.e., more tied to a local construction of "Eastside" or "Westside" of the metro-Atlanta area, and more personal. In some cases, rivalries would arise by affiliated roller rinks as attendees would argue that their preferred rink had the best music or the best skaters. Regardless, the experience of attending an Atlanta roller rink came with a kind of ubiquity: they each featured a large oblong skating rink with an elevated DJs booth on one side, standing between a gaming and dining area at one end near a small accessories shop and skate rental booth at the other. Another pervasive facet of the roller rink scene was the way the patrons related to and transformed the space, which would, eventually, become a driving force in Atlanta hip-hop aesthetics.

Dance-skating was a seminal feature of these spaces. The purpose of the rink was not simply to travel the circle en masse, but to do so with considerable style and flair; it was, in essence, a dance floor on wheels. Those who were able to skate backward, do spins, splits, and steps, who could incorporate popular dance moves in their skating, maintain balance and momentum while weaving through the crowd, had a great amount of cachet in the rink.

Throughout the 1980s in metro-Atlanta, the most skilled skaters formed competitive crews at the roller rinks. These groups, usually consisting of between two and six members, would zip around the rink in highly choreographed unison. There was little room for improvisation in this format as the prestige of the group hinged on its ability to maintain formation and to move as one. The best crews circulated through all the rinks, challenging other crews in other areas to better them in coordination, style, creativity, and athleticism. Around this time, something else began to happen. Some of the crews began to transition their routines from skates to sneakers. While some crews zipped around the rink, others would be on the sidelines or in the center of the rink, practicing or performing routines as (un-wheeled) dance moves.

A Brief History of Yeeking

There is currently no literature on yeeking and there is very little on the roller rink culture from which it emerged. Much of my research, therefore, relies on the stories of my interlocutors to construct an account of a moment, a culture that eluded decades of documentation in an effort to restore prestige and material gains to the people who created yeeking and who keep the scene alive today. This effort to produce, perfect, and capitalize upon yeeking as the definitive Atlanta hip-hop dance style extends back to the early years of Atlanta hip-hop history. The story of yeek is bound to the story of Atlanta. The following is a composite of oral histories put forth by people from the scene.

When questioned about the history of yeeking, participants identify specific waves or eras that are affectively tied to important moments and spaces. The first wave was sometimes referred to as the roller rink era. This era, temporally assigned to the early 1980s, was defined by the first attempts to establish a dance culture in the roller rinks of Atlanta. During this wave, the first competitive skate-dancing crews were created, establishing the roller rinks as a central space for Atlanta's budding hip-hop culture. This would have also been the time that crews, after practicing their routines without their skates, began engaging in the signature coordinated dances that would later be known as yeeking.

The second wave/era, the late 1980s to early 1990s, is sometimes referred to as the talent show era. During this time, politicians and schools invested in talent showcases for Black youth to incentivize high-school-aged Black youth to refocus their leisure time on "productive" efforts; this was especially important since national conversations about social health, especially regarding recreational drug use and violent crime, placed the blame squarely on under-stimulated antisocial Black youth as the central culprits. The sudden presence of talent showcases allowed yeek dancers to reconceptualize their routines for the stage and, importantly, raised the stakes for rivalries between competing crews and/or neighborhoods. Recordings of these showcases provide some of the earliest video evidence of yeeking.

The third wave/era encompasses the early-to-late 1990s and coincides with the peak years of Atlanta's largest Black youth party event, Freaknik. While Freaknik began in 1982 (Thompson 2007: 27), it would not emerge as one of the city's largest events until the mid-1990s, with a peak of about 200,000 attendees in 1994 (ibid.: 28). During these years, yeeking and its accompanying music, Atlanta bass, dominated the city's hip-hop party scene, which increased interest in the style. Many of the music videos and concert performances coming out of Atlanta during this era featured yeeking. There was no discussion of a fourth wave of yeeking as its popularity went into decline in the late 1990s with party culture shifting to the more mosh-oriented movements of crunk. But there is a concerted effort to revive yeeking today. Dancers from the original three waves perform and offer classes to younger people in an effort to keep the dance style alive, to highlight the ways that it is responsible for some of the elements of contemporary hip hop and to, hopefully, inspire a new generation to yeek.

As interest in the dance moves intensified, more crews emerged to compete against each other for bragging rights, each with its own name, brand, and style. Spontaneous contests would emerge in the center of rinks and, at some locations, would temporarily take over the entire rink for dance battles. Audiences gathered around these ciphers, at the center of which groups would be executing their routines with perfect synchronicity. Onlookers would cheer and chant along with the music, calling upon an emergent vocabulary of heretofore nonsensical exclamations with a particularly impressive move or sequence was executed. Dancers and watchers alike would yell "AY!", "YUED!", and "YU!" to affirm the people in the center and, most importantly "YEEK!" when a concluding move hit just right, usually on the final beat of the sequence. To get the audience to yell "YEEK!" was tantamount to a victory knell—a collective declaration of the dancers' virtuosity, if not triumph, in the moment. So, it is fitting that later, the dancers who engaged this style would take on this word as its name.

As indicated by the name of the second era of yeeking, talent shows were another important performance site that ultimately shifted the performance format again. While schools commissioned some of these contests, it seems that others were more spontaneous or youth-organized events where the audience evaluated the talents of competitors and voiced their approval, or conversely their disapproval, with their immediate responses. This amplified the stakes for performance. While there is theoretically some cover when crews performed at the rink, with skaters circling and people there enjoying the arcade and gift shop, transitioning to a stage meant creating a kind of showcase that necessitated absolute focus. This new context brought with it a desire to amp things up, in terms of the moves, the music, the costuming, and the intensity. By the mid-1990s, yeeking was a central feature of dance showcases, public party events, Atlanta-based music videos, and nightclubs: at that point, it epitomized Atlanta hip-hop style.

The Movements of Yeek

The basic movement of yeeking is a side-to-side step. At the opening of every dance routine (whether improvised or pre-choreographed) dancers begin with the same left-to-right motion, the pendular moment of which generally continues throughout the routine. This motion is a holdover from yeek's start in roller dancing. Just as skaters propel in a zig-zag pattern as weight shifts from one leg to the other, so too does yeeking. In maintaining that central motion, even in relatively neutral positions, yeeking harkens back to its origins in the roller rinks of Atlanta.

The names of the moves and the moves themselves work somewhat syntactically, a pool of well-known fragments that can be broken apart and recombined in new sequences that insiders can perform in unison if guided by a leader calling them out. To borrow from Saussure's linguistic frame of langue and parole, yeek dancers pull from a shared "vocabulary" of movements (langue) that find meaning when they are strategically and knowingly sequenced in ways that convey meaning (parole), or more importantly for their purposes, expressions of aesthetic pleasure. While most yeek competitive routines were meticulously choreographed and practiced beforehand, this ability to coordinate on the fly expedites the choreography process. Furthermore, in improvised performances, the ability to follow a leader's call and perform in unison would allow a crew to maintain formation either on the dance floor or skating around the roller rink. These calls were part of the soundscape. Almost rapped, they have a rhythm to them that fits with the music and becomes part of what is expected of the performance. Even at times when the choreography is settled upon before the performance, the dancers would interject vocalizations, not unlike those that the audience would contribute at the rink competitions, as a means of articulating their moves. In short, yeeking is a kind of dancing, but a major component of the performance is the voice, both as a communicative tool in emergent choreography and as an exclamatory punctuation. On different occasions, the established yeek dancers offered some historical context for the moves they taught, usually referencing a specific person that was known for the move. The implication is that the canon of yeek movements grows directly out of the competitive dancers' drive to put forth something new; however, as most of these histories indicate, one crew/person might have invented the move, but it was often transformed and standardized by another.

While both improvised and pre-planned routines are specific regarding the unison sequencing of movements, the music seemed to be somewhat interchangeable. I witnessed the same routine performed with different songs, even with different tempos. Sometimes, the dancers would go through several songs searching for the right tempo and feel to match their energy for the night. If the song had a 4/4 time signature, had a moderate-to-fast tempo, and a strong bass line, any yeek routine, improvisational or through-choreographed, could be performed to it.

As carefully crafted as the choreography is, and as rigidly synchronized as the dancers must be, yeeking maintains a sense of explosive spontaneity. Most of that comes from small gestural amendments each dancer makes to the moves, enough to express a kind of individuality. These decisions, nearly imperceptible to those unfamiliar with the format, are a part of how the dancers in this scene evaluate each other. In a dance where everybody moves in unison, where every group pulls from the same pool of movements, the *how* becomes a central means of earning prestige, a method of formulating a signature. Additionally, this latitude for micro-adjustments allows for a slight imprecision that ultimately adds to the feeling that each dancer is truly expressing their "every explosive klimax!" in a way that is incapable of being fully contained.

One additional consistent component of the dance style is the big finishing move. It manifests differently each time, but usually represents some forceful gesture: a stomp, a jerk to one side, or a full body crunch. But its purpose is to punctuate the sequence. To follow our syntactical metaphor, the closing move is the exclamation point that marks the end of the sentence. This move is always accompanied by a collective vocalization by both performer and audience; a loud and full-chested "YEEK!" This exclamation preceded the official naming of the dance style; in fact, as indicated earlier, what became known as yeeking existed without a specific name for years. But the importance of this moment in the performance imbued the word "yeek" with special significance, which is how it eventually became the defining referent.

Yeek Musicality

In my interviews, dancers who were on the scene when it first emerged spoke nostalgically of songs that were played on heavy rotation at the rink. The ones that they selected for practice most frequently included "Planet Rock" by Afrika Bambaataa, "Din Daa Daa" by George Kranz, "Panic Zone" by N.W.A. and "Set It Off" by Strafe. To my surprise, the selected music only occasionally included more local, i.e., Atlanta, artists. This mix, however, makes sense for referencing the genesis of yeeking. Atlanta did not have a well-established hip-hop party sound in the first half of the 1980s and roller rink DJs would have, undoubtedly, pulled dance records from non-local artists to establish and maintain the party. The early yeek dancers skated to this music, but as the dance style broke free of its skate-dancing origins, performers began to demand something different from the standard roller rink repertoire. According to the dancers I spoke to, the first musical shifts for yeeking occurred when some dancers complained that the tempo of most music was too slow. Since the dancers no longer had to coordinate moves with the pragmatics of skating, they were free to incorporate more acrobatics, more elaborate footwork, and, importantly, faster speeds. Crews resolved to get somebody to physically force records to play faster by pushing the record along with their fingers. The familiar hip-hop and R&B songs would become faster, hovering around 140–175 bpm, higher-pitched, and timbrally tinnier. Additionally, the acoustics and crowd noise, or more appropriately the vocal contribution of the audience and performers, combined to create the unique sound of yeek. The desire for this musical aesthetic and this tempo drove many yeek dancers to branch into music making.

Many of my interlocutors from the yeeking scene had at some point become involved in making hip-hop music, be it as singers, rappers, producers, or DJs, but the driving force behind their music always revolved around creating something to dance to. There were several music producers that started out as crew members. For example, DJ Taz and DJ Kizzy Rock, two of Atlanta's local celebrity producers, were central in forming and producing the subgenre of Atlanta bass; they credit yeeking with inspiring their composition methodologies. At a public forum on yeek's history, Atlanta hip-hop artist and producer Kizzy Rock spoke specifically of a yeek dancer who inspired the texture of one of his most successful hits, "Whatz Up Whatz Up," performed by Playa Poncho and LA Sno:

> The first record I produced... 'Whatz Up Whatz Up'... the whole concept came from yeeking and the dancers. It was about the talk. You heard what [Ted, a yeek dancer] just did? When he came out here? 'Got damn. Unh. What's up [performed with yeek-style hand gestures with a sparse rap-style vocal]... it came from that and that one lit-

tle thing... so when Playa Poncho [the featured artist] talking about ideas and shit, he a lying muthafucka. That's some real shit... The dance-offs. That's where it came from. I got it from Ant [another yeek dancer]. That nigga talk like a muthafucka. More than anybody. He'll be like 'What's up... Ya grandmamma too... Get some... Unh!... Suck a dick nigga...' [performed as before]. I could give it to you over and over. But I got the whole concept of 'Whatz Up Whatz Up' from the dance talking. For real. (Personal observation February 2016)

Kizzy Rock's track for "Whatz Up Whatz Up" is typical of Atlanta hip-hop party music of the mid-1990s. The beats featured extended sections of chant and/or voiced interjections that mirrored the yeeking soundscape; it was part of the underlying sonic texture of Atlanta's hip-hop dance music. The incorporation of the sonic and performative features that are specific to yeeking marked the style as distinctly Atlanta hip-hop party music. The patterns of call-and-response in this song and others bring focus onto the role of the audience's performance in hearing. "Whatz Up Whatz Up" is essentially yeeking disembodied, packaged, and redistributed for hip-hop dance styles, yeeking and others, to be performed and vocalized with.

Kizzy Rock's contention that Playa Poncho is a "lying muthafucka" for claiming to be the driving force behind the song's format highlights a fundamental rift between perceptions of creation/ownership in traditional hip hop and the collaborative/democratic gestural and compositional methodologies that were most prominent on the yeek scene. As the primary rapper on the song, Playa Poncho is the one most credited with it, just as the vocalists on many mainstream hip-hop songs are often considered the "owner" or the individual most responsible for the song's gravitas. The notion that meaning and impact are most attributable to the rapper is, at least in part, due to a text-centric evaluative approach that likens hip-hop music to poetry. From this perspective, the importance of the chanted section and its connections to the scene to which it refers is diminished if not disregarded; or conversely, such a section, as is the case of "Whatz Up Whatz Up" is understood as an extension of the rapper's creativity. In asserting that the composition of the song is based upon the sonic experience of yeeking, the vocalizations of both the dancers and the crowds, Kizzy Rock directly challenges the focus on a singular narrative-style vocal performance of the rapper. In this subtle way, Kizzy Rock articulates that Atlanta bass was about two things: a cathartic body and collective voicing.

Conclusion

Dance has always been central to discussions of meaning in hip hop. From its earliest moments, the presence of people moving acrobatically, audaciously was an important part of the establishment of hip-hop space. Accordingly, from the earliest writings that would eventually form the area of hip-hop studies, the rhythms and gestures of breaking and b-boying have been seminal inclusions to theorizations of hip hop's cultural intervention. And yet, breaking and b-boying are far from the only iterations of social dance that hip hop yields. As our theoretical scope expands ever farther beyond the hip hop that germinated in 1970s New York, so too must our frames for theorizing and historicizing hip-hop embodiment and dance.

Yeeking is a manifestation of hip hop's radical embodiment that somehow fell through the cracks; it evaded much documentation or theorization throughout the decades, despite its impact on Atlanta's hip-hop party aesthetics. That could possibly be attributed to how visually different yeeking is from breaking and b-boying. Or perhaps it is because hip-hop scenes in the US South have only recently garnered much focus in academia, and even still that focus remains primarily concentrated on rappers. Whatever the reason, the elusiveness of yeeking has not lessened its potency.

Given that yeeking has eluded being the subject of research or even much journalism, how does knowledge of yeeking contribute something useful to hip-hop discourse? The answer is threefold. First, yeeking is arguably at the core of Atlanta hip-hop party music. It was the driving force behind many Atlanta hip-hop artists' first foray into music-making and led many of them to form compositional techniques that became signatures of Atlanta's style. Atlanta-based hip hoppers have been a major force in the market in the 21st century, so understanding contemporary hip hop necessitates delving into this movement. The second reason yeeking must be entered into discourse has to do with the investment of the people on the scene. Many of the interviews I conducted included some summation of yeek's importance to their lives or, in some cases, their survival. A recurrent theme was the extremely limited opportunities in poor and working-class Black neighborhoods for Black youths' recreational time. They each shared a sense of malignant stagnancy, a feeling that had it not been for yeeking, they might have succumbed to a more treacherous path. In a city that sought to restrict, rather than protect, Black youth during a crisis of missing and murdered children, yeeking in roller rinks and at talent showcases was one of the few activities through which the Black youth of Atlanta could express a sense of agency in defining space and cultural particularity. And the third is that yeeking offers an apt case study for entering embodiment in discussions about meaning in hip-hop music, which has implications for other subgeneric movements in hip hop.

What I offer here is not an exhaustive history, but rather a brief sketch of some of the sociopolitical phenomena that imbue yeeking with its performative resistance. Each of these moments fundamentally impacted a generation of Black Atlantans' relationship to the right to occupy public space for their own purposes. Atlanta's own Civil Rights era slogan, "a city too busy to hate," falls back on a neoliberal idea of capitalism as a meritocratic equalizer; one which notably stood in stark contrast to the lived experience of Atlanta's first generation of hip hoppers. For them, safety and freedom were leveraged against their willingness to navigate life in respectable silence, diminishing their (raced and classed) presence, and they responded by creating music and dance that was purposefully loud and grounded in the Black body expressing "Your Energetic Explosive Klimax," YEEK!

Discography/Videography

Afrika Bambaataa and the Soul Sonic Force. "Planet Rock." *Planet Rock: The Album*. Tommy Boy, 1982, vinyl.

Goodie Mob. "Cell Therapy." *Soul Food*. LaFace Records, 1995, compact disc.

Goodie Mob. "Goodie Mob – Cell Therapy." Goodie Mob. Posted on February 26, 2014. YouTube video, 4:20. https://www.youtube.com/watch?v=OGy4bmG5SJw.

GWA Liko. "Yeet!!!! New dance." GWA Liko. Posted on February 12, 2014. YouTube video, 0:15. https://www.youtube.com/watch?v=ExAaaXH090w&t=7s.

Kranz, George. "Din Daa Daa." Personal Records, 1983, vinyl.

Meatball. "YEET Dance (Original Video)." PM Productions. Posted on April 13, 2014. YouTube video, 0:06. https://youtu.be/57053eGYwZ4?si=w-IfFy55Q3PFTuzw.

Playa Poncho and L.A. Sno. "Whatz Up Whatz Up". *Whatz Up Whatz Up–EP*. Columbia, 1995, compact disc.

Playa Poncho. "Playa Poncho, LA Sno – Whatz Up, Whatz up (Official Video)." PlayaPonchoVEVO. Posted on October 25, 2009. YouTube video, 3:54. https://www.youtube.com/watch?v=KLvxu6pHasU.

Silentó. "Silentó – Watch Me (Whip/Nae Nae) (Official)." SilentoVEVO. Posted on June 25, 2015. YouTube video, 3:22. https://youtu.be/vjW8wmF5VWc?si=SrJbdzq3M4ig-sCW.

Strafe. "Set It Off". *Set It Off*. Jus Born Records, 1984, vinyl.

We Are Toonz. "We Are Toonz – Drop That #NaeNae." WeAreToonzVEVO. Posted on April 23, 2014. YouTube video, 4:45. https://youtu.be/I_e3G3X-CYA?si=fws096pSPYojESlb.

References

Allen, Frederick. 1996. *Atlanta Rising: The Invention of an International City, 1940–1990*. Lanham: Taylor Trade Publishing.

Dickson, EJ. 2019. "Atlanta Child Murders Case Has Been Reopened." *Rolling Stone*, August 20, 2019. https://www.rollingstone.com/culture/culture-news/atlanta-child-murders-case-reopened-mindhunter-874051/.

Hobson, Maurice J. 2017. *The Legend of the Black Mecca: Politics and Class in the Making of Modern Atlanta*. Chapel Hill: University of North Carolina Press. https://doi.org/10.5149/northcarolina/9781469635354.001.0001.

Holt, Kevin C. 2018. "On Politics and Performativity in Atlanta Hip Hop Party Culture, Or How to Get Crunk with (Body and) Words." In *The Oxford Handbook of Hip Hop Music*, edited by Justin D. Burton and Jason Lee Oakes. Oxford: Oxford University Press. https://doi.org/10.1093/oxfordhb/9780190281090.013.30.

Hunter, Marcus Anthony, and Zandria Robinson. 2018. *Chocolate Cities: The Black Map of American Life*. Berkeley: University of California Press. https://doi.org/10.1525/california/9780520292826.001.0001.

Ritzen, Stacey. 2018. "What Does 'yeet' Mean and How Did It Become a Meme?" *Daily Dot*, September 13, 2018. https://www.dailydot.com/unclick/what-does-yeet-mean/.

Rutheiser, Charles. 1996. *Imagineering Atlanta: The Politics of Place in the City of Dreams*. London: Verso Books.

Thompson, Krista A. 2007. "Performing Visibility: Freaknic and the Spatial Politics of Sexuality, Race, and Class in Atlanta." TDR/The Drama Review. MIT Press – Journals. https://doi.org/10.1162/dram.2007.51.4.24.

Urban Dictionary. 2017. "Yeet." December 28, 2017. https://www.urbandictionary.com/define.php?term=Yeet.

Identity Transgressions as Transgressions of the Art Form
The Case of Frank Ocean

Martina Bratić

Abstract *Hip-hop culture, known for upholding heteronormative values and sometimes displaying homophobic tendencies, is also notably characterized by its strong focus on masculinity, which can be attributed to different historical, social, and cultural factors. Heavily influenced by traditional notions of masculinity, this cultural circle primarily revolves around resilience, assertiveness, and a confrontational stance of rebellion; the one that discourages expressions of gentleness, sensitivity, and tenderness.*
Frank Ocean's persona and artistic contributions paved the way for an alternative male presence within the hip-hop realm. This marked a departure from the established norms of (Black) male identity in performance, giving rise to fresh creative horizons, novel modes of artistic creation, and diverse forms of engagement and audiences. The noteworthy aspect of Frank Ocean's case in particular lies predominantly in his act of transgression: defying conventional gender norms on one hand and breaking free from artistic genre constraints on the other. Just as queer identity rejects fixed definitions, Ocean's music resists easy categorization within a specific genre.
This chapter seeks to emphasize Frank Ocean's nonconformity in the context of resistance culture, wherein the experience of the marginalized becomes the new artistic- and identity currency.

Frank Ocean is one of those figures in popular music who has built his fan base almost as much through his award-winning music as through the prism of an artistic persona, of a personality Ocean gathers and performs in the realm of his own notion of a celebrity.

His musical beginnings are today the object of a romanticized idea of a Black creative youngster, whose creative zeal was there in the background of many performers of stellar status at the time. Christopher Edwin Breaux, the artist Frank Ocean, was born on October 28, 1987, in Long Beach, California. At the age of five, his family moved to New Orleans, where he spent a significant part of his childhood. Ocean became deeply involved in NOLA's vibrant jazz music scene and its rich history from an early age, and his biographies regularly highlight the influence of his mother's love for R&B on his music.

In his teenage years, Ocean ventured into producing music and took on several odd jobs to finance his studio sessions. Following his high school graduation in 2005, he enrolled at the University of New Orleans, though his time there was short-lived when the region was hit by Hurricane Katrina in August of that same year, causing widespread destruction, with Ocean's recording studio severely damaged by flooding and looting. It was at this point that he decided not to pursue further academic endeavors, but to turn the rudder towards his future musical career. Immediately after this event he departed to Los Angeles, another decisive turning point, where he recorded demos in the studios of his friends and acquaintances. This secured him a songwriting deal that would soon lead to him ghostwriting for Brandy, Beyoncé, Justin Bieber, and John Legend (Kellman, n.d.). Under the songwriting alias Lonny Breaux (he legally took the name Frank Ocean in 2015), he had already established himself as a creator with incredible attention to detail, including his vivid and relatable lyrics touching on universal themes, with harmonies that leave "listeners entranced" (Blanchet 2020). Still, Blanchet recounts that his writing, which had significantly influenced those who worked with him during his earlier prolific period, could be seen as presaging Ocean's later approach to work: characterized by secrecy, seclusion, and enigma, occurring in distant realms, whose manifestations remain unpredictable in terms of timing and content.

This more restrained mode of presentation continued for Frank Ocean through his affiliation with the LA-based hip-hop collective Odd Future, of which he was a member from 2010 until 2014. In its rotating roster of performers, with a prominent inclination towards the DIY principle of creative work, Odd Future provided Ocean with a safe and creative zone of action, but also a direct entry point into the pop-culture domain, which, almost paradoxically, gave way to a proportionately invisible, secretive story of existence. As time has shown, the mode of personal secrecy permeated deeply with the reception of his music, of him as an artist and of his every artistic expression. In hindsight, it can be said that the professional steps in Frank Ocean's career was carefully aligned with impulses from his private life, in a mutually reinforcing nexus that stands at the center of this chapter.

The chapter aims to shed light on the interdependent relationship between Frank Ocean's personal life and his artistic output, by exploring the possibility of the narrative of Ocean's (sexual) identity having influenced his music and artistic expression. By analyzing his lyrics, interviews, public appearances, and general artistic presence, the chapter seeks to provide a deeper understanding of how Ocean's personal life and transgressions in relation to normative (Black) masculinity have shaped his artistic identity. This text will delve deeper into the topic of masculinity from a socio-psychological perspective, while specifically exploring the various connotations and implications of the term within the context of hip-hop culture, which serves as a unique platform for the construction and practice of diverse sexual, racial, and class identities.

Moving forward, my attention will be centered on the song "Bad Religion" (2012) from the album *Channel Orange*. Through an original in-depth analysis of the song's musical and textual elements, I aim to explore how it addresses and challenges conventional notions of gender and sexuality, asserting that the song can serve as a poignant reflection of Ocean's personal identity—or at least, what he chooses to serve us as this enigmatic artistic persona.[1] Here it is worth out-

---

1   I would like to emphasize that the scholarly output on the study of Frank Ocean so far is not significant. It mostly consists of individual articles that mainly ex-

lining the methodological framework of this study, which is based on the textual and musical analysis of Frank Ocean's original material, which with the exception of primary sources, are mostly found online. A principle platform in this regard is the Genius website—formerly Rap Genius—an online community that focuses on annotating and explaining song lyrics, poetry, and other forms of text. I use these annotations as telling insights into the meaning, wordplay, cultural references, and background information behind the analyzed materials proved fruitful for this study. In this regard, I primarily draw upon content analysis, examining the themes and language—as well as narrative analysis—that focuses more on the storytelling aspects of lyrics; that is, their potential in character creation and plot development. In this sense, the Genius platform is used as a valuable starting reference point for further analysis in the chapter.

Deconstructing Masculinity in Hip-Hop Culture: From Hegemony to Resistance

What it began as is a story of secrecy, of the inability to articulate one's own self, of the incapacity to send it out to the world in all its identity networks and meanings. This identity cross-linking and networkedness is what determines each of us,[2] it is what reassembles the particles of

---

amine him with a focus on racial narratives (e.g., B. Lewellyn-Taylor's 2018 article "The Free Black Artist: Frank Ocean Through a Decolonial Lens") and narratives related to his sexual orientation and coming-out. Interestingly, the latter topic is most prevalent in bachelor and master-level papers, which attests to the fact that the youngest generations have chosen to approach it from a theoretical perspective in an effort to gain a more nuanced understanding of the ways in which Ocean's identity can influence his musical expression. This chapter therefore tries to respond to the gaps in the understanding of the music of Frank Ocean through the prism of identity and sociocultural contexts.

2   The existent discourses on these matters are wide-ranging and multifaceted, for example, in: Foucault (1976); Butler (1990); Harrison and Cooley (2012); and Kaufman and Powell (2014).

our identity, our own sexuality, and sexual preferences as *what we are*. However, some intrinsically 'agreed' arrangements are more or less correspondingly molded into a sociocultural given or, better said, construction. Within this constellation, the heteronormative framework encompasses sexuality which does not necessarily need to be emphasized or talked about because it is normal, standard, as well as normalizing and standardizing. On the other hand, everything outside the matrix of the heterosexual blueprint is unnecessary to hear for one side (the normative one), unnecessary to mark and acknowledge, and is yet nothing less than vital for the other.

Such dynamics are further fueled within the context of same-sex, or any other 'non-normative'—or let me go with the over encompassing term *queer*, here—desire. This context is framed largely by this idea of resistance to hegemony, by its rejection of dominant power structures and norms, including those related to race and social class, in addition to gender and sexuality. In particular, the breeding ground of hip-hop culture significantly draws from the heteronormative, hypersexual, and hypermasculine concept of *the Subject*,[3] namely, the male subject. With prevalent elements of vulgarity, bravado, and braggadocio, the homophobic, misogynistic, and violent undertones[4] set the foundation

---

3   Herein, I refer to the philosophical definition of the concept of the subject, which denotes the individual self, self-awareness, and identity, and which as such should not inherently reflect any truth about gender, but which in the (Western) history of society is almost synonymously equated with the masculine identity, as a result of many historical and cultural biases. In the same vein, Simone de Beauvoir writes in her seminal book *The Second Sex* (1949): "[Woman] is determined and differentiated in relation to man, while he is not in relation to her; she is the inessential in front of the essential. He is the Subject; he is the Absolute. She is the Other" (2011 [1949]: 6).

4   Here one could highlight Juvenile's track "March N***a Step" (1999); Nelly's remix "Tip Drill," particularly the music video that was criticized for its themes of misogyny; or Eminem's *The Marshall Mathers LP* album (2000), which thematically and lyrically feeds on the themes of violence, misogyny, and homophobic slurs.

for the "toxic forms of masculinity," as Christal Daly (2019) argues.[5] Further, Matthew Oware contextualizes these forms of demeanor as "a particular presentation of self" that "emerges due to the limited opportunities that many Black males face in their daily lives" (2011: 23). He continues by referencing Mark Anthony Neal (2006) and Majors and Billson (1992) in disclosing how the masculine aesthetic of the "Strong Black Man" started with its genesis 400 year ago "due to the enslavement, violence, and continued economic exploitation of this group. As a result, black males created a 'functional myth' to help them handle their plight. ... [A]lthough black males defined their manhood similarly to white males—provider, breadwinner, procreator, and protector—they did not have the necessary resources to fulfil those roles" (Oware 2011: 23). This results in a form of masculinity that is ritualized and created in a chain of "carefully crafted performances" interwoven with "unique patterns of speech, walk and demeanor," among other instances (ibid.). An additional stream to this discussion can be found in Raewyn Connell's thoughts, who, in referring to Robert Staples and his 1982 book *Black Masculinity: The Black Male's Role in American Society*, writes that "the level of violence among black men in the United States can only be understood through the changing place of the black labor force in American capitalism and the violent means used to control it. Massive unemployment and urban poverty now powerfully interact with institutional racism in the shaping of black masculinity" (2005: 80).

Taking a few steps back from these ideas and considering masculinity as a kaleidoscope of socio-psychological factors, which are nevertheless subject to a certain systematization, could allow us to break down the particularities of each individual group or their intersections. A starting point can be taken from the most common reference for the classification of masculinity, that of the above-mentioned Raewyn Connell, in-

---

5   Of course, here it is necessary to refer to the fact that it is difficult, especially with more contemporary performing practices and aspirations, to subsume all hip hop under the above-mentioned categories. And it would be unfair not to keep in mind the antipodes in the form of conscious and political hip-hop subgenres.

cluded in a more general discussion of gender and power models in her 1987 book *Gender and power*, with a more comprehensive approach in the 1995 publication *Masculinities*.

For Connell, masculinity branches out into four tenets (2005: 76–81); *the hegemonic form*, as the dominant one, one that is implied and expected by Western society, then *the complicit form*, where the subject may not fit into all the features of the hegemonic form and norm, but still tries to somehow reflect it. The third type for her is *the marginalized* model of masculinity, in which the dominant feature is the inability to penetrate the hegemonic norm, due to specific instances such as race. The last form is *the subordinate masculinity*, with the subject projecting characteristics in polar opposition to the ones proscribed by the hegemonic model. Still, it is important to have in mind that Connell's proposed nomenclature by no means implies absolute qualities. She argues that these are "not fixed character types," but rather "configurations of practice generated in particular situations in a changing structure of relationships. Namely, any theory of masculinity worth having must give an account of this process of change" (2005: 81).

Further, especially through considering the latter two forms—the marginalized and the subordinate practice of masculinity—their precarious positions are what constitutes them in a greater sense. Yet, Connell's understanding underlines one big difference, and this is the fact that marginalized groups are specifically engaged in changing the narrative, while strongly adopting the dominant features of the hegemonic model. Additionally, in trying to compensate for the inability to penetrate this domain, the marginalized and subordinate groups will amplify features such as aggression and combativeness, and at the same time suppress emotions and overall self-reflection, as Connell argues (2005: 46, 102–103). Somewhere within this cleft of attempting to reshape the narrative while simultaneously embracing hegemonic aspects, we should consider the dominant masculinity trait of hip-hop culture, which, from the 2000s onwards has nevertheless changed in some ways: it became less violent, on the one hand, but on the other, there are practices of oversexualization of women that are still very much pronounced through its cultural production, as many authors have noted.[6] This phenomenon in particular, may be interpreted as reflecting a certain compensation for one's own marginality in relation to hegemonic male Whiteness. The relation of the positive and its negative other, in the discussion of gender identities in hip-hop music, can be broken down on many levels. Kai Arne Hansen explains the logic of their precise pairing well:

> At the extreme, the dichotomy between hegemonic and nonhegemonic—or negative and positive—masculinities adhere to a binary logic that resembles the one that underpins the naturalization of masculinity and femininity as opposing categories. The shortcomings of any dichotomy relate to its exclusionary dimensions, by which I mean that dichotomies tend to hide from view whatever does not correspond to either of their mutually exclusive parts. (2021: 18)

In relation to this, besides urban structural inequalities paired with systematic racism, one needs to keep in mind that Black hip-hop culture emerged in part as a response to the Black masculinity crisis,[7] beginning in the 1970s. The initial currents of hip hop not only provided essential social commentary but also served as a significant platform for male rappers to respond to the multifaceted challenges facing Black men of that era. These challenges encompassed social, economic, and political

---

[6] I will herein point to articles by Adams and Fuller ("The words have changed but the ideology remains the same: Misogynistic lyrics in rap music," 2006); Aubrey and Frisby ("Sexual objectification in music videos: A content analysis comparing gender and genre," 2011), but also to songs such as Major Lazer ft. Tyga, 2Chainz, Bruno Mars et al.'s 2013 "Bubble Butt," 2Chainz ft. Kanye West and their track "Birthday Song" (2012), and Future's "My Collection" from 2017. Additionally, the issue of hypersexualization should not be unequivocally attributed to male rappers. Female rappers, such as Cardi B or Megan Thee Stallion, have embraced sexual objectification and promote it themselves. On the one hand, this can be interpreted as a common advertising tactic of 'sex sells,' but also as a strategy for female empowerment and sexual self-awareness.

[7] Among many sources writing on this matter, I would highlight Robert Staples' *Black Masculinity: The Black Male's Role in American Society* (1982), and Mark Anthony Neal's *New Black Man*, with its first edition in 2006.

issues, particularly prevalent in urban America. It is important to recall the stark realities of that time: rampant poverty, soaring unemployment rates, pernicious negative stereotypes, and the consequential dearth of opportunities afflicting Black communities, with a particular impact on Black men in The Bronx from the 1970s on.[8] This crisis may not have been acknowledged or recognized by mainstream society at the time, which could have contributed to the development of hip-hop culture as a means for Black men to express their experiences and assert their identities in ways that were not otherwise available to them. Having to come to terms with the fact that the Western society's cultural notion of the dominant form of masculinity or manhood in the first instance is that of "a white, heterosexual, largely middle-class male" (Ezeifeka 2019: 389), the subordinated classes or ethnic groups' marginalized position is always read as "relative to the *authorization* [original emphasis] of the hegemonic masculinity of the dominant group" (Connell 2005: 80–81).

The divide between the normative male subject and his subordinate counterpart presents a complex narrative that touches upon the realms of both marginality and relativity. However, this very rupture simultaneously serves as a fertile ground for individuals to express themselves and assert their identities.

---

8   This interpretation must not be understood unilaterally when it comes to the gender structure of hip-hop culture in its beginnings. Namely, early female participation in hip hop, which undeniably existed right from the outset and had its share of valuable social commentary, carried a distinct and predominantly female perspective (Roxanne Shanté or Queen Latifah might be referenced as perhaps the most well-known names that marked this early wave). It functioned, in essence, as a counterpoint to the prevailing male narrative, predominantly celebrating themes of empowerment and self-expression. These trailblazing women in hip hop presented a compelling perspective, highlighting the resilience and strength of females as they established their distinct presence in a genre undergoing rapid evolution, often diverging significantly from the predominant 'male voice.' A good overview of such streams can be found in publications such as Kathy Iandoli's 2020 book *God Save the Queens: The Essential History of Women in Hip-Hop* or Clover Hope's *The Motherlode: 100+ Women Who Made Hip-Hop* (2021).

Identity Negotiations I: Textual Analysis of "Bad Religion"

From this summarized overview of Raewyn Connell's schemata of masculinities in Western societies, I believe it becomes evident that the hegemonic model is taken as *the* model towards which the other three forms relate and establish themselves in a more or less direct way, with the latter mostly considered *unfavorable* derivatives. Drawing from this relation between the dominant, hegemonic image, and its resultants, all the non-hegemonic forms of masculinity are therefore seen and practiced as a specific deviation from the norm. Such a system of hierarchy, in whichever cultural-political context, builds its internal structure on the principle of strictly limited spaces, practices and identity markers. It is a system that is unfavorable to 'let' the spokespeople of one's culture, in this particular context that of hip-hop culture, to transgress the prescribed or expected gender/sexuality norms.[9] Yet, in the case of Frank Ocean, this transgression was indicated first, ostensibly by chance, by alluding to his own non-hegemonic Black male sexuality, only to turn him, with time, into a destroyer of the dam that clearly marked the boundary between hip-hop culture and the territory of non-normative sexual identities and desires.

The first such transgression is evident in the track "Oldie" by Odd Future from 2012, where Ocean's verse includes a line in which he says that he is high, and he is bi, but wait—he will say—I meant to say I am straight,[10] a play on words, for which an annotation on Genius[11] (Odd Future 2012) claims are a triple entendre. The reference reads:

---

9   XinLing Li claims the consequences of such prospects are far reaching: "homophobia in hip-hop survives on the dearth of out rappers, a phenomenon that has its roots in gay men's lack of participation in traditionally masculinised sites of sociopolitical discourse" (2019: 11).

10   Owing to copyright issues, this chapter exclusively paraphrases song lyrics. See Odd Future (2012) for direct lyrics.

11   The last edited version of the annotation was written in 2018, by the user AndrewGar.

a) "I'm hi and I'm bye" refers to the way he is with people (women), where he just gets in and gets out no drama;
b) However, it could also be, "I'm high and I'm bye," as in high and drunk ("I'm bye" as in "I'm so gone"); and
c) With the recent news of Frank Ocean's bisexuality this line is a reference to that as well.

The annotation continues, "This line was Frank casually putting one over all of our heads. Most people when they heard that song just thought it was a witty play on words, rather than an allusion to his actual bisexuality. Frank Ocean basically came out in this verse, and it went unnoticed because no one really believed that he meant it at the time."

Such a hint to his sexuality, albeit accidental and not semantically exclusive, experienced its full actualization in the further professional step Ocean made that same year with the release of his first commercial album, *Channel Orange*, on Def Jam Records, an event that coincided with the singer's coming-out letter posted on Tumblr, entitled "thank you's" (Ocean 2012a). However, here it is important to note that he never explicitly made a statement, or put a precise label on his sexuality, a concept he strongly rejected whenever asked about it. However, the groundbreaking Tumblr post should nevertheless be considered as a specific statement in expressing his same-sex desires in the public arena. In his *GQ* interview from 2012, published some four months after the post, when asked directly if he is bisexual, Ocean gave a response provided here in part:

> You can move to the next question. I'll respectfully say that life is dynamic and comes along with dynamic experiences, and the same sentiment that I have towards genres of music, I have towards a lot of labels and boxes and shit. ... People should pay attention to [the following] in the letter: I didn't need to label it for it to have impact. Because people realize everything that I say is so relatable, because when you're talking about romantic love, both sides in all scenarios feel the same shit. As a writer, as a creator, I'm giving you my experiences. But just take what I give you. You ain't got to pry beyond that.

> I'm giving you what I feel like you can feel. The other shit, you can't feel. You can't feel a box. You can't feel a label. (Wallace 2012)

Despite a certain impression of detachment and objectification of such a strong identity instance as one's sexual orientation, such a bold statement has stuck an unbreakable patch on Ocean's persona that marks his semantic field of sexuality as the primary identifier. In other words, by legitimizing his sexuality as out-of-the-norm, that specific identifier became synonymous with his public figure, making him a paragon of the queer hip-hop artist. How significant and influential that move was, not only for the perception of his public significance, but also for the broader discussion of hip-hop culture, can certainly be witnessed by one example from his direct circle of activity; it is Lil Wayne's (Dwayne Michael Carter, Jr.) track "Turn On the Lights" from the same year (2012), where he raps in the last hook about how he skateboards like a real man. Basically, he is not Frank Ocean; he is straight (Lil Wayne 2012).[12]

Exactly this need to stay out of the boxes, out of the categories our surroundings and other more formal structures prescribe, can be argued is present in Frank Ocean's creative expression as well, where eluding any clean categorizations becomes the imperative. Beyond the binary norms, beyond the hegemonic masculinity grid, beyond the one-way Black rapper's expression,[13] beyond the violent, homophobic, or sexist matrix hip-hop culture was long characterized and reprimanded for. On the other hand, what makes the issue of gender in the case of Frank Ocean even more surprising, or simply confusing, is its relative absence as a major theme or narrative in Ocean's oeuvre. Namely, the role of gender in his

---

12 See Lil Wayne (2012) for direct lyrics.
13 The one that is inescapably "constructed in white-supremacist capitalist patriarchy" (hooks 2004: x). Although she would point to the "undeniable sense of freedom hip-hop manages to provide to Black men, ... tied to intellectual growth and camaraderie," Crystal Belle would also agree that "an unemotional persona lies at the heart of Black masculine performances. This is often an act, a performance of sorts that asserts a manhood that is dominant and deviant, attempting to define itself in a world that has often tried to deny the very existence of Black men" (2014: 288–289).

work remained relatively unimportant and was by no means elevated to a central theme or a platform for activism. In other words, one might expect that such a bold step of disclosing his non-normative sexuality would make gender more than a nominal category for Frank Ocean. Tiq Milan (2016) underlines this as the following:

> His art centralizes a queer sensibility while queer identity is still being navigated as a margin. It doesn't feed the social media frenzy or follow a cookie cutter formula. His music betrays genres in the same way queers challenge gender. There are few gender signifiers in his love ballads but that doesn't make it any less poignant.

Nevertheless, Frank Ocean's characters can generally be viewed through an intersectional lens. However, even the 'unfavorable' aspects are integrated into his writing, serving as reflections of his own experiences and the collective consciousness shared by his entire generation. Namely, even though "Ocean's production of a vulnerable musical space subverts the hypermasculine, hypersexual, hyper violent stereotypes of Black men in hip hop that define emotional vulnerability as a weakness," as Josephine Blanchon (2020: 83) claims, I would point to the fact that this vulnerable, honest, self-reflective man is not a one-sided position Ocean speaks from and to. His man is also the ruthless pimp (in the song "Pyramids" from *Channel Orange*, the narrator switches between the voice of the affectionate lover to his beloved queen, Cleopatra, to becoming a manipulator who is only concerned about his stripper paying his bills), and using the derogatory term "bitch" in the song "Chanel," in a way "conforms to the expectation of misogyny in heteronormative masculinity from the 1990s" (Blanchon 2020: 83). Namely, "by using this term, Ocean attempts to draw on traditional expectations of strength in masculinity ... by conforming to his audience's expectations" (ibid.).[14]

---

14   In all fairness, the term "bitch" in "Chanel" might also be interpreted as a metaphor for the music industry, as Ocean wants to conquer it, to humiliate it; therefore, it/she should grind on his belt, as the lyrics say. Also, one of the reviewers of this article, to whom I am very grateful, directed me to the lyrics of Jack Harlow's track "Churchill Downs" (2022), featuring Drake, who in his verse

Alex Layton (2017) also forewarned about Ocean's "using of females as social capital" as reproducing the sexist rhetoric. Herein, I would also point to the song "Chanel" (2017), which has become an emblematic topic in discussions about the gendered statements in his oeuvre. With the hook saying how he sees both of the two sides, just like Chanel, and, further, how he, sort of, operates on both sides,[15] the track was unanimously accepted among scholars as a statement on Ocean's bisexuality, a sort of a bisexual anthem of a generation.[16] In the subsequent discussion, however, I direct my focus to the track "Bad Religion" (2012), from the *Channel Orange* album, the musical and textual organization of which I believe approaches the issue of gender and sexual identity through a multi-layered intersectional filter.[17]

In his storytelling manner, Frank introduces us to the story through a self-perspective. He sits in the taxi driver's car and asks, in complete anonymity, for him to act as his shrink for an hour. He makes it clear to the taxi driver that he has demons to deal with, setting "the song's overall tone of reflective, pseudo-religious angst," as the user Elizabeth Ayme

---

raps, "When I say bitch I'm very rarely referring to women, Most of the bitches I know are n****s they not even women." However, the term 'bitch' as an interchangeable currency again carries the asymmetry of power and even so when it is addressed to men or boys, 'bitch' takes on a different connotation and becomes a derogatory term implying subservience, weakness, or cowardice; that is, being/acting as a woman would.

15 See Ocean (2017) for direct lyrics.
16 Among the authors who have tackled the duality of the lyrics and the musical setting of the song, I would point readers to the honors thesis of Josephine Blanchon from 2020 *Representations of Black Queer Masculinity in Contemporary Popular Music: A Close Analysis of Tyler, The Creator and Frank Ocean*. Furthermore, Blanchon's text can serve as a good delineation in outlining individual Frank Ocean songs from the perspective of gender and masculinity (I rely on her dualistic reading of the song "Chanel" in my text), although she focuses on illuminating the changes and developments that the category of Black masculinity has undergone in the last fifty years in contemporary popular music, which significantly diverges from the aims of my chapter.
17 See Ocean (2012) for direct lyrics.

(Ocean 2012) in the annotation on Genius suggests. His taxi driver, however, comes from a different religious background, and Ocean responds to his "Allahu Akbar" with a plea not to curse him, ruminating out loud on this ever-thematized topic of unrequited love: be it his lover, be it society, be it religion in this example (possibly as a metaphor for society in a more general sense). One of the most potent lines in the song, the chorus line that reads: that, which brings someone to their knees, cannot be but bad religion (Ocean 2012), touches on the topic of the weight of endurance of what faith puts before us: the weight of dealing with the expectations of the society which assesses the strength of one's faith or belonging to a religion and its practices in general. It is a line applicable to the widest possible notion of 'deviation' from that same set of rules; it might refer to the dialectic of sin and forgiveness, which from the angle of one's sexuality and in the realm of religion, can be considered a painful and traumatic experience. In that sense, our protagonist's love for God becomes an unrequited one. This line echoes some of the sentiments from Frank Ocean's 2016 open letter that was published in response to the Orlando mass shooting in a gay club (released on June 21, the same day the shooting occurred). The Genius annotations also discuss this, and the letter questioned why "some religious people believe that God wants them to hurt, even kill, others for not following what they believe to be God's law" (user Elizabeth Ayme [Ocean 2012]).

The question of determining what this love means for him, that is, towards whom it is directed and from whom it is unrequited, he once again decides on ambiguous strategies of expression. Further, how he can never make him love him (Ocean 2018: 02:18) says the line from the last chorus, which is the most downright allusion to his love for another man on *Channel Orange*, one could argue. Be that as it may, playing many sides in his lyricism and allusions, this "him" may also be interpreted as "Him," with a capital "h," alluding to Frank being unable to make "a God that frowns upon homosexuality love him" (user Ashley Chittock on Genius [Ocean 2012]).

In verse two, Ocean admits to the taxi driver how he balances three lives, three different living experiences, as a heavy burden, a precariousness which he compares to steak knives lingering just above a person's head. This is another line that points to the impossibility of reaching an equilibrium between the roles he must fulfil and the lives he wants to live: the private Frank seen from the prism of publicity, the Frank who is someone's love/lover and the Frank whose love life may not be in accordance with hegemonic-normative social expectations and the public eye. This is especially telling in the context of him still not having written the infamous Tumblr post when this song was recorded, "hence his 'disguise' that he mentions in the next line," as user Elizabeth Ayme believes (Ocean 2012). And this confession is another powerful vehicle in transmitting what lies deeply hidden within him; Ocean says he cannot tell the driver (or the listener?) the truth about his identity, that is, about his disguise, as he cannot trust anyone. This loudly underlines the predicament he is in, where everyone becomes an enemy with even the slightest blunder or slip of the tongue, leaving him vulnerable to exposing his true self.

Identity Negotiations II: Musical Analysis of "Bad Religion"

Musically, Ocean depicted this confessional *Lacrimosa* statement accordingly. In terms of form, it is a perfect formula of a verse-chorus-verse-chorus-outro. In a procedure we find very frequently in his music, we have an intro, this time the sound of an organ in a descending major (almost) tetrachord (as he shifts to the subdominant), announcing something solemn, frightening, but worthy of celebration. The protagonist entering the taxi and having to confess something echoes the frightening church space and the daunting organ resonance, recorded in two-channel. This sets the tonal and melodic foundation for the verses, with Ocean's confession and appeal to the taxi driver. In this call, Ocean's voice is on the brink of breaking, conveying the intensity and anguish he feels, as well as the weakness of his spirit.

Of note is the musical arrangement of the chorus, questioning what compels Ocean to fall on his knees and then immediately offer a response to this quandary. Namely, this melodic ascent unfolds along secondary dominants (Ocean 2018: 0:44–0:48) culminating in a resolution in the antithesis, asserting that only a bad religion can evoke such a surrender, beautifully captured in the tonic (ibid.: 0:49–0:52). This musical journey symbolizes the author's ultimate acceptance and harmony with the seemingly unacceptable aspects of the environment, society, and religion as a whole. The verse, I would say, breaks in two, which Ocean marks by an overall change in his voice: from a full-blooded throat singing reminiscent of a church call, he switches to a barely audible, uncertain, and timid conjecture about unrequited love and the question: can he become worthy of his, that is "His," with a capital "h," love?

This overt depiction of same-sex desire is musically hinted at in a concealed manner, as if he poses a question to himself and God, that he hopes his shrink on four wheels will not hear. On this aspect of employing two voices, as in two levels of vocal delivery, in her analysis of the song "Chanel," Josephine Blanchon sees a duality "that might be seen as representing two facets of Ocean's sexuality as the listener hears his voice from two perspectives; the two voices depict him as part of 'both sides' literally" (2020: 80). Later, Blanchon notes how "the two voices can be understood as alluding to his attraction to both men and women and as portraying Ocean as a man divided within himself" (ibid.).

In its second delivery, this exact place in the second portion of the verse (Ocean 2018: 1:52–2:00) is accompanied by bass and amplified strings, and the mechanical rhythmic bass has this metallic sound that evokes the coldness of the ostinato death march. Herein, supported musically, Frank opens up completely, and reaches the finale in the highest tone of the song, through a throaty falsetto (ibid.: 2:26). These "belting notes that reach the outer threshold of his chest voice," is for Blanchon "another musical decision that is often seen as weak" (2020: 82). Their intention, she states, is to "express his vulnerability regarding his love interest," but to stretch it a bit further, she claims these "higher notes also have a sexual undertone due to the strain involved in reaching [them]" (ibid.), to which I would not agree. Rather, I see these uncontrolled vocal gestures as a reflection of the impossibility of controlling one's own subject before what is above us: either our sexuality, or religion.

In the outro, Ocean still ruminates on his predicament, in a melodic scope of a third, with a full voice that has given up on the subject of their desire. The sentiment spreads to unrequited love *to anyone*, really, in the line from the outro, which points to the hurdle of harboring affection for someone who could never reciprocate another person's love (Ocean 2018: 2:31–2:37). The "someone" is apostrophized, the only part of the text recorded in a multiplied voice, as a sign of universality, in a plagal harmonic relationship of tonic and subdominant. This harmonic correlation is in fact another framework Ocean's music stays within, often avoiding the relationship of tonic and dominant, culturally, and historically charged with, gender tension dualism and polarity. Another good example would be the track "Pink Matter" from *Channel Orange*, which, once again, touches upon the difference between the male and female subject, as a terrain of his desires and social norms that are put upon him and stays almost completely in the framework of the aforementioned harmonic relationship.

Navigating Identity, Ambiguity, and Social Commentary: Concluding Remarks

In the pursuit of a postmodern paradigm and the goal of exposing culturally gendered practices, particularly within the genre of pop songs, Frank Ocean diverges from subgenre categorizations and instead experiments with form. This allows him to expand the meaning of his work beyond traditional boundaries and explore topics such as educational content and critique of toxic masculinity and violence against women, all from a deeply personal perspective. Ocean's approach has earned him the label of "carefree-masculinity" (Milan 2016); but also, criticism for his lack of political engagement, particularly in light of the Black Lives Matter movement (cf. King and Powers 2016).

One, of course, needs to look at his work in the context of maneuvering the boundary between the commercial artist and the indie scene: Ocean opted for a "non-traditional route when promoting his music, by not participating in the major social media platforms such as Twitter,

Instagram, or Facebook" (Gardias 2019: 30). In addition, it should not be overlooked that his project trajectories always seem to follow the same route: taking as much time as he needs for delivering a new album or new track, this "young man [is] on no one's timeline but his own" (Scott 2016), while at the same time leaving his audience cryptic messages on his Tumblr account or Instagram,[18] catering for specific user groups. In general, one could argue that Frank Ocean's "deliberate ambiguity" (Blanchon 2020: 81) potentially contributes to the increased market appeal of his creations. This notion aligns with Josephine Blanchon's argument, where she highlights a conventional trope within hip-hop culture, that of materialism, through her analysis of the song "Chanel."[19]

Certainly, Frank Ocean's enigmatic and elusive persona in the realm of pop culture, coupled with his unconventional marketing tactics, has led to a significant increase in his overall marketability. This leads me to my final point, which is somewhat alluded to in Blanchon's text, and has caused me to reconsider the potential impact of Frank Ocean's identity crisis as a means of speaking out on social and political issues, as well as creating art that is heavily influenced by this experience. Namely, the most forthright signal of this symbiosis came hand in hand with the mass-marketing 101 lesson, as Ocean posted about his same-sex love on his Tumblr six days before *Channel Orange* came out. I bring this text to a

---

18   Despite Katharine Gardias pointing out Frank Ocean's departure from contemporary social media promotion practices, particularly on Instagram, it is worth noting that the singer did create an Instagram account in 2017 under the username "blonded." To date, this account has amassed 4 million followers, yet there has not been a single post retained on the account. Occasionally, Frank does share cryptic or suggestive posts or stories when he chooses to engage with the platform; these are either deleted or expire after twenty-four hours.

19   To turn the focus toward the gender discussion, I will herein quote Nayo Sasaki-Picou, who also evaluated Ocean's statement about his sexuality as unproblematic in his further perception, precisely because of his performance of masculinity which does not take away from the desired, hegemonic form: "Frank Ocean's public performance of hegemonic masculinity suggests that this constructed version of black masculinity remains as the socially acceptable norm, despite his 'coming out'" (2014: 103).

close with a quote by Matt Donnelly, and his *Los Angeles Times* article that rather provocatively opens up the possibility of Ocean's intimate lament which thereafter became his "exclusive right" (I am here referring mainly to *GQ* magazine's abrupt refusal to discuss it further): "Maybe his fans enjoy the coded morsels in his song lyrics about heartbreak or Ocean is learning in advance to keep the juicier parts of his identity close to the vest. But if his sentiment on 'prying' makes anything clear, he's holding the cards—along with cash, industry cred and a *GQ* Man of the Year title. Content indeed" (Donnelly 2012).

In hindsight, now more than ten years after his bombastic coming out, it seems more than justified to discuss these pivotal events in the light of a broader marketing strategy. To this day, his coming-outs (in the sense of appearing in the public light, because let us remember—fans often wonder if Frank Ocean is alive at all) still happen in amplitudes, like some seismological panorama of his public pulse. Sometimes it is here, sometimes it is not, but mostly nowhere to be seen or found. Yet, when he does emerge, he engages in discussions on significant topics, whether personal or societal. The buzz around him consistently arises as a response to what Ocean chooses to share in a particular moment, including the strategic elements of marketing. Ultimately, Ocean has maintained a deliberate ambiguity surrounding his sexual identity, resisting being confined to labels or categories, but also mixing different perspectives of sexual orientation and interests, never giving us a clear and unambiguous answer. This refusal to conform has had a significant impact on Frank Ocean's public image, on how he is perceived, and what is expected of him in advance, making him a prominent figure in the discussion of pop-culture icons, and queer hip-hop artists in particular.

Discography/Videography

Ocean, Frank. 2018. "Bad Religion." Blonded. Posted on October 30, 2018. YouTube video, 2:55. https://www.youtube.com/watch?v=JMpypbtrcCg&ab_channel=FrankOcean-Topic.

References

Belle, Crystal. 2014. "From Jay-Z to Dead Prez: Examining Representations of Black Masculinity in Mainstream Versus Underground Hip-Hop Music." *Journal of Black Studies* 45 (4): 287–300. https://doi.org/10.1177/0021934714528953.

Blanchet, Brenton. 2020. "An oral history of Frank Ocean's former songwriting alias, Lonny Breaux." *The Face*, March 4, 2020. https://theface.com/music/lonny-breaux-frank-ocean-songwriting-midi-mafia-oral-history.

Blanchon, Josephine. 2020. "Representations of Black Queer Masculinity in Contemporary Popular Music: A Close Analysis of Tyler, The Creator and Frank Ocean." Honors thesis, Bates College. https://scarab.bates.edu/honorstheses/326.

Connell, Raewyn. 2003. *Gender and Power: Society, the Person and Sexual Politics*. Cambridge: Polity Press-Blackwell Publishers Ltd.

Connell, Raewyn. 2005. *Masculinities*. Berkeley: University of California Press.

Daly, Christal. 2019. "How Frank Redefines Masculinity Through His Music." Medium, December 11, 2019. https://medium.com/@cdaly0225/how-frank-redefines-masculinity-through-his-music-f1b958fe95ba.

de Beauvoir, Simone. 2011 [1949]. *The Second Sex*. New York: Vintage Books.

Donnelly, Matt. 2012. "Frank Ocean and the art of identity crisis." *Los Angeles Times Online*, November 20, 2012. https://www.latimes.com/entertainment/la-xpm-2012-nov-20-la-et-mg-frank-ocean-sexuality-gq-men-of-the-year-story.html.

Ezeifeka, Chinwe RoseAnn. 2019. "Patriarchal Legitimization Strategies in Igbo Gender-Related Taboos: A Case for Critical Discourse Analysis." *Advances in Social Sciences Research Journal* 6 (3): 383–400. https://doi.org/10.14738/assrj.63.6229.

Gardias, Katharine. 2019. "A Dip Into Frank Ocean's Music and Marketing." Senior project, California Polytechnic State University. https://digitalcommons.calpoly.edu/cgi/viewcontent.cgi?articl e=1109&context=musp.

Hansen, Kai Arne. 2021. *Pop Masculinities. The Politics of Gender in Twenty-First Century Popular Music.* Oxford: Oxford University Press. https://doi.org/10.1093/oso/9780190938796.001.0001.

hooks, bell. 2004. *We Real Cool: Black Men and Masculinity.* New York: Routledge. https://doi.org/10.4324/9780203642207.

Kellman, Andy. n.d. "Frank Ocean Biography." AllMusic. Accessed May 6, 2023. https://www.allmusic.com/artist/frank-ocean-mn0002592086/biography.

King, Jason, and Ann Powers. 2016. "Detangling Frank Ocean's 'Blonde': What It Is And Isn't." National Public Radio, August 22, 2016. https://www.npr.org/sections/therecord/2016/08/22/490918270/detangling-frank-oceans-blonde-what-it-is-and-isnt.

Layton, Alex. 2017. "Frank Ocean: Challenging Hip-Hop's Hyper-Masculinity." *Prindle Post,* September 26, 2017. https://www.prindleinstitute.org/2017/09/frank-ocean-challenging-hip-hops-hyper-masculinity/.

Li, XinLing. 2019. *Black Masculinity and Hip-Hop Music: Black Gay Men Who Rap.* Singapore: Palgrave Macmillan. https://doi.org/10.1007/978-981-13-3513-6.

Lil Wayne. 2012. "Turn On the Lights." Genius. https://genius.com/Lil-wayne-turn-on-the-lights-lyrics.

Milan, Tiq. 2016. "Opinion: Frank Ocean Is the Perfect Model of 'Carefree Black Masculinity.'" NBC News. https://www.nbcnews.com/feature/nbc-out/opinion-frank-ocean-perfect-model-carefree-black-masculinity-n642051.

Ocean, Frank. 2012. "Bad Religion." Genius. https://genius.com/Frank-ocean-bad-religion-lyrics.

Ocean, Frank. 2012a. "thank you's." Tumblr post, July 4, 2012. https://frankocean.tumblr.com/image/26473798723.

Ocean, Frank. 2017. "Chanel." Genius. https://genius.com/Frank-ocean-chanel-lyrics.

Odd Future. 2012. "Oldie." Genius. https://genius.com/Odd-future-oldie-lyrics.

Oware, Matthew. 2011. "Brotherly Love: Homosociality and Black Masculinity in Gangsta Rap Music." *Journal of African American Studies* 15 (1): 22–39. https://doi.org/10.1007/s12111-010-9123-4.

Sasaki-Picou, Nayo. 2014. "Performing Gender. The Construction of Black Males in the Hip-Hop Industry." *Contingent Horizons: The York University Student Journal of Anthropology* 1 (1): 103–107. https://doi.org/10.25071/2292-6739.50.

Scott, Shaun. 2016. "Frank Ocean is the Unapologetic Prophet of America's New Masculinity." *Paste Magazine,* September 2, 2016. https://www.pastemagazine.com/politics/frank-ocean/frank-ocean-is-the-unapologetic-symbol-of-americas/.

Wallace, Amy. 2012. "Frank Ocean: On Channel Orange, Meeting Odd Future, and His Tumblr Letter." *GQ,* November 20, 2012. https://www.gq.com/story/frank-ocean-interview-gq-december-2012.

Afro-Cosmopolitanisms
Discourses on Race and Urban Identities in Brazilian Hip Hop

Eliseo Jacob

Abstract *Hip hop is a cultural practice in which Black youth in Brazil's working-class, urban communities have explored and expressed their lived experiences. For this chapter, I will examine how contemporary hip hoppers have developed an urban cosmopolitanism characterized by a Black aesthetic rooted in a working-class ethos that responds to the racial discrimination and social marginalization they experience. These hip hoppers, in particular during the 2010s and 2020s, incorporate expressions of Blackness into their work as they seek to not only publicly denounce racial and class prejudices, but espouse new forms of Black pride: they call upon the American notion of the ghetto to espouse a Black urban cultural identity rooted in their lived experiences in the* favelas *(slums) and* periferias *(working-class outskirts); they frequently reference Afro-diasporic historical figures and Black pop culture; and they follow in the practice of Afro-Brazilian cultural productions from previous generations by calling upon African-based cultural, religious, and spiritual traditions as a way to celebrate their ethnic heritage. Ultimately, this newer generation of Brazilian hip hop problematizes how Blackness has been minimized and marginalized in Brazil through meta-narratives like racial democracy by situating itself within a global Black urban cultural practice.*

On May 13, 2012, Afro-Brazilian rapper Emicida was arrested in the Brazilian city of Belo Horizonte at the conclusion of his show. He sent out a tweet regarding the incident stating that "I was arrested for disrespect to authority after a show in BH [Belo Horizonte] due to the song 'Dedo na ferida' [Finger in the Wound]" (@emicida: 2012). The song was dedicated to the victims of the *favelas* (slums or shantytowns) of Moinho, Pinheirinho, Cracolândia, Rio dos Macacos, and Alcântara (the majority of whom are Afro-descendant and working class) who were displaced by violent police action in São Paulo. A spokesperson for the military police claimed Emicida was arrested for inciting the public to make obscene gestures to the police who were policing the event as well as politicians. Emicida was eventually released the next day; however, the incident along with the song at the center of the controversy—which was released on Emicida's blog in March of that same year—speaks to larger power dynamics related to race and social class imbued within Brazilian society. The rap song and the police's violent reaction to it, in a way reveal what anthropologist João Vargas identifies as the hyperconsciousness of race, in which Brazilians and the Brazilian state go to great lengths to repeatedly deny the central role race has played in the country's social formation even though ideologies like racial democracy[1] have been used to create the myth of harmonious social relations between different races and social classes (2005: 15). Emicida's

---

[1] Racial democracy was an idea developed during the 20th century to describe racial relations in Brazil. It was advanced by scholars, in particular Gilberto Freyre, who wrote about racial formations in Brazil in his 1933 book *Casa Grande e Senzala* (The Masters and the Slaves). The idea of racial democracy is rooted in the notion that Brazil is beyond racism and racial discrimination due to the mixing of different races and ethnic groups throughout its history. Contemporary scholars have pointed to the problems of racial democracy in that state apparatuses have used this ideology to argue that while other forms of discrimination may exist, racism is not an issue for Brazilian society, thereby making it difficult for individuals and organizations to effectively address problems to do with racism in civil society. For additional analysis on the relationship between race and national identity in Brazil, see Thomas Skidmore's seminal work *Black into White: Race and Nationality in Brazilian Thought* (1992).

song and performance speak to how Brazilian rap is disrupting these social norms by addressing issues relating to racism and inequality in a direct manner by evoking Afrocentric cultural traditions and histories that create a Black identity not limited to the dictates of hegemonic cultural norms that have a vested interest in maintaining existent racial and social hierarchies.

Emicida's body of work represents a larger trend taking place among certain sectors of contemporary Brazilian rap in the 21st century, namely achieving commercial success while staying committed to an Afrocentric aesthetic that situates it within the larger African diaspora both within and beyond Brazil. He, along with other contemporary Brazilian rappers like Baco Exu do Blues, Rincon Sapiência, Drik Barbosa, Tássia Reis, and BK, compose raps that center the Black experience in Brazil by focusing on issues that range from racism, state violence, and social inequality to topics that celebrate the importance of their African ancestry. Like the Golden Age of hip hop in the United States (mid-1980s to early, mid-1990s),[2] they are currently part of the mainstream hip-hop scene in Brazil but continue to experiment with different rhythms and frequently use rap as an artistic and poetic medium that addresses important social issues and cultural traditions related to Afro-Brazilian communities through an Afrocentric lens.

Hip hop has a long history in Brazil, going back to the early 1980s and changing through different phases during the last thirty-five years. Because Brazil has the largest Afro-descendant population outside of Africa, hip hop has always been framed by concerns with racial inequality and reaffirming pride in one's ethnic identity. Hip hop has been a space where Afro-descendant youth in Brazil's working-class, urban communities have been afforded the opportunity to explore and express their experiences as marginalized citizens. One of the foremost scholars on Brazilian hip hop, Derek Pardue, has observed how this

---

2   See Tricia Rose's *Black Noise: Rap Music and Black Culture in Contemporary America* (1994) and Imani Perry's *Prophets of the Hood: Politics and Poetics in Hip Hop* (2004) for a more detailed analysis of the social and cultural impact of rap during the Golden Age era in the United States.

musical genre and cultural practice has brought race to the forefront in Brazil through the categorization of what he views as the four phases of *negritude*[3] in Brazilian hip hop (2011: 98). For this chapter, I will be examining how hip hoppers that have emerged during the fourth phase (1999–present), which is characterized by a Black aesthetic rooted in a working-class ethos, employ a dialectical response to the racial discrimination and social marginalization they experience (Pardue 2011: 115–16). I would even argue that there is a fifth stage, which combines Afro-Brazilian roots, rhythms and references to other Afro-diasporic icons, images, and new forms of rap like trap with a strong political message that now has commercial success through self-created recording labels.[4] These hip hoppers, in particular during the 2010s and early 2020s, incorporate what I observe as three key types of expressions of *negritude*, or Blackness, into their work as they seek to not only publicly denounce racial prejudices, but espouse new forms of Black pride: they call upon the image of the American Black ghetto as a way to address poverty and social inequity in Brazil's major cities; they reference key historical figures from the African diaspora and Black American pop culture, which they have developed into what I label as an urban Afro-cosmopolitanism; and they follow in the practice of Afro-Brazilian cultural productions from previous generations by calling upon African-

---

[3] Derek Pardue argues that there are four moments of rap music in Brazil tied to discourses on *negritude*, or Blackness: The first takes place from 1987 to 1992 and promotes a *união* (unity) ideology. The second takes place between 1992 and 1996 and focuses on using a resistant Afro-Brazilian ideology, which generates a *negritude* discourse in working-class Black communities. The third takes place from 1996 to 1999 and shifts to a marginal aesthetic with narratives about *periferia* (urban periphery) life. Moment four takes place between 1999 and the present, in which a tension between *periferia* narratives and *negritude* ideology can be found in Brazilian rap.

[4] Emicida created his own record label, Laboratório Fantasma (Ghost Lab), in collaboration with his family. Baco Exu do Blues also created his own label, 999, to increase the representation of rappers from the Brazilian state of Bahia. Rincon Sapiência has the label MGoma, which is a reference to the term *ngoma*, which are musical instruments used by the Bantu peoples in Brazil. The term derives from the Kongo word for drum.

based religious and spiritual traditions to situate rap and hip hop within the larger trajectory of Afro-Brazilian culture and history. Ultimately, the dynamic nature of how this new generation of Brazilian rappers construct their identity comes about through political rhetoric, which problematizes how Blackness has been minimized and demonized in Brazil through meta-narratives like racial democracy and references to Afro-Brazilian traditions that ultimately situate themselves within a larger, global Black tradition.

In this chapter, I will be examining the body of work of two rappers who have emerged as key players in the Brazilian hip-hop scene during this fifth phase, and who embody these more complex constructs of Blackness in Brazil: Baco Exu do Blues and Emicida. Born Diogo Álvaro Ferreira Moncorvo, his stage name Baco Exu do Blues contains several references to Black culture. Exu is an *orixá* (deity in Afro-Brazilian religions), who is the messenger that communicates with humans on behalf of the other *orixás* and opens paths for humans. Blues refers to the African American musical tradition, which always interested Baco due to its history and mythology. He has become a leader of the hip-hop scene in his hometown of Salvador, Brazil's fourth-largest city, which is known as *Roma Negra*, or Black Rome, for having a population that is over 80 percent Black. His focus on promoting rap music from Salvador and other areas of Brazil's Northeast region can be seen in the creation of his music label, 999, and in one of his first recorded songs, "Sulicídio" (Southicide), which criticizes how Brazilian rap has historically been concentrated in the Southeast region in cities like São Paulo and Rio de Janeiro. Emicida is the stage name for Leandro Roque de Oliveira, a rapper from São Paulo's urban periphery. His name combines the words MC and homicide in reference to his ability to destroy his opponents in MC battles when he was an up-and-coming young rapper. He also has his own record label, Laboratório Fantasma, which produces not only his music but other rappers from São Paulo. The commercial success of both Baco Exu do Blues and Emicida via their own labels has allowed them to maintain a strong focus on themes in their rap music that center the experiences of Afro-Brazilians. However, before examining the three key elements of how they construct an Afrocentric aesthetic through rap, it is important to provide some historical context to better understand the racial dynamics, political tensions, and hip-hop formations that have occurred in Brazil during the last four decades.

Historical and Political Context of Brazilian Hip Hop

Hip hop's emergence in Brazil can be traced back to the rise of Black soul and power movements in major cities like São Paulo, Salvador, and Rio de Janeiro in the late 1960s, which were influenced by the transnational flow of Black music from abroad. Because of the limited economic opportunities and the political repression of the Brazilian military dictatorship in 1964–85, Afro-Brazilians organized informal parties, which resulted in the development of a nightclub circuit, particularly in São Paulo (Pardue 2011: 36). These dance parties were known as *bailes black* (Black dances) where sound system teams would play international Black music, primarily funk and soul music from the United States (Santos 2016: 167). It was common for thousands of people to show up for a *baile black*. One of the most well-known sound system teams, ChicShow, would organize some of the largest *bailes black* in Brazil at the time, including one where James Brown performed in 1978 (Santos 2016: 167). These gatherings became important spaces for the circulation of not only Black music, but the introduction of ideas related to Black Power consciousness. Ideas by Black writers like Angela Davis and Malcolm X in the US, images of Black celebrities both in Brazil and abroad, and even film scenes with African Americans were projected at *bailes black*, thereby sharing information about Black pride movements throughout the African diaspora that instilled a sense of Black pride among participants (Santos 2016: 168). The impact of Black consciousness can be observed with the sound system teams as they took on names like Black Power, Zimbabwe, Soul Grand Prix, and *Atabaque*[5] to reflect an Afrocentric positioning.

---

5   *Atabaque* is a drum used to maintain the rhythm for the music and singing performed at a *roda*, or circle of practitioners of *capoeira*, an Afro-Brazilian martial art.

The circulation and commercialization of rap in Brazil was due to the sound systems that provided a space for it in the nightclubs. The nightclubs that initially hosted the *baile blacks* began to give space and time for rap music and break dancing. Brazilian sound teams that hosted *bailes black* provided opportunities for local MCs to perform as well. Derek Pardue noted that one of the most well-known sound system teams, Chic Show, "was the first crew to explicitly incorporate a time slot for rap during the dance parties called the rap club (*clube do rap*)" (2011: 36). And some of these sound teams, like Zimbabwe, also proved key in producing some of the foundational rap records of the late 1980s and early 1990s, including one of most important early rap compilations: *Consciência Black* (1989), which included songs by Racionais MCs, one of the most important rap groups of all time in Brazil (Pardue 2011: 37).

The introduction and circulation of Black music from abroad, including rap, coincided with the rise of the Black political movement in Brazil during the 1970s. The late 1970s and early 1980s in Brazil were known as the *Abertura* (opening) as the country transitioned from a military dictatorship to a democratically elected government. During this time, Black political groups like the *Movimento Negro Unificado* (Unified Black Movement) became prominent in addressing institutional racism. Rappers and posses mirrored these political movements by narrating in their music the everyday problems impacting their communities (Weller 2011; Pardue 2011).

This political militancy can be seen in the early albums of Brazilian hip hop, in particular with Racionais MCs. The 1989 album *Consciência Black* (Black Consciousness) in which they contributed two songs, echoes the *bailes black* of the 1970s and early 1980s that mimicked African American funk, soul, and rap with names like Grandmaster Rap Junior, Criminal Master, Sharylane, and Frank. In 1990, Racionais MCs released their first album, *Holocausto Urbano* (Urban Holocaust), which focused heavily on a militant aesthetic, addressing the stark realities of living in São Paulo's urban periphery. Their focus was on using rap as a political tool, and they did not want to mix in Brazilian rhythms or focus on images of celebration at a time when violence and poverty were negatively impacting their communities. This tension between a focus on the harsh life of the urban periphery and the privileging of an Afrocentric lens continued through the 1990s until the turn of the 21st century, when the fourth phase as defined by Derek Pardue combined the narratives of urban life with a *negritude* ideology (2011: 115).

Emicida and Baco Exu do Blues build on this long tradition in Brazilian hip hop of addressing social inequality while centering Black culture. Both artists frequently produce songs that address the realities of living in *favelas*[6] and urban peripheries (state violence, racism, social inequality) juxtaposed with a rhetoric that calls upon their African ancestry and rich cultural traditions. They both created their own record labels to not only produce their own music, but identify and highlight other Black rappers, visual artists, and writers. They see themselves not only as rap artists, but as cultural producers of Black art, music, and literature. Therefore, the focus of this chapter is to examine how their rap music reflects a larger trend in contemporary Brazilian hip hop of creating dynamic and complex constructs of Black identity in Brazil.

Ghetto/Gueto

The first of the three Afrocentric expressions that I categorize in Emicida and Baco Exu do Blues's work, the adoption of the term *gueto*, has to do with publicly denouncing racial prejudices and social inequity. Jennifer Roth-Gordon, in her study of everyday language in urban Brazil in relation to race notes that "the globalization of hip-hop culture has made urban space particularly salient, and the ghetto (or the 'hood') is arguably one of US hip hop's most visible exports, iconically linking Blackness to urban space" (Roth-Gordon 2009: 65). One way in which urban youth do this is by renaming buildings after the boroughs of New York City. In the

---

6   *Favelas* are informal, working-class communities that started to build up in Brazil's major cities during the 20th century as people were displaced from city centers and others migrated from Northeast Brazil to São Paulo and Rio de Janeiro. These communities historically have experienced income inequality and state violence.

case of rappers, they adopt a language that creates a narrative that mimics the experiences of the Black American ghetto to highlight the state violence that Afro-Brazilians from marginalized communities experience.

Returning to Emicida's song introduced in the chapter's introduction, "Dedo na ferida" (Finger in the Wound), I examine how his use of language tied to the ghetto references the displacement of predominately Black and Brown communities and calls upon the legacy of slavery to critique the state's continued oppression of these communities. The song starts with Emicida dedicating it to "the victims of Moinho, Pinheirinho, Cracolândia, Rio dos Macacos, and Alcântara and all the *quebradas* devasted by greed." Meanwhile, the music video displays clips of actual residents from these communities and police in riot gear attempting to displace them. Emicida's *quebrada*, which is equivalent to the term "the hood" in American English, is a word commonly used by rappers, artists, and everyday residents from *favelas* and *periferias* in Brazil's major cities. While it is meant to evoke an urban space that has experienced social marginalization, the term can also be used as a form of pride in which the user of the word indexes their community origin.

The first stanza of the song addresses how residents of contemporary *quebradas* are being displaced due to larger economic interests valued by the state and property development companies and have no political power to stop the destruction of their communities:

Vi condomínios rasgarem mananciais	I saw condominiums tear up springs
A mando de quem fala de deus e age como satanás	Under the command of who speaks of God but acts like Satan
(Uma lei) quem pode menos, chora mais,	(A law) who has less, sobs more,
Corre do gás, luta, more, equanto o sangue corre	Run from the gas, fight, die, while the blood flows
É nosso sangue nobre, que a pele cobre,	It's our noble blood, that our skin covers,

Tamo no corre, dias melhores, sem lobby	We're in the daily grind, better days, no lobbyists
Hei, pequenina, não chore	Hey, little one, don't cry
TV cancerigena,	Carcinogen TV,
Aplaude prédio em cemitério indígena	Applaud for the building on the indigenous cemetery
Auschwitz ou gueto? índio ou preto?	Auschwitz or ghetto? Indian or Black?[7]
(Emicida 2012)	

"Tear up springs" refers to environmental and social impacts of city expansion, specifically gated communities (known in Brazilian Portuguese as *condomínio fechado*) being developed in recent years in the suburbs of São Paulo. The suburbs have historically been populated by working-class communities, but upper-middle-class and wealthy residents have looked to the outskirts as a place where they can create planned communities that are far from what they view as urban problems like traffic congestion and crime. However, these new real estate developments urbanize previously natural areas and displace poor communities that are forcibly removed from their homes by the police, which Emicida comments on when these residents must "run from the gas, fight, die." He also criticizes the hypocrisy of politicians, in particular evangelical politicians who have gained political power in recent years in Brazil and frequently invoke God in their campaigns but support the passage of laws that favor these condominium and shopping development projects to the detriment of *favela* residents. This difference in treatment of Brazilian citizens based on class, race, and location (*periferia* and *favela*) has a long history in Brazil, especially in São Paulo, from the later half of the 20th century to the present (Holston 2008).

---

[7] All translations of lyrics to English are completed by the author, Eliseo Jacob.

"Noble blood" evokes the long history of resistance by Afro-Brazilians fighting against the necropolitical state that has manifested itself through unjust laws initiated during the colonial period with slavery to the outlawing of Afro-Brazilian cultural practices at the turn of the 20th century and the current economic exploitation, and state sanctioned violence in the urban periphery of São Paulo. "Auschwitz or ghetto" is a powerful image comparing the *favelas* to the concentration camps and Black American ghettos. Emicida highlights what many Afro-Brazilian activists and scholars have observed: that there is a Black genocide taking place in contemporary Brazil through poor living conditions and police violence. Jaime Alves refers to this genocide in São Paulo's urban periphery as the double negation of Afro-Brazilians as citizens (person) and as humans (individual) (2014: 11–12).

Baco Exu do Blues' song "Tropa do Babu" echoes Emicida's commentary on the ghetto as a metonym of Black genocide in Brazil. The song was included on his third album, *Não tem Bacanal na Quarentena* (There's no Bacchanalia in Quarantine), which was released during the early months of the pandemic.[8] "Tropa de Babu," or Babu's Crew, refers to Afro-Brazilian singer and actor Babu Santana, who has played an important role in promoting Black musicians and artists. Babu was born and raised in the *favela* Morro do Vidigal (Vidigal Hill),[9] which overlooks Ipanema beach in

---

8   The album was originally titled *Bacanal* (Bacchanalia), but with the arrival of the COVID-19 pandemic in early 2020, it was updated to reflect the drastic changes occurring in the world. All the beats used in the songs and the guest artists who participated in the album were produced virtually due to the pandemic.

9   Many *favelas* in Rio de Janeiro are located on hills and mountainsides, thereby including the word *morro* (hill) in the community's name like *Morro do Vidigal* is common. In the Zona Sul (South Zone) of Rio de Janeiro, there is a stark class divide between the upper-class communities in neighborhoods like Copacabana and Ipanema and the *favela* residents who live in the hills above them. There is a common expression in Brazilian Portuguese that refers to the geographic divide, which emphasizes the social inequality between the rich and poor: *do morro* (from the hill) and *do asfalto* (from the asphalt).

the south zone of Rio de Janeiro. He began his acting career with the theater group, Nós do Morro (Us from the Hill), a *favela*-based company and school founded in 1986 in the *favela* where he grew up. The song title expresses a sense of solidarity among young Black men throughout Brazil who are linked to Babu due to their experiences of being raised in the *favela*—Brazil's equivalent of the ghetto. Babu has also starred in multiple Brazilian films and television series with narratives tied to the *favela* and urban periphery, including the films *City of God* (2002), *Something in the Air* (2002), *City of Men* (2007), *Maré, Our Story of Love* (2008) and the series *City of Men* (2002), *Mais X Favela* (2011–14), *I Love Paraisópolis* (2015), and *Os Suburbanos* (2015–18). Therefore, by referencing him as the namesake of the group, Baco Exu do Blues is making it clear that this is a crew from Brazil's ghettos.

The refrain, which opens the song, and the first stanza reiterate a sense of pride in being from the ghetto and engaging in politics of resistance to outside social and economic forces that attempt to silence the voices of young Black men from historically marginalized communities in Brazil:

Todos meus manos são preto	All my homies are Black
Tropa do Babu, tudo preto	Babu's Crew, all Black
Mato esses hippies sem medo	I kill those hippies without fear
Olha, meu irmão, vim do gueto	Look here brother, I'm from the ghetto
--	--
Não me desculpe, negrão mó rude	I don't apologize, super rude Black dude
Vignado amigos, Boyz In The Hood	Avenging friends, Boyz in the Hood
Tipo Eazy-E, Doctor Dre e Ice Cube	Like Eazy-E, Dr. Dre and Ice Cube
999, pretos com attitude	999, Blacks with attitude
Tá na minha cidade e me odeia, então se mude	You're in my city and hate me, so leave
(Baco Exu do Blues 2020)	

"I kill hippies" refers to the foreigners that visit and inhabit Salvador. Despite Salvador being a predominately Black city, Afro-Brazilians have had little political and economic power there, commonly seen as a population meant to project Brazil's cordial diversity in the cultural tourism industry by propping up Salvador as the "capital of happiness," despite being one of the most violent cities in Brazil for Black youth (Smith 2016: 3–4). The references to the movie *Boyz in the Hood* (1991) and the members of the rap group NWA, several of whom are originally from Compton and South Central Los Angeles, point to the impact of the image of the Black American ghetto in the imaginary of Black youth from Brazil's *favelas* and urban peripheries. Baco mimics NWA's confrontational positionality by not apologizing for not having a deferential attitude.

Baco Exu do Blues echoes the issue of Black genocide in Brazil that Emicida addresses in his songs. He concludes the song by using Babu's words to discuss the state violence that takes place in the *favelas*:

O mundo passa por cada coisa	The world has experienced everything
Você ainda se surpreende com o mundo?	You still are surprised by the world?
O quê que foi o nazismo? O quê que foi o nazismo?	What was Nazism? What was Nazism?
O quê que foi a escravidão?	What was slavery?
Voce ainda se espanta com o mundo?	You still are surprised by the world?
O quê que são as favelas?	What are favelas?
E você ainda se espanta com o mundo?	And you still are surprised by the world?
Não se espante! Segure na sua convicção	Don't be shocked! Be firm in your convictions
Que o mundo precisa de pessoas com convicções	That the world needs people with convictions
(Baco Exu do Blues 2020)	

The final verse is an excerpt from an interview Babu gave where he was commenting on the legacy of genocide in Brazil, the Black Atlantic, and globally. He links what has been taking place in the *favelas* to larger scale mass genocide during the Transatlantic slave trade and the Jewish Holocaust during World War II. How he concludes his response is important in that he recognizes that genocide is a never-ending cycle, and for it to end we need people to not be silent in the face of such violence.

Afro-Cosmopolitanisms in Brazil

The second characteristic that defines this generation of current rappers and hip hoppers has to do with the creation of an Afro-cosmopolitanism in which they reference key historical and political figures from the African diaspora, call upon African American pop culture and musical traditions, and demonstrate a deep understanding of global Black political movements. I use the term Afro-cosmopolitanism because it points to these rappers being conscious of shared experiences and histories with other communities, both within Brazil and abroad, which are a part of the larger African diaspora.[10] They are developing narratives in their raps that are not confined to the traditional, Eurocentric forms of cosmopolitanism, but instead focus on alternative forms of cross-cultural exchange, namely Afrocentric in nature, which illustrate the development of a diasporic citizenship that goes beyond the confines of national borders (Koshy 2011: 594).

Emicida makes conscious decisions in the way he frames his songs to make them connect to a larger body of knowledge tied to the African diaspora. He accomplishes his goal through the composition of song titles that reference key historical Black figures, thereby exposing listeners to content related to global Black history. The figures he references

---

10   In the article "Funk and Hip-Hop Transculture: Cultural Conciliation and Racial Identification in the 'Divided City,'" Shoshanna Lurie provides insight into how cassette tapes of funk and hip-hop music from the US were circulated in Brazil (2000).

span different corners of the African diaspora from Brazil to Africa and even Asia. In 2015, the song "Mandume" was released on his second studio album, *Sobre crianças, quadris, pesadelos, e lições de casa* (About Children, Hips, Nightmares and Lessons from Home). The song title is a direct reference to Mandume ya Ndemufayo, who was the last king of the Oukwanyama kingdom, which was located in southern Angola and northern Namibia. He was known for resisting Portuguese and German colonists until his death in 1917 during battle with South African armed forces. Interestingly, the lyrics to the song have no direct reference to Mandume. However, the themes Emicida and his guest artists address related to cultural resistance tie back to Mandume's legacy as a figure of resistance to Western colonial rule. Another song, "Yasuke (Bendito, Louvado Seja)," was produced for a fashion show Emicida organized with his brother for their clothing line—also named Yasuke—at the 2016 São Paulo Fashion Week.[11] The song was later released as a single in 2017. Yasuke was an African brought to Japan in 1579 by the Portuguese in service of a Jesuit missionary and eventually became a samurai. Emicida and his brother chose Yasuke as the name of the song and clothing line because Brazil has the largest Afro-descendant population outside of Africa and the largest Japanese community outside Japan; therefore, they wanted to merge those two important influences on Brazilian culture into their music and fashion (Emicida 2016). Emicida also names songs in honor of historical Afro-Brazilian figures. His 2018 single with the eponymous title "Inácio da Catingueira" gives visibility to a lesser-known person. Inácio (1843–1879) was an enslaved African from Northeast Brazil who was known as the "artist slave" or "genius slave" for his artistic abilities in poetry and music (de Oliveira 2020: 393). Despite being illiterate, he was known for his ability to improvise verses

---

11   For more information on Emicida's project at the 2016 SPFW, see the following report by AfroPunk: https://afropunk.com/2016/11/brazilian-designers-defy-gender-norms-showcases-body-type-diversity-and-models-with-vitiligo-in-their-yasuke-collection-at-sao-paulo-fashion-week/ (Boateng 2016), and a video of the fashion show: https://www.youtube.com/watch?v=mvgwJf3rpjU&ab_channel=LaboratorioFantasma (Laboratório Fantasma 2016).

and became famous in his region for being able to beat other poets in contests known as *pelejas* (verse exchanges) using the *literatura de cordel* (Cordel Literature) poetic tradition (Nunes and Nogueira 2015). Emicida named the song in his honor since he saw many parallels in his own life as an artist and rapper producing music in the face of adversity. The way in which Emicida incorporates references to these historical figures points to how they serve as a model for how he and other Afro-Brazilians can excel in the face of racial inequality. He is also dialoguing with these historical figures through his music to position himself within the larger pantheon of Black leaders and artists found throughout the African diaspora.

Brazilian rappers have made frequent references to African American culture and history in their music, including the civil rights movement of the 1960s, highlighting important intellectual and community leaders and Black American pop culture references (Pardue 2011; Santos 2016). Baco Exu do Blues follows in this tradition by centering the contributions of African American music and culture to the African diaspora in his music. His stage name includes a direct reference to blues music, which he has repeatedly stated is "the first rhythm to make Black people rich" (Cavalcanti 2018). The privileging of blues and African American music can be observed in his second studio album, *Bluesman* (2018), in which four of the nine tracks on the album make direct references to African American music: "Bluesman," "Me Desculpa Jay-Z" (Excuse Me Jay-Z), "Kanye West da Bahia" (Kanye West of Bahia), and "BB King." According to Baco Exu do Blues, the genesis of the album "was to have a blues album without playing the blues" (Cavalcanti 2018). Alluding to blues music and its legacy while maintaining being a rap album, in particular Brazilian rap music, highlights the shared histories and rhythmic structures Baco can make between Afro-Brazilian and African American musical traditions. The first track on the album, the eponymous "Bluesman," functions as Baco's thesis for why blues music is foundational to Black musical traditions. The song's first verse functions as a preface where Baco discusses the importance of Blues music to the

African diaspora. Muddy Waters' song "Everything's Gonna Be Alright"[12] plays in the background as Baco shares his views on blues music:

Eu sou o primeiro ritmo a formar	I'm the first rhythm to form
pretos ricos	rich Blacks
O primeiro ritmo que tornou pretos livres	The first rhythm that made Blacks free
Anel no dedo em cada um dos cinco	Ring on the finger of all five
Vento na minha cara, eu me sinto vivo	Wind in my face, I feel alive
A partir de agora, consider tudo blues	From now on I consider everything blues
O samba é blues, o rock é blues, o jazz é blues	Samba is blues, rock is blues, jazz is blues
O funk é blues, o soul é blues	Funk is blues, soul is blues
Eu sou Exu do Blues	I'm Exu do Blues
Tudo que quando era preto, era do demônio	Everything when it was black was of the devil
E depois virou branco e foi aceito	And later it turned white and was accepted,
Eu vou chamar de Blues	I'll call it blues
É isso, entenda, Jesus é blues	That's it, understand, Jesus is blues
(Baco Exu do Blues 2018)	

---

12   Born and raised in Mississippi, Muddy Waters is considered the father of modern Chicago blues.

Stating everything is blues, Baco is recognizing a shared genealogy of Black music not just in Brazil, but the larger diaspora. Blues music's roots go back to the 19th century in the US American South with the incorporation of African American spirituals, work songs, and chants. The call-and-response structure is also key to blues music, which is a common musical pattern found in musical traditions with ties to Africa. Blues music did not come before all other musical forms in the African diaspora, but by stating that "samba is blues, funk is blues, soul is blues," and so on, Baco Exu do Blues is making a keen observation that all the musical forms listed have a shared history in rhythmic structures that can be traced back to African-based forms. Additionally, the final lines of the stanza point to the history of Black music being marginalized, but then experiencing appropriation by White artists, who then circulate it into mainstream popular culture, which is not unique to African American culture. Afro-Brazilian musical forms, like samba, have roots in the legacy of slavery and African rhythms, passed through periods of criminalization, and then eventually became appropriated and seen as part of Brazil's national identity. Blues music, therefore, becomes a metaphor for understanding the complex, rich, and at times violent history of Black music in the Americas.

Afro-Brazilian Cosmologies

The final characteristic that defines the Afrocentric focus of this current generation of rappers and hip hoppers has to do with how they situate themselves in relation to previous generations of Afro-Brazilian musical and cultural traditions with a common practice of calling upon African-based spiritual and cultural practices. Different Black artists and musicians have commonly given reference to Afro-Brazilian cosmologies through the *orixás* of Afro-Brazilian religions like *Umbanda* and *Candomblé*.[13] *Orixás* are deities or spirts that were originally rooted in the

---

13   *Umbanda* is a hybrid religion that brings together beliefs and practices from African religions, Roman Catholicism, and Indigenous beliefs. It is common

religion of the Yoruba peoples of West Africa and are now commonly found in Latin American religions rooted in the African diaspora, including Brazil, Cuba, Puerto Rico, and the Dominican Republic. These African-based religious practices are currently very active in Brazil and have become a part of certain aspects of Brazilian popular culture and music. However, despite their vibrancy in Brazil today, these religions still experience discrimination by politicians and by certain sectors of civil society, in particular from specific Evangelical sects that have gained prominence in Brazil in recent years, especially with the election of Jair Bolsonaro in 2018. Therefore, incorporating references to religions like *Candomblé* has two purposes: to publicly acknowledge their ethnic identity as Afro-Brazilians and as a form of cultural resistance against White supremacy.

Emicida's song "Ubuntu Fristaili" from his 2013 album *O Glorioso Retorno de Quem Nunca Esteve Aqui* (The Glorious Return of Who was Never Here) positions the idea of the cypher within the context of Afro-Brazilian spiritual rituals. *Ubuntu* is a well-known African concept—I am because we are—and *Fristaili* is the phonetic spelling of the word freestyle for native Portuguese speakers. The idea of the cypher as a group of people who gather to watch an impromptu rap battle or performance parallels the gathering of followers of *Candomblé* in the *terreiros* (temples or religious houses), where spiritual rituals and practice take place. Within the song, Emicida performs a rap that references how followers of *Candomblé* interact with each other and invoke the *orixás* tied to their religion:

---

in this religion for the *orixás* to have been syncretized with Catholic saints. *Candomblé* is an African-based religion that emerged in Brazil during the 19th century. Like *Umbanda*, it is a mix of West African religious traditions with Roman Catholicism. Veneration of the *orixás* is a central tenet of *Candomblé*. Each practitioner has a patron *orixá* that chooses them when initiated into the religion. For more information on the transnational nature of *Candomblé*, see J. Lorand Matory's *Black Atlantic Religion: Tradition, Transnationalism, and Matriarchy in the Afro-Brazilian Candomblé* (2005).

A África está nas crianças, e o mundo?	Africa is in the children, and the world?
O mundo está por fora	The world is on the outside
Então saravá Ogum, saravá Xangô, saravá	So saravá Ogum, saravá Xangô, saravá
Saravá vovó, saravá vovô, saravá	Saravá grandma, saravá grandpa, saravá
Saravá mamãe, saravá papai,	Saravá mother, saravá father,
De pele ou digital, tanto faz é tambô	Made of skin or digital, it doesn't matter it's a drum
Eu meto essa memo, eu posso	I get into it, because I can
Eu tô pr aver, algo valer mais que um sorriso nosso	I'm worth seeing, is something worth more than our smile
Graças ao quê, graças aos raps	Thanks to what? Thanks to raps
Hoje eu ligo mais quebradas do que o Google Maps	Today I connect more hoods than Google Maps

(Emicida 2013)

The expression *saravá* is a common greeting used by followers of *Candomblé* and *Umbanda* and can be synonymous to other terms like *salve* (save) and *bem-vindo* (welcome). In the song, Emicida is greeting or welcoming not only family members, but two important *orixás*: Ogum and Xangô. Within the Candomblé religion, Ogum is the deity tied to iron, metal, technology, and war. Ogum is also known among Yoruba religions as the first *orixá* to descend to Earth to search for an adequate home for humanity. Xangô is the deity of thunder and fire and is also known as the founder of the cult tied to the *eguns* (spirits of the deceased). Therefore, Emicida's reference to these two *orixás* is not by chance due to their spiritual and cultural importance.

The importance of rhythm and beats in the cypher becomes tied to the central role of music found in Afro-Brazilian religions as explored in the second half of the stanza. Emicida alludes to how percussive instruments, whether digital or physical, serve the same purpose in both hip-hop culture and *Candomblé*. Drums are used during rituals in the *terreiro* and are frequently used in Afro-Brazilian musical traditions that call upon the *orixás* not only as a spiritual practice, but to express one's cultural heritage tied to the African diaspora.

The hybrid nature of Afro-Brazilian cosmologies comes to the fore in Baco Exú do Blues's raps as he explores the intersections between African-based religious practices and Western influences. The title of his first solo album, *Esú* (2017), highlights the importance of the *orixás* in his work as a hip hopper and his identity as an Afro-Brazilian. While his stage name has the Portuguese spelling (Exu) of the key *orixá*, the album uses the Yoruba language spelling of the deity. As previously noted, Exu is one of the most important *orixás* due to their role in providing communication between the *orixás* and humanity. In the eponymous titled song, "Esú," Baco makes multiple Afro-Brazilian and Western cultural references, thereby illustrating that his cultural and religious identity is syncretic in nature:

Componho pra não me decompor	I compose so I don't decompose
Poeta maldito perito na arte de Arthur Rimbaud	Cursed poet specialist in Arthur Rimbaud's art
Garçom, traz outra dose, por favor	Waiter, bring another round please
Que eu tô entre o Machado de Assis e o de Xangô	'Cause I'm Between Machado de Assis and Xangô
Soneto de boêmia, poesia, melancolia	Sonnet of Bohemian poetry, melancholy
Eu sou do tempo onde poetas ainda faziam poesia	I'm from the time when poets still made poetry
Saravá, o canto de Ossanha vem me matando	Saravá, Ossanha's song is killing me
...	...

Aqui, se escuta o batuque do trovão	Here one can hear the thunder's rhythm
Thor e seu martelo, Jorge e seu dragão	Thor and his hammer, George and his dragon
Ciranda do céu, rave de tambor	Ciranda from heaven, drum rave
Os deuses queriam chorar por amor	The gods wanted to cry for love
Aqui, se escuta o batuque do trovão	Here one can hear the thunder's rhythm
Os deuses queriam chorar por amor	The gods wanted to cry for love

(Baco Exu do Blues 2017)

"Between Machado de Assis and Xangô" refers to Machado de Assis—who scholars consider to be the most important writer in the history of Brazilian literature and was of African descent and participated in White, lettered society—in dialogue with the *orixá* of lightening, fire, and justice. The juxtaposition of these two figures reveals an existential question that the rapper poses to himself as to how to gauge his approach to society: be more conciliatory within the norms of White society or be more confrontational rooted in an Afrocentric positionality. This tension between western culture and his African roots continues throughout the stanza as he makes references to the influences of French poetry in his education, the Marvel universe, and Catholic saints. Thor's role as the God of thunder ties back to the *orixá* Xangô, and St. George is frequently associated with the *orixá* Ogum due to both figures' use of metal weapons to combat their adversaries. Ultimately, Baco Exu do Blues' ability to juxtapose his exposure to popular culture, western literature, and Catholicism with his Afro-Brazilian identity highlights how contemporary rappers belong to the rich tradition of Afro-Brazilian artists' evocation of deities and practices tied to African-based cosmologies.

Emicida and Baco Exu do Blues are just two of many contemporary Brazilian rappers who engage in an Afrocentric aesthetic and discourse;

however, by providing an in-depth analysis of their raps, a deeper understanding to how these three iterations of Black cultural expression manifest within the current hip-hop scene becomes clearer. While previous generations of Brazilian hip hoppers have also incorporated a *negritude* ideology, what makes Emicida, Baco Exu do Blues, and other rappers of this current generation unique is the creative control they have through their independent recording labels that have not only provided commercial success but enabled them to explore what it means to be Black in Brazil in more nuanced and complex ways. Ultimately, their musical productions reflect a hip-hop community in Brazil that sees itself as part of a larger Black cultural tradition that goes beyond the limits of their national identity.

Discography/Videography

Baco Exu do Blues. "Esú." *Esú*. Baco Exú do Blues, 2017, Spotify.
Baco Exu do Blues. "Bluesman." *Bluesman*. Baco Exú do Blues, 2018, Spotify.
Baco Exu do Blues. "Tropa do Babu." *Não tem bacanal na quarentena*, Baco Exu do Blues, 2020, Spotify.
Emicida. "Ubuntu Fristaili," featuring Felipe Vassão. *O glorioso retorno de quem nunca esteve aqui*. Laboratório Fantasma, 2013, Spotify.
Emicida. "Mandume," featuring Drik Barbosa, Amiri, Rico Dalasam, Muzzike, and Raphão Alaafin. *Sobre crianças, quadris, pesadelos, e lições de casa*. Laboratório Fantasma, 2015, Spotify.
Emicida. "Inácio da Catingueira." Emicida. Posted on September 18, 2018. YouTube Video, 4:01. https://youtu.be/kBIwIvzFlpM.
Emicida and DJ Duh. "Yasuke (Bendito, Louvado Seja)." Emicida. Posted on February 3, 2017. YouTube Video, 5:51. https://www.youtube.com/watch?v=kvAWTrLUpok.
Emicida and Renan Samam. "Dedo na ferida." Emicida. Posted on March 7, 2012. YouTube Video, 4:04. https://youtu.be/QdvYAjQYdIs.

References

Alves, Jaime. 2018. *The Anti-Black City: Police Terror and Black Urban Life in Brazil*. Minneapolis: University of Minnesota Press. https://doi.org/10.5749/j.ctt2oh6vpx.

Alves, Jaime Amparo. 2014. "Neither Humans nor Rights: Some Notes on the Double Negation of Black Life in Brazil." *Journal of Black Studies* 45 (2): 143–62. https://doi.org/10.1177/0021934714524777.

Cavalcanti, Amanda. 2018. "Baco Exu do Blues fala das inspirações que fizeram 'Bluesman.'" *Vice*, November 23, 2018. https://www.vice.com/pt/article/wj3xex/baco-exu-do-blues-fala-das-inspiracoes-que-fizeram-bluesman.

de Oliveira, Antonio Martins. 2020. "O ilustre escravo Inácio da Catingueira e a sua peleja contra o império da escravidão no sertão da Paraíba." *Cadernos Cajuína* 5 (3): 392–411. https://doi.org/10.52641/cadcaj.v5i3.366.

Emicida (@emicida). 2012. "Fui preso por desacato a autoridade após o show em BH por causa da música dedo na ferida." *Twitter*, May 13, 2012. https://twitter.com/emicida/status/201809119127154689.

Freyre, Gilberto. 1977. *Casa-grande & senzala: formação da família brasileira sob o regime da economia patriarcal*. Rio de Janeiro: J. Olympio.

Koshy, Susan. 2011. "Minority Cosmopolitanism." *PMLA* 126 (3): 592–609. https://doi.org/10.1632/pmla.2011.126.3.592.

Lurie, Shoshanna. 2000. "Funk and Hip-Hop Transculture: Cultural Conciliation and Racial Identification in the 'Divided City.'" In *Brazil 2001: A Revisionary History of Brazilian Literature and Culture*. Dartmouth, MA: Tagus Press.

Pardue, Derek. 2011. *Brazilian Hip Hoppers Speak from the Margins: We's on Tape*. Reprint edition. New York: Palgrave Macmillan.

Roth-Gordon, Jennifer. 2009. "Conversational Sampling, Race Trafficking, and the Invocation of the Gueto in Brazilian Hip Hop." In *Global Linguistic Flows: Hip Hop Cultures, Youth Identities, and the Politics of Language*, edited by H. Samy Alim, Awad Ibrahim, and Alastair Pennycook, 63–78. New York: Routledge.

Santos, Jaqueline Lima. 2016. "Hip-Hop and the Reconfiguration of Blackness in Sao Paulo: The Influence of African American Political and Musical Movements in the Twentieth Century." *Social Identities* 22 (2): 160–77. https://doi.org/10.1080/13504630.2015.1121573.

Smith, Christen. 2016. *Afro-Paradise: Blackness, Violence, and Performance in Brazil*. Urbana: University of Illinois Press. https://doi.org/10.5406/illinois/9780252039935.001.0001.

Vargas, João H. Costa. 2005. "Genocide in the African Diaspora: United States, Brazil, and the Need for a Holistic Research and Political Method." *Cultural Dynamics* 17 (3): 267–90. https://doi.org/10.1177/0921374005061991.

Weller, Wivian, Marco Aurélio, and Paz Tella. 2011. "Hip-Hop in São Paulo: Identity, Community Formation, and Social Action." In *Brazilian Popular Music and Citizenship*, edited by Idelber Avelar and Christopher Dunn, 188–204. Duke University Press. https://doi.org/10.1215/9780822393603-011.

"Ich lebe für Hip Hop"
German Hip-Hop Music, Cultural Hybridities, and the "Berlin Moment"

Martin Lüthe

> "Wu-Tang and Graffiti on the wall in Berlin..." *(GZA 2000)*

Abstract *This chapter argues that the performances of hybrid, transcultural identities mark a cornerstone of hip hop and inform the debates within and about hip hop as a movement, practice, lifestyle, or culture. As hip hop is in essence about belonging and practice, about "doing something somewhere," it is also crucially about "doing identity," about creating a self in a world that is as much for you as it is against you. In the case of Berlin rap, hip-hop music videos enter a complex relationship with US hip hop and its repository of cultural gestures in their aspiration to put Berlin rap music on the map (roughly in the first decade of the 21st century). Ultimately, of course, this generational conflict hinges on a notion of performing and remixing authenticity that hip-hop culture had itself transported into the world and on the tension that arises when transcultural engagement meets 'keepin' it real.'*

This contribution looks at the transcultural and transatlantic relationships and connections hip-hop culture has facilitated since it became a powerful (and global) pop cultural and youth cultural force in the early-to-mid 1990s. Hip hop allows us to conceive of it as decisively transcultural in the way that "it invites us to consider the intermingling of presumably distinct cultures and the blurry lines between them" and "individuals, communities, and societies that increasingly draw from expanded, tremendously pluralized cultural repertoires," as Afef Benessaieh (2010: 11) defines transculturality. More specifically, I set out to enhance our understanding of the significance of a specific set of performative gestures that have traveled the globe as part of hip-hop culture's rise to worldwide mainstream visibility. I use visibility in both senses of the term: to denote the global recognition of hip hop and, more specifically, the way the culture came to be represented, and represented itself, in the audiovisual media of the time.

My focus here is German rap music's relationship with the United States, and I relate this connection to the pervasiveness of the hip-hop music video as a media form. Music videos are themselves entangled with MTV becoming an international brand and outlet in the 1980s and 1990s, and to the more recent global "YouTube-ification" of pop cultures since roughly the mid-2000s. In Germany, MTV and its companion network Viva made the music video available to their target audience of teenage music fans in the early 1990s, and thus began to disseminate the performative gestures and styles of hip-hop culture and the hip-hop music video (Müller 1999: 74ff).

As hip hop is in essence about belonging and practice, about doing something somewhere, it is also crucially about "doing identity," about creating a self, or many selves, through (trans)cultural practice or performance. In New York City, Los Angeles, or Berlin, hip-hop culture—and the audiovisual gestures it disseminates—inform who we are, who we aspire to be, and how we belong; here, transcultural hybridity reigns supreme![1]

---

[1] Early scholarship on hip hop emerged in the early 1990s and the study of hip hop constituted itself as a field right around the heyday of the boom bap era, see Gilroy 1993; Bartlett 1994; Rose 1994; and Potter 1995. A second wave of scholarship began to focus on, among other things, the question of hybridity, space, and religion in hip hop culture in general, see Forman 2002; Sylvan 2002; Perkinson 2002; and Miyakawa 2005. For an in-depth exploration of transcultural hip hop, or hip hop as a transcultural phenomenon in Delhi,

One of the ways in which hip-hop culture becomes transcultural is that it takes foot in a variety of heterogeneous locales as it travels the globe. Germany's history of hip hop began in close proximity to US army bases, including Heidelberg, Frankfurt, Stuttgart and then a little later Hamburg, Cologne, Bochum, Dortmund, and the Ruhr Area. In the German hip-hop imaginary of the 1990s, Germany's capital and largest city, Berlin, was strikingly absent. This, of course, is not to say that hip-hop culture had no footing in Berlin, it just did not figure prominently in how the rest of Germany conceived of the Berlin music scene: the techno clubs and the Love Parade defined Berlin's place on the German pop music map.

Ultimately, however, hip hop in Germany came to be defined by an emerging scene and style from Berlin, namely its brand of so-called *Straßenrap* (street rap, or rap from the streets).[2] So what happened and what was at stake, I wonder, when Berlin-style street rap took on the German scene defined by an earlier generation? Performers like Kool Savas, Sido, and Bushido accused artists of a previous generation and from different places of being bourgeois, harmless, and ultimately weak, specifically because of the previous generation's affinities with (African) American styles. This, I will show, took shape through a renegotiation of crucial signifiers not only of the first and second generation of German hip-hop practitioners as originators, but also vis-à-vis some of the formative gestures of hip-hop culture typically associated with African American styles and an appreciation of so-called "Black style(s)" in the Black Atlantic World. Ultimately, of course, this generational conflict

---

India, see Singh 2021. For an earlier example of the role of American-ness or Americana in Black traveling culture, see Fleetwood 2005.

[2] In analogy to, for example, the "post" in postcolonial studies, I believe—with M.K. Asanti 2008, the younger one—that we find ourselves in a post-hip hop moment. Not in the sense that hip hop is dead, has vanished, or lost its potential entirely, but rather in the sense that it might now be harder than ever to identify where hip-hop culture ends and pop culture starts. That being said, hip hop is still very much relevant and indeed, its pervasiveness as a pop-cultural phenomenon makes it all the more interesting to be addressed, analyzed, and criticized form within and without.

hinges on a notion of performing authenticity, which hip-hop culture had itself transported into the world, and on the tension that arises when transcultural engagement meets "keepin' it real."

The heterogeneous cultural forms and practices we consider hip hop are themselves embedded within the Black Atlantic and the Black Pacific. These realms provide a dynamic space for cultural performances that are distinctly non-textual but put bodies in movement on screens and make them legible for different audiences across the globe. This performative realm I consider the complementary sphere of the Black Atlantic: the "Black(face) Atlantic" within it. I take my cues from the expansive and interdisciplinary scholarship on blackface performances; I specifically utilize the principal ideas put forth in Eric Lott's *Love and Theft: Blackface Minstrelsy and the American Working Class* (1993) and W.T. Lhamon's *Raising Cain: Blackface Performance from Jim Crow to Hip Hop* (2000) and bring them in conversation with each other and with hip hop itself. To be clear though, I do not attempt to dispute the origins of hip-hop culture as firmly rooted in African American and (Black) Caribbean cultural idioms, practices, and performances, or the specific culturally hybrid locales in NYC in the late 1970s and early 1980s. Rather, I wish to take seriously the complexities that are at play, once these gestures travel the globe to different audiences. Global audiences engage with these gestures to make sense of who they are, and they enact their identities in close correspondence with what they believe these idioms and performative gestures signify.

I will specifically build on one crucial element of Eric Lott's argument here as a point of departure, namely Lott's assessment of the complex drive of blackface as a simultaneity of fear and desire, a coinciding vilification and appreciation. According to Lott, it is these "contradictory racial impulses" (Lott 1993) that blackface reproduces, expresses, and brings to the stage and the cultural fore. I find this insight meaningful in two ways: on the one hand, Lott aspires to understand the cultural work blackface performances fulfill regarding their audiences, rather than only focusing on the shows' crude and racist mechanics. On the other hand, he allows this cultural work to be decisively messy, at times self-contradictory in terms of what we would now call affect and effect. This,

I believe, becomes especially true in the processes of hip-hop music's transculturalization in the German contexts I analyze here, which are emblematic of the intersecting transatlantic and cross-racial desires at play in Black cultural performances in the Atlantic world.

"Isch lebe für Hip Hop":[3] Transcultural Performativity and the Hip-Hop Music Video

While German language rap music and hip-hop culture established itself firmly on the two German music TV stations, namely MTV (Germany) and VIVA, during the 1990s, the origin of mainstream *Deutschrap* (German rap) is somewhat surprising and seemingly eclectic. The general consensus is that the success of German-language rap music would hardly be the same had it not been for the four White middle-class men from Stuttgart who called themselves Die Fantastischen Vier (The Fantastic Four) and had released their hit single "Die da" (Her, there) in 1992.[4] Towards the middle of the decade, Stuttgart also brought forth the collective that referred to itself as Die Kolchose (The Kolkhoz), consisting of the mainstream darlings Freundeskreis (Circle of Friends),

---

3   "Ich lebe für Hip Hop" translates as "I live for hip hop"; I intentionally misspell the title of the song here to indicate what the chorus sounds like when rapped in German by the featured artists from the US. This pronunciation already alludes to the complex processes of gestures within hip-hop culture, and rap music specifically, when they travel to different locales across the globe.

4   A case can be made that German music television would not have been the same without the success of "Die da" and the group behind it, partly because they not only put German rap on the proverbial map, but also because their "silly" video clip and their over-emphatic performance of what hip-hop culture meant to them ignited a debate about the status of hip hop, of rap, and about the rules and politics of the culture as subculture. This debate fits the Zeitgeist of a reunified Germany and the overall aesthetic and performance logics/agenda of German-language music television for a teenage audience, which really served as a laboratory for the business of private cable television in the newly reunified country. For more on the significance of "Die da" and on the exaggerated performance within it, see Breitenwischer (2021: 64ff).

who nonetheless managed to credibly claim an anti-mainstream attitude with the help of fellow crew Massive Töne (Massive Tones) and the Afro-German rapper Afrob. Beyond Stuttgart, Heidelberg, Frankfurt, and Hamburg served as hubs of German rap, and Munich was largely considered to be home to the more quirky, ironic, and wordplay-based styles of acts like Blumentopf (Flower Pot) or Main Concept. Cologne and the cities of the Ruhrpott (the Ruhr area) proudly represented German-language rap's underground scene with crews like STF (Cologne) or RAG and Creutzfeld & Jacob (Dortmund/Bochum). Their music videos mostly aired during the shows dedicated to hip-hop culture and rap music, *Freestyle* (1993–1995) and later *VIVA Word Cup* (1996–1999). This simplified, eclectic map of hip-hop music in Germany during the first golden era of German-language rap from roughly 1996 through 1999, arguably showed little room for artists from Berlin.

This apparent absence of Berlin-based rappers in the German mental map of rap changed dramatically and quickly around the turn of the millennium. In 2000, two German DJs/producers released tracks and albums that would irrevocably put Berlin on the map for two very different reasons and with very different styles:

a) The Düsseldorf-based DJ Plattenpapzt (Record Pope) recorded an album, which featured established and lesser-known rappers on the tracks, and a Turkish-German rapper's contribution to the album was chosen to be released as a single: the song was titled "King of Rap" by a lesser-known rapper from Berlin by the name of King Kool Savas (KKS), born Savas Yurderi. On the slick production, boom bap-type, head-nodding beat, KKS spit two verses, two different bridges, and rapped two choruses, fundamentally changing German rap. The flow, the slang, the ruggedness of the language, and the message that Savas had come for the throne made everything before it sound immediately "old," "tame," and "weak," in Savas's own words. At the same time, however, a Berlin-based DJ/producer by the name of DJ Tomekk produced and released music for the first time with a slightly different angle than Plattenpapzt.

b) Tomekk's debut album proudly claimed to mark the *Return of Hip Hop* and was released in 2000 after two of the previously released singles had garnered much attention and success. Strikingly, even though Tomekk was from Berlin, he decided to feature a variety of MCs on his tracks, none of whom represented Berlin. In fact, Tomekk's unique style was to produce danceable, slick, and booming beats and to bring together German-language rappers with American rappers (of significant standing) on the album, often on the same track.

Accordingly, his first single featured legendary Public Enemy crew member and hype man Flava Flav alongside German rappers Afrob and MC Rene. The latter being one of the originators of German-language rap who had all but disappeared from cultural visibility in the late 1990s. The music video clearly underscored Tomekk's intention to connect New York and Germany, as the song's hook repeatedly lets audiences know. The opening shot of the video clip shows Afrob walk through an airport in Berlin, as emphasized by an on-screen caption, before he is held in custody by German police and uses his one phone call to call a payphone in NYC. Tomekk answers, only to put Flava Flav on the line later. The MCs rap their verses through the landline and thus connect New York and Germany lyrically and visually through the wire. In hindsight, it seems that the music video and its commercial success established a formula for Tomekk, both in terms of song production, artist collaboration, and music video aesthetics.[5]

Echoing or anticipating the tenets of discussions in debates about transculturality, Stuart Hall (1992: 28) identifies Black diasporic cultural forms as always already "the product of partial synchronization, of engagement across cultural boundaries, of the confluence of more than

---

5   There is a lot to unpack here, but the topoi of transatlantic travel, the power of hip-hop culture as a practice to transculturally connect practitioners from different places across the globe, a somewhat shy but explicit reference to Tomekk's Berlin base, and the concept of English and German verses alternating on a single track in a call-and-response style served as the crucial ingredients of Tomekk's style around the turn of the millennium.

one cultural tradition," and as "hybridized from a vernacular base" in his essay "What Is This 'Black' in Black Popular Culture?" In hip hop, we find this excessively in Wu-Tang Clan's oeuvre, and in the way they fused Asian Kung fu movie lore with their immediate environment. Wu-Tang Clan interweaves the Kung fu aesthetic and outlook with the landscape of NYC, as well as with the belief system of the Five-Percent Nation of Islam. This becomes especially evident on their 1997 sophomore album *Wu-Tang Forever*. These gestures gain an additional layer when hip-hop culture then travels to other locales, and White German rappers and producers collaborate with hip-hop culture in general and Wu-Tang Clan specifically. One member of Wu-Tang Clan, GZA a.k.a. the Genius, played a crucial role in putting Berlin on the German hip-hop map in Tomekk's second music video release, "Ich lebe für Hip Hop." This featured GZA, Sunz of Men, Curse, and Stieber Twins: artists from NYC, Minden (Westfalia), and Heidelberg.[6] The video is set in Berlin and the mise-en-scène crucially contributes to the plot of the video, in which—once again—the MCs are portrayed as heroes, with the German police as villains trying to impede the success of hip-hop culture. The latter is represented by a tape circulating from artist to artist in an obvious allusion to the selling of drugs on the street.

In a sense then, Wu-Tang Clan and Sunz of Men—like Flava Flav and KRS-One on other feature tracks in the Tomekk oeuvre—contributed in two ways as ambassadors of "the culture." This is how the video for "Ich lebe für Hip Hop" frames them: they are rapping in a setting resembling the United Nations, providing much needed aid to local artists. Thus, Tomekk not only brings these US heavyweights to Germany, but he specifically places them in Berlin. The lyrics to these songs frequently establish a connection between NYC and Berlin, at times metonymically to represent the birthplace of hip-hop culture, with the US on the one hand, and Germany—as the transcultural continuation of hip hop's course—on the other.

---

6 I am on the fence about how these videos and the tracks have aged, but I think one thing is for sure: it is part of a cycle of hip-hop music videos shot in Germany that put Berlin on the German rap map.

What is more, the songs' structures, such as the call-and-response between English verses by US artists and German verses, alongside the plots in the respective videos, underscore the relationship between US and German hip-hop culture, rap, and lyricists. Let us also take the significance of the lectern seriously here: GZA might be preaching to the choir, but he is most certainly spreading the word and might also be performing hip-hop development assistance. The video translates the call-and response pattern into the lecture hall/church when Chris Stieber gets up on his chair and raps his response from the audience. This audiovisual choice strikes me as emblematic of the processes at play in transcultural hip hop, where local artists often inhabit a space we could refer to as the "production/reception nexus."

Three observations regarding the video clip from "Ich lebe für Hip Hop" strike me as additionally relevant to my argument:

1. The emphasis on hip hop as a culture that is bigger than just rap music: the frequent displays of graffiti specifically, but also the status of the DJ and the cuts and breaks he delivers on the turntables.
2. The way in which the video alludes to some classics of the genre and, for example, places Curse and German rapper Afrob—in a different DJ Tomekk video of the time, namely "1,2,3,... Rhymes Galore" (1999)—in altercations with the German police (fig. 1 and 2). This setting serves as a visual reference to the notorious "Straight Outta Compton" video clip by NWA, which figuratively and literally put Compton on the map.
3. The race/class intersection, which the video represents, brings to the fore the German discourse within and about hip-hop culture at the time.

Figure 1: Curse rapping toward/at the police

(Modul/BMG, 1999/2000)

Figure 2: Afrob being held in custody by the police

(Modul/BMG, 1999/2000)

While observation 1 is quite straightforward in a song called "Ich lebe für Hip Hop," it is noteworthy how the video captures Berlin's graffiti culture and some of its street culture in the plot point related to the circulation of the tape. Again, the status of the police in fig. 2 strikes me as an adaptation of a familiar hip-hop video trope to the German context; in fact, Curse's "in your face rap" vis-à-vis the police is not only reminiscent of the aforementioned classic "Straight Outta Compton," but it also evokes the Roots' ironic how-to manual for rap videos in their clip of "What They Do." What these citations hint at is the more general, at times complex, processes of adaptation, identification, and appropriation in hip-hop videos.

I use adaptation as the most innocent, descriptive term here to indicate the use of a performative gesture familiar from elsewhere: here, German rappers make use of literal anti-police rap to claim their authenticity as (German) rappers. Adaptation implicitly performs a sense of a shared reality or lifeworld with those who deployed the set of gestures originally. In this sense, they enact a sense of identification with other rappers. This, of course, happens across the board in pop music: audiences and performers alike identify with other performers when they engage with their material; or, to put it more eloquently in Simon Frith's terms:

> My argument here, in short, rests on two premises: first, that identity is *mobile*, a process not a thing, a becoming not a being; second, that our experience of music—of music making and music listening—is best understood as an experience of this *self-in-process*. Music, like identity, is both performance and story, describes the social in the individual and the individual in the social, the mind in the body and the body in the mind; identity, like music, is a matter of both ethics and aesthetics.[7] (Frith 1996: 109)

---

[7] We identify with the heartache of Adele, the Backstreet Boys, or Boyz II Men, the anger of Metallica or Slipknot, or the layered emotionality of Beyonce. However, I would add that I take the term identify very seriously in the way it relates to "the creation of a sense of self."

And because authenticity—realness and keeping it real—operates as the fundamental currency in much of hip-hop culture, these performances of identification become a complex issue: is Curse performing his anti-police rap based on his own experience, or as part of a repertoire of gestures rap and hip-hop culture have provided him? Both might be the most satisfactory answer, but the complexity of identification remains, and it speaks to the third observation regarding the video: the race/cultural appropriation nexus. Appropriation is a complicated term and is now commonly used to designate a lack of authentic experience in a person's self-fashioning with the help of cultural gestures they adapt.[8]

I consider two things crucial to keep in mind here: historically, pop cultures have always been syncretic, hybrid, layered, but still blatantly racist at the same time. These processes are not mutually exclusive. Second, I read hip-hop culture's obsession with the "real" and "realness" not only or primarily as a response to late postmodernism (as some critics have done), but as a floating self-awareness of the impossibility of Black subjectivity in a world of racial capitalism, following the trajectory from Patricia Hill Collins (2000) and Cedric Robinson (1983; 2019) to Achille Mbembe (2017) and Ruth Gilmore (2022). A racial capitalism that has, since the mid-1960s decisively turned towards the exploitation of Black bodies and Black expressive cultures for the purpose of entertainment, while simultaneously disposing of and killing Black bodies in the name of profit and policing. In that sense, racial capitalism with its undergirding evil of a racist carceral state, i.e., Black mass incarceration, has never stopped keeping it real.

So, when Tomekk, Curse, and Afrob make use of allusions to the carceral state in the German context, the transcultural complexities of hip-hop culture really become evident. Strikingly, while Tomekk was considered neither "real" nor "really from Berlin," his efforts to connect

---

8   For a White German American studies person, this of course opens a whole can of worms, and I am not here to judge individual examples; but, yes, the history of hip hop's success in the world also serves as a reminder of the appropriation of Black cultural gestures across the globe; this is also why I utilize the idea of a "Black(face) Atlantic."

hip-hop music with German street culture make him a valid example of what happened when Berlin put itself on the German rap map. Arguably, one of the most crucial differences between what Savas and Tomekk represented can be found in the way they viewed the African American impact on German rap and hip hop. After all, while Tomekk courted New York big-shot-MCs to rap on his tracks, Savas rapped, "Deutscher Rap ist dick schwul [sic] und bitet Ami-Müll aus Angst."[9] So, even though Kool Savas had only moved to Kreuzberg as a kid, he encapsulates the specific Berlin-bravado perfectly and made it visible to the rest of Germany and hip hop specifically.

"Du wärst der schwäbische Nelly": Hip-Hop Hybridity and the Streets of Berlin

The more descriptive sections above already hint at the argument I am trying to make in this final section: I read Tomekk's collaborative music videos from roughly the first three years of the new millennium as representative of a German and Western European infatuation with African American cultural idioms, and so-called Black music specifically, which was formative and remained important throughout the first decade of German-language rap in Germany. This, then, marks the first and largely affirmative period in German-language rap as a transcultural phenomenon and practice. The move towards Berlin as Germany's epicenter for rap music, which Tomekk's music contributed to, also inaugurated a new relationship with the African American "Ur-text" of rap and a second period of German-language rap as transcultural. In other words, when Berlin became known for its brand of so-called *Straßenrap* (street rap, or rap from the streets) the performative identities not only

---

[9] My translation, which does not flow at all, would be, "German rap is fat gay and bites US trash out of insecurity." I retain the homophobic slur here because I do not feel the German word for gay, "schwul," should be naturalized as an insult, although it is clearly used in that manner. I sincerely hope that this decision makes sense and does not offend any readers.

took on the German rap scene as bourgeois, harmless, and ultimately weak, but actually—in true Berlin style—claimed a unique identity at least in part based on a decisive break from North American rap music and hip-hop culture.

When Savas claimed a place for himself, his crew M.O.R, and Berlin on "King of Rap," he not only aspired to rid himself and German rap from a long-standing admiration of American styles and trends, but also dissed some of the grandees of German-language MCs, most notably Advanced Chemistry's Torch. The generational conflict between the first one-and-a-half generations of German-language MCs and the new generation became apparent on "King of Rap" and continued to become even more pronounced and evident as more rappers from Berlin reached commercial visibility.

Even though Kool Savas was never signed to the independent label Aggro Berlin, it quickly emerged as a household name and as the epicenter of commercially visible street rap from Berlin. The artists and executives utilized the familiar narratives of hardcore rap and independent labels (ironically, typically situated in the US), hinging on creative freedom and a rags-to-riches attitude. With street rap, the streets also entered the boardrooms of the recording industry in Germany. The videos by rappers signed to the label put forth a very distinct aesthetic and two artists especially, Sido and Bushido, reached impressive and lasting mainstream success, also because the bourgeois critics and gatekeepers of print media outlets took to scandalizing German street rap and marking it as potentially harmful to young listeners, as obviously vulgar, misogynistic, and violent. Here, of course, the German critics unintentionally echoed the conservative concerns of the previous decade during the culture wars in the US. The German *Leitkulturdebatte* (our culture wars) was thus also premised on the mainstream visibility and success of previously marginalized folks in the media. So, as the Berlin street rappers rhetorically aspired to distance themselves from the US, and to stake their claim based on their unique positionalities within the city of Berlin, discussions with the rappers and subsequent debates about them replicated debates familiar to US audiences of hip-hop music. Bushido, arguably more so than Sido, explicitly engaged in a one-man battle with the culture of hip hop, which he now wished to fully make his own. There is an obvious tension here, as the title of one of his early singles released in 2005 gives away, "Nie ein Rapper" (Never a Rapper). This is not an insult targeting an imaginary foe, but rather a proud self-expression; Bushido and SAAD rap: "Ich war nie ein Rapper, ich hab' für die Straßen gekämpft!" (I never was a rapper, I was fighting for the streets!)

The video utilizes familiar performative gestures from the canon of the hip-hop music video genre: the camera angle, even the gritty black-and-white aesthetics, the urban terrain, and two young men rapping at the camera clothed in what Germans have deemed "streetwear," including athletic sweaters, loose-fit denim, baseball caps, hoodies, name-brand sneakers, and sweatpants. Lyrically, however, the claim of the song's hook that the two were "never rappers" introduces the crucial distinction between themselves and the hip-hop scene in Germany associated with the previous generation. The lyrics create a whole array of assumed antagonists: among them the police, but also, and crucially, other rappers and the German and transnational hip-hop scene. The close affiliation between German bourgeois rappers and the way they collaborated with and idolized North American rappers emerge as less intuitive reasons for SAAD and Bushido to diss the scene. Arguably, this provides Berlin rappers, and especially those associated with the labels Royal Bunker, Aggro Berlin, and later ErIsGuterJunge (HeIsGoodboy), with their claim to an authentic identity beginning around 2005.

The transcultural hybridity proposed by the Berlin rappers cannot be found in the infatuation and appreciative copying of North American rap. Rather, the in-between-space SAAD and Bushido claim to make them who they are is the German hip-hop scene and, by extension, Germany at large. Strikingly, this articulation of a self not belonging here or there resonates with hip-hop culture and has arguably fueled hip-hop culture in the US and elsewhere since its inception. Even though Bushido's dad is Tunisian, the visual representation of the Lebanese flag, which coincides with the line "Einer von denen, die es niemals schaffen, ihre Heimat zu sehn" (I am one of those, who will probably never see their home country/country of origin). This designates a return to a hybrid German identity, which had been part of German hip-hop culture from the get-go. However, there are obvious differences between Torch's insistence that he indeed holds a German passport, "Ich hab nen grünen Pass, mit nem goldenen Adler drauf!" (I hold a green passport with a golden eagle on it!), his identity as a "Heidelberger Haitianer" (Haitian from Heidelberg), and Bushido's amalgamation of an identity strongly rooted in the streets of Berlin while being strongly out of place in Germany and "homeless," despite hip-hop culture. The promise of hip-hop culture for the first generation of German hip hoppers had, after all, always been that it might become a home away from home: a place of belonging despite not belonging anywhere else, with hip hop as a transcultural community. This is what Bushido's identity operates in opposition to: German hip hop does not provide a home for him or his peers, the streets of Berlin do. Of course, this serves as yet another example of an uneasy translation of a trope in hip hop's cultural imaginary, namely the North American ghetto transposed to a European context.

Thus, the self-stylization of Berlin rappers since what I refer to as the "Berlin moment" is also based in fashion. The new style cannot be part of global hip-hop aesthetics, but only loosely premised on the streetwear idiom. This is why Bushido obsesses over baggy pants, he detests them as a gimmicky appropriation of African American styles by White, middle-class Germans. As Moritz Ege has demonstrated, Bushido's affiliation with Picaldi, a then-Berlin-based fashion label, speaks to another pop cultural conjuncture. Ege calls this "the post-Prolet era," (the post-pleb, post-prole) which he localizes and dates in Berlin and within the very scene I engage with (2013). I have argued elsewhere that the cultural pervasiveness of a German *Gheddo* (ghetto) in rap music of that time (and arguably up to today) provided, and continues to provide, German culture with one of the few discursive spaces in which the increasing wealth and income gaps, poverty, migration, and class are addressed frequently, rigorously and with a powerful affective regime attached to it (Lüthe 2019).

Of course, here Bushido plays the game of realness, and the problem of authenticity informs his every move. Bushido does not formulate a critique of the capitalist appropriation of Black styles, but he shares a sense of unease with the acts of transculturation within hip hop, which at times also inform leftist critiques of hip hop's global success story. Still, Bushido only ups the ante of one of the driving forces of hip-hop culture: its claim to provide an authentic voice to the disenfranchised and forgotten. In addition, the neoliberal rags-to-riches fantasy that Eko Fresh around the same time begins to call "The German Dream," serves as a cornerstone of hip-hop-based youth culture of post-Hartz-reform Germany. These reforms initiated by the Social Democratic Party arguably, and somewhat ironically, represent Germany's complete embrace of the neoliberal pro-austerity political practice of cutting welfare and social safety nets in general (McManus 2022: 68ff). In addition, even though this might be simplistic or crude, Bushido and his German/Berlin-Dream affiliates have introduced a crucial component to hip-hop identities this side of the pond, namely that of the businessman and the neoliberal "proletarian" entrepreneur of the self. The message is "we do not belong, we should not have succeeded, but because we kept it real as gangsters, we are now rich." "Vom Bordstein zur Skyline" (From the Pavement to the Skyline), the title of Bushido's first solo album, thus makes all the sense in the world, and the album pursues similar world-making aspirations as some of the most successful German male rappers today, such as Capital Bra, RAF Camora, and 187 Straßenbande (187 Street Gang). On the level of lyrical content and music video aesthetics, this is Aggro Berlin reinvented, updated, and taken to the extreme for today's youth. The music sounds different, and the drugs are new as well.

Bushido's ten-minute-long diss track against former protégé Kay One, "Leben und Tod des Kenneth Glöckner" (Life and Death of Kenneth Glöckner), provides insight into his self-fashioning. He is equally disgusted by Kay One's initial poverty and economic dependence as he is with his selling out (his snitching): the "sin" that made Bushido record the track in the first place. What is more, however, Bushido reads the fact that Kay wanted to be a German/Swabian version of Nelly in baggy pants and a doo-rag as the real mirror into the empty soul of his opponent. Kay One's only claim to identity, according to Bushido, is that it is non-existent.[10]

These German diss tracks condense the affective allure of gangsta rap across the world. They thus encapsulate the intrinsic connection between a sense of self and other to firmly position oneself in opposition to and the simultaneous affective regimes of anger, aggression, angst, superiority, and belonging. Hip hop has maybe always been about expressing a self that is rooted within hip-hop culture; a self that belongs there, where others do not.

In Lieu Of a Conclusion: Affect, Generation, and Post-Realness?

Tricia Rose's foundational text *Black Noise: Rap Music and Black Culture in Contemporary America* (1994) not only introduces hip hop as a scholarly object but raises a variety of intersecting concerns that I revisit here in conclusion: my triad of affect, generation, and post-realness serves as a clumsy nod to Rose's prisms of "flow, layering, and rupture" in *Black Noise*. She writes:

> What is the significance of flow, layering, and rupture as demonstrated on the body and in hip hop's lyrical, musical, and visual works? Interpreting these concepts theoretically, one can argue that they create and sustain rhythmic motion, continuity, and circularity via flow; accumulate, reinforce, and embellish this continuity through layering; and manage threats to these narratives by building in ruptures that highlight the continuity as it momentarily challenges it. These effects at the level of style and aesthetics suggest

---

10   This specific diss of Kay One having no real identity to fall back on references one of the most popular and respected diss tracks in German-language rap's history: Kool Savas's 2005 diss track against the aforementioned Eko Fresh, in which he raps: "Player-, Lover-, Türken-Rap oder Gangster, entscheide Dich; Du weißt es nicht, den Du hast keine Identität!" (Player-, Lover-, Turkish-Rap, or Gangster, make a decision; oh, you can't, 'cause you have no identity!).

affirmative ways in which profound social dislocation and rupture can be managed and perhaps contested in the cultural arena. Let us imagine these hip hop principles as a blueprint for social resistance and affirmation: create sustaining narratives, accumulate them, layer, embellish, and transform them. (Rose 1994: 39)

None of the above becomes meaningful unless used "as a blueprint for social resistance" (ibid.: 39). The "social" that Rose is interested in is crucially produced and policed by experiences rooted in racialization, with its ultimate pseudo-neutral signifier of Whiteness, but also in the ways hip hop itself has impacted the social and cultural performances within its communities across the globe and, as a shortcut, has made audiences "feel" what it is to be within this world.

In terms of affect then, hip-hop music and culture have a lot to offer: graffiti writing not only enables artists to consider themselves artists, but also provides the effect of the thrill of the illegal and the outcome of writing oneself into being. Breakdancing openly celebrates a sense of belonging, both with the crew and in the cypher, and offers a similar affective attachment as, for example, other sports and activities premised in physical competition: excitement, working-out, exhaustion. Making music and listening to it shapes who we are, who we want to be, and how we feel about being in the world.

"Hip Hop in Deutschland, ich frag mich, wer bellt da; wisst Ihr morgen noch, wer heute Euer Held war?" (Hip Hop in Germany, look who is barking; do you today remember who your hero was yesterday?), as Torch had it on one of his features on a Tomekk-track (2000). And whether or not we and the current generation have forgotten about our heroes of the past, the trailblazers of German-language rap and hip-hop culture of the 1990s, the current scene is more diverse than ever. Following the success of SXTN, in 2019 Berlin rapper Juju released the most successful German rap album by a female artist. The contribution of female rappers ranging from the styles of Shirin David via Schwesta Ewa all the way to Sookee, indicates that we are currently witnessing an age of increasing visibility of female German-language rappers in Germany. While not all these rappers continue the long tradition of Black feminist and womanist voices in rap music (Collins 2000/2009), Sookee, for example, brings gender and queer studies consciousness to the German rap stage. This, I believe, has a lot to do with the changing generational outlook of German rap.

Some of the transcultural concerns of early rap—how German am I, how German can hip hop be in the first place, does hip hop need to be translated to the German context in order to be palpable?—have all but vanished. Capital Bra now proudly declares that he is "Capital aus Ukraine und nicht Drake aus Canada" (Capital from Ukraine and not Drake from Canada) in one of his songs "Benzema" (2018). On the whole, then, the uneasiness that haunted early hip hop in Germany, especially regarding Whiteness, German-ness, and the US as a place of origin seem to have taken a back seat and maybe intergenerational conflicts have taken its place. After all, the history of hip hop in Germany and the variety of identities it has enabled to be articulated and performed is so rich by now, that the necessity to engage with US American and African American originators has all but disappeared.

In the 21st century, the internet and YouTube have replaced the army bases and the youth centers and the need to root hip-hop identities in Germany in the local. Massive Töne's and Freundeskreis' "Mutterstadt" (Mother Town) has given way to Tua's "Vorstadt" (suburb): a place that could be anywhere in Germany (even though it is also in Stuttgart).[11] Strikingly, the latter, a song about growing up and growing out of the suburb, lyrically and musically trace German rap history from the suburbs of the 1990s to the contemporary moment in the third verse of the

---

11   Arguably, Tua's "Vorstadt"—the German suburb—sits at the intersection between what the suburb signifies in US culture, its imagined racial homogeneity/Whiteness, its alleged peacefulness, its relationship with private property and homeownership, and what the suburb signifies in French cultural history in the notion of the "banlieu" as an ethnically diverse, economically precarious, and isolated place outside of the city. The lyrics delineate this complexity and tension between the suburb as harmless and dangerous, as both connected to urban life and as distinctly not part of the city, as representing a more limited spectrum of diversity typical of mid-size German towns and cities.

song, which is also set apart musically through a choppy, cloud-style beat and rap.

In this chapter, I focused on the first and second generation of male German rappers and how they performed transcultural hip-hop sensibilities for German-speaking audiences. If we take the street rap era and the Berlin take-over of German rap to have formed the second generation of German-language rap, we find ourselves now in a third-generation moment of German hip hop. Sookee, SXTN, die Orsons, Edgard Wasser & Fatoni, and Danger Dan & the Antilopen Gang can rightfully assume that their audiences long for new perspectives and identities within rap music. The carnivalesque Orsons, the self-ironic and meta-aware Fatoni and Edgar Wasser, and the queer activist Sookee explicitly articulate identities vis-à-vis the older generations, who now primarily serve as emblems of hip hop's past and of days gone by. Age has become an issue in Germany, too. When Edgar Wasser jokes about the fact that his comrade Fatoni caters to a generation of old White German critics of rap music in their 2021 song "Künstlerische Differenzen" (Creative Differences), it makes me feel old, too.

It begs the question, of course, what does it signify that a whole generation of German hip-hop practitioners—like me—do not get tired of sharing what hip hop means to them? Have we become the old White dudes in German society that hip hop once potentially enabled us to criticize? Maybe growing up with rap music and hip-hop culture is still easier than growing old with it. And maybe the "can't stop, won't stop" mentality of hip-hop culture forces us to still do what we do and to continue to be who we are: as part of, and thanks to, hip-hop culture and the world it created.

Discography/Videography

Bushido. *Vom Bordstein bis zur Skyline*. Aggro Berlin, 2003, compact disc.
Bushido. "Leben und Tod des Kenneth Glöckner." Ersguterjunge. YouTube video, posted in 2013. (The music video has since been deleted from the artist's channel.)
Bushido and Baba SAAD. "Nie ein Rapper." *Carlo Cokxxx Nutten II*. Ersguterjunge, 2005, compact disc.
Capital Bra. "Benzema." *CB6*. Bra Musik, 2019, compact disc.
Die Fantastischen Vier. "Die Da." *Vier Gewinnt*. Columbia Records, 1992, compact disc.
DJ Tomekk vs. Grandmaster Flash featuring Afrob, Flava Flav and MC Rene. "1,2,3,... Rhymes Galore." *Return of Hip Hop*. Modul/BMG, 1999/2000, compact disc.
DJ Tomekk featuring Curse, GZA, Sunz of Men, Stieber Twins. "Ich lebe für Hip Hop." *Return of Hip Hop*. Modul/BMG, 2000, compact disc.
DJ Tomekk featuring KRS One, MC Rene, Torch. "Return of Hip Hop." *Return of Hip Hop*. Modul/BMG, 2000, compact disc.
Fatoni and Edgar Wasser. "Künstlerische Differenzen." *Delirium*. LoL Records, 2021, compact disc.
King Kool Savas. "King of Rap." *Full House* (Plattenpapzt). Jive, 2000, compact disc.
Massive Töne featuring Afrob and Freundeskreis. "Mutterstadt." *Kopfnicker*. MZEE Records, 1996, compact disc.
Massive Töne. "Das Urteil." *Die John Bello Story*. Optik Records, 2005, compact disc.
Tua. "Vorstadt." *Tua*. Chimperator Productions, 2019, compact disc.
Wu-Tang Clan. "Bring Da Ruckus." *Enter the Wu-Tang (36 Chambers)*. Loud Records/BMG Music, 1993, compact disc.

References

Asante, M.K. Jr. 2009. *It's Bigger Than Hip Hop: The Rise of the Post-Hip-Hop Generation*. New York: St. Martin's Griffin.

Benessaieh, Afef, ed. 2010. "Multiculturalism, Interculturality, Transculturality." In *Amériques transculturelles – Transcultural Americas*: 11–38. Ottawa: University of Ottawa Press. https://doi.org/10.2307/j.ctt1ch78hd.4.

Breitenwischer, Dustin. 2021. *Die Geschichte des Hip-Hop: 111 Alben*. Ditzingen: Reclam.

Collins, Patricia Hill. 2009. *Black Feminist Thought: Knowledge, Consciousness, and the Politics of Empowerment*. New York: Routledge Classics.

Ege, Moritz. 2013. *"Ein Proll mit Klasse": Mode, Popkultur und soziale Ungleichheit unter jungen Männern in Berlin*. Frankfurt/New York: Campus.

Fleetwood, Nicole R. 2005. "Hip-Hop Fashion, Masculine Anxiety, and the Discourse of Americana." In *Black Cultural Traffic: Crossroads in Global Performance and Popular Culture*, edited by Harry J. Elam, Jr. and Kennell Jackson, 326–45. Ann Arbor: The University of Michigan Press.

Frith, Simon. 1996. "Music and Identity." In *Questions of Cultural Identity*, edited by Stuart Hall and Paul Du Gay, 108–127. London: Sage Publications. https://doi.org/10.4135/9781446221907.n7.

Gilmore, Ruth Wilson. 2022. *Abolition Geography: Essays Towards Liberation*. London: Verso Books.

Hall, Stuart. 1992. "What Is This 'Black' in Black Popular Culture?" In *Black Popular Culture*, edited by Gina Dent, 21–33. New York: Dia Center for the Arts.

Lhamon, W.T. 2000. *Raising Cain: Blackface Performance from Jim Crow to Hip Hop*. Cambridge: Harvard University Press.

Lott, Eric. 1993. *Love and Theft: Blackface Minstrelsy and the American Working Class*. Oxford: Oxford University Press.

Lüthe, Martin. 2019. "Bedrooms, Bathrooms, and Beyond? MTV Cribs, Hip Hop und Reichtumsperformanzen im privaten Kabelfernsehen in den 2000er Jahren." In *Reichtum in Deutschland: Akteure, Räume und Lebenswelten im 20. Jahrhundert*, edited by Eva-Maria Gajek, Anne Kurr and Lu Seegers, 272–285. Göttingen: Wallstein Verlag. https://doi.org/10.5771/9783835343276-272.

Mbembe, Achille. 2017. *Critique of Black Reason*. Durham, NC: Duke University Press.

McManus, Ian P. 2022. *The Repoliticization of the Welfare State*. Ann Arbor: The University of Michigan Press.

Müller, Eggo. 1999. "Populäre Visionen. Ein Sampler zur Debatte um Musikclips und Musikfernsehen in den Cultural Studies." In *Viva MTV! Popmusik im Fernsehen*, edited by Klaus Neumann-Braun, 74–91. Frankfurt: Suhrkamp

Robinson, Cedric J. 1983/2000. *Black Marxism: The Making of the Black Radical Tradition*. Durham: The University of North Carolina Press.

Robinson, Cedric J. 2019. *On Racial Capitalism, Black Internationalism, and Cultures of Resistance*, edited by Ed. H.L.T. Quan. New York: Pluto Press.

Rose, Tricia. 1994. *Black Noise: Rap Music and Black Culture in Contemporary America*. Hanover, NH: University Press of New England.

Singh, Jaspal Naveel. 2021. *Transcultural Voices: Narrating Hip Hop Culture in Complex Delhi*. Bristol: Multilingual Matter.

Producing Hip-Hop Culture and Identity
How a Youth Recording Studio Supports Well-Being

Bronwen Low and Édouard Laniel-Tremblay

Abstract *Montreal, Canada, is a vibrant multicultural and multilingual city, within which, unfortunately, racialized youth grapple with discrimination and marginalization, shaped by a confluence of institutional, cultural, and political forces. However, the dynamic realm of hip-hop culture provides a transformative avenue for emerging artists, offering alternative spaces of belonging. In this chapter, we build on previous scholarship on hip hop as a site of social and cultural redefinition for marginalized identities. Our study explores how music creation and community-building at a recording studio can foster youth well-being. Located in a free after-school youth center, the studio supports well-being through the development of community, critical perspectives, self-expression, and performative hip-hop identities. We argue that this positive hip-hop identity is anti-essentialist and that it challenges reductive and exclusionary models of Quebec identity and belonging. Our methods are ethnographic, including participant observation and interviews with nine youths aged 18 to 21.*

In August 2022, the Réseau express métropolitain (REM), an electric train network under development in Montreal, posted to their TikTok account a freestyle created by rapper Maky Lavender commissioned to promote the new transit option. The video was widely criticized and then deleted due to criticisms that Lavender, a Black bilingual MC, rapped only in English. The Quebec government agency in charge of the REM had hired Lavender to perform as part of a publicity campaign a year prior and recorded this freestyle at that time. The agency explained that they removed the post because "the video did not meet their publication criteria on sharing information regarding the electric train" (Leavitt 2022), despite them having the English language video for a year. While the REM sought out Lavender for his coolness and credibility among youth, they gave him no instructions, abandoned him and the project as soon as there were concerns raised, and asked him to stay quiet: "It was so easy for them to pull the plug. It was so easy for them to be like, 'yeah we'll just take it off—don't talk to the press'" (Kassam and Caruso-Moro 2022). This event speaks to anti-English language politics in the province as well as attitudes towards rappers, and particularly Black men, as expendable.

These politics and attitudes shape the lived context of the youth in our study, who all attend NBS Studio (NoBadSound Studio), a free-access community recording studio. The studio is housed in Chalet Kent, a not-for-profit community center for youths aged 11 to 18, located in a very culturally diverse neighborhood of Montreal. Chalet Kent describes itself as being "dedicated to inspire and empower youth through various projects and programs and allow for young people to build meaningful relations, engage in critical thinking, and (re)imagine more sustainable futures" (Chalet Kent, n.d). Many of the youth who make music at NBS are deeply invested in hip-hop culture. The quality of NBS Studio's facilities and equipment, combined with the director's musical and interpersonal skills and profound commitment to empowering youth, have made this free-access studio a focal point for emerging artists in the Montreal hip-hop community. Here, youth create and record music and can develop positive identities grounded in hip-hop culture.

In this chapter, we first set the stage for our ethnographic inquiry by describing the political and cultural context in Quebec, including its hip-hop history, as well as some literature on hip hop, youth and well-being, and the hip-hop alter-ego. We then describe our study of nine young people who attend NBS Studio and explore how music making there can support well-being through the development of community, critical perspectives, self-expression, and performative youth identities. Youth can counter and challenge negative discourses about racialized and immigrant adolescents in Quebec by exploring and celebrating these otherwise marginalized identities in the spaces, both physical and digital, of the studio and international hip-hop culture.

The Politics of Belonging in Quebec

Identities in Quebec

Members of our research team have previously described the dominant model of belonging in the province in terms of "Québéquicité," in which

> two intersecting continua, sight, and sound... are the most important elements: having or not Whiteness is the first fact to be noted about any newly encountered individual in Quebec. The other, unseen but clearly heard, element that goes to make up Québéquicité in our theoretical framework is language: specifically, speakers in Quebec being perceived as having or not having the 'right' kind of French. (Sarkar, Low, and Winer 2007: 357)

These elements are legacies of Quebec's history. After the Treaty of Paris in 1763, French elite settlers left New France and English-speaking settler elites took control of the economy being built upon indigenous territories, eventually forming the nation-state of Canada (Bouchard 2012:14–15). French settlers lived mainly along the St. Lawrence River and continued to be part of the colonial project, testified by French toponyms across North America (Bouchard and Lévesque 2014). At the same time, they were marginalized based on economic, social, and political factors; however, their social status was in no way comparable to that of indigenous peoples facing the first stages of genocide (Austin 2010: 19) and Black peoples oppressed by chattel slavery, segregation, and other manifestations of antiblackness (Howard 2020: 128). In the 1960s, during the Quiet Revolution, a cultural upheaval which saw the rise of secularism and heightened social and economic development, the population of what is called "old stock" Quebeckers, who are White, francophone, and (sometimes only culturally) Catholic, became the economic, political as well as cultural dominant group. This dominance has been maintained in part by exclusive discourses, policies, and practices which can serve to separate "us" from "them." For instance, some political parties and media instrumentalize fears of the disappearance of the "old stock" francophone population in light of immigration and population growth, mobilizing language and identity politics for political gain.

For example, in the Fall 2022 provincial political campaign, the incumbent (and now re-elected) premier François Legault indicated that accepting more than 50,000 immigrants a year would be "a bit suicidal" until "we have stopped the decline of French." A week later the then immigration and labor minister Jean Boulet said, "80 percent of immigrants go to Montreal, don't work, don't speak French or don't adhere to the values of Quebec society" (Nerestant 2022).[1] Language and identity politics also shape recent pieces of legislation restricting the wearing of religious symbols in the public sector, including for teachers, with negative consequences for Muslim women and others (Low et al. 2021), and restricting access to English language services in the public sector (including health care, the courts, and college education) and business. Fighting discrimination is complicated by the fact that the premier does not recognize systemic racism in the province (Banerjee 2020).

This brief socio-historical description highlights aspects of the sometimes-hostile climate facing racialized and indigenous peoples in Quebec, as well as those who immigrate to the province, including many members of the Quebec hip-hop scene (particularly those based in Montreal, the largest city).

---

1   While the premier criticized these remarks and said that Boulet, the minister in question, would be removed from this position if his party were re-elected, Boulet had been in the position for almost a year and was re-elected in his riding.

Hip-Hop Histories in Quebec

Hip-hop culture started to appear in Quebec towards the end of the 1970s (Lamort 2017: 11). The history of hip hop in Quebec is marked by the appearance and development of networks on the fringes of conventional circuits. As performance scholar Annette Saddik reminds us, hip hop must be understood in relation to a continuity of Afro-American forms of performative expression in constant renewal (2003: 120), including Caribbean, Latin, and African traditions. Hip hop was introduced to Quebec through cultural exchanges between the Caribbean and Afro-American diasporas of Montreal and New York, and this, from the beginning of the emergence of the hip-hop movement in the late 1970s (Low, Sarkar, and Winer 2009: 66). During the 1990s, hip hop started becoming more popular in Quebec's francophone music scene while remaining very close to, and sometimes imitating, what was popular in France (Fortin, Lasse, and Roy 2007; Desfossés 2020). At the end of the decade, a paradigm shift started to occur when rap artists in Quebec stopped imitating the French rap artist accent, and began to use their own local slang, expressions, and prosody in their songs (Sakar and Winer 2006: 176; Lesacher 2012). These developments paved the way to more fluidity, freedom, and variety in language use after the turn of the millennium.

Since the 2010s, hip hop has been on the rise and undergoing new transformations in Quebec. While some speak of "post-rap" (Pagliarulo-Beauchemin 2016), the term "Rap Québ" or "Rap Keb" is beginning to be used to designate the hip-hop scene in Quebec (Arbour-Masse 2017). The controversy over Franglais—French infused with words borrowed from English—in Quebec hip hop (Savard Moran 2019; White 2019) has brought attention to hip-hop culture in the mainstream media landscape.[2] However, not all artists benefit from the same recognition; as

---

2   In an interview by Renaud, Laniel-Tremblay explains, "this controversy addressing the state of French in Quebec was rather a way of circumventing terms which may be even more controversial, but which are nevertheless necessary to name in this context—for example the influence of the racialized

scholar Néméh-Nombré has argued, the hip-hop artists receiving the most media attention are French-speaking White men (2018: 39–44). Racialized artists also get less support from institutions (media, festivals, funding) and may sometimes be subject to police surveillance (Arbour-Masse 2018). We should also keep in mind that hip hop holds high cultural prestige, a rare domain in which young, racialized people's identities are valued, positioning them as trendsetters (Fortin 2006; Kitwana 2005). Yet, throughout hip-hop history in Quebec, accounts of hypervisibility and erasure illustrate the difficulties of addressing the presence of racialized people in the public space (Ferah 2019; Néméh-Nombré 2018: 39–44).

Previous research from our team members on the hip-hop scene in Quebec has analyzed how some in the community challenge dominant language and identity politics through richly diverse membership and practices, including multilingual code-switching or "translanguaging" in their lyrics (Low and Sarkar 2014; Sarkar 2009). We have examined the ways this "parler hip hop" challenges Quebec official monolingual language policies and Québéquicité as a model of belonging. We argue that the Montreal hip-hop community creates its own language and identity standards from the bottom-up, a kind of resistance vernacular that reflects the ways language is lived in very diverse neighborhoods. A rich literature exists on the hip-hop community in Quebec (White 2019; Lesacher 2014) with a focus on youth (Atséna Abogo 2019; Leblanc et al 2016; Laabidi 2012). Less has been researched on the spaces (in as well as out of school) that nurture and support the Montreal hip-hop community and its particular linguistic and cultural practices; this chapter extends our recent study that seeks to fill this gap (Laniel-Tremblay and Low 2022). In the literature from outside Quebec on nonformal hip-hop

---

communities [on the evolution of the spoken language] which brings new vocabulary and speech practices in the public space" (Renaud 2021, translation by Laniel-Tremblay). The case of Franglais in hip hop highlights how languages are often instrumentalized in Quebec to talk indirectly about races and identities.

programs, Dimitriadis' (2009) multi-year study of a hip-hop-based program in a youth center in the United States explored its impact on youth identities and community building. More recently Levy et al. (2021: 221–222) conducted a study in a community center with children aged 8 to 11 participating in a hip-hop and spoken word therapy program. The results highlighted gains in self-confidence, the ability to express difficult topics, and improvement of a sense of a community.

While hip hop includes four well known elements (Mcing, Djing, break dancing, and graffiti), to which some add knowledge as the fifth (Alim 2009: 2; Laabidi 2006: 168), NBS Studio focuses on music production and personal growth, including knowledge of self.

Hip Hop and Youth Well-Being

In contexts with a glaring lack of mental health resources, hip-hop music-making and listening can be important outlets and supports (Harper and Jackson 2018: 114; Heath and Arroyo 2014: 31–38; Chang 2005). The central art forms of hip-hop culture—rap lyric writing, deejaying, dancing, and beatmaking—have been gaining traction in wellness-focused settings for their abilities to engage young people in the process of actively working through life challenges (Elligan 2000) as culturally sustaining forms of expression, self-knowledge, and community-building (Paris and Alim 2017). For these reasons, scholars have developed a literature connecting hip hop and mental health. This corpus opens the door to rethinking and adapting therapeutic practices (Hadley and Yancy 2012). For instance, hip hop therapy relies on "the deliberate integration of elements of hip-hop culture into a therapeutic context to achieve a cathartic state that contributes to psychosocial development" (Alvarez 2012: 122). Similarly, scholar Raphael Travis says that "hip-hop empowerment strategies suggest that deliberate and purposeful engagement in musical experiences (and other empowering aspects of hip-hop culture) help the evocation, modulation, or termination of emotions, and subsequently promote health development through the cascading and reinforcing aspects of development" (2016: 128–131).

Key to hip hop's therapeutic value is rap lyric writing. The exercise of putting feelings, emotions, thoughts, and aspirations to paper is a core principle of rap and can be extremely positive and beneficial for the development of the participants (Levy, Cook, and Emdin 2018: 2–6). As Low (2011: 118) reminds us, the centrality of language and poetry, speech and words, in hip hop is embodied in the acronym rap (rhythm and poetry). Exploring the emotional impact of writing lyrics, social behavioral scientists Lepore and Smyth (2002) demonstrate how writing can reduce health risks by promoting socio-cognitive and socio-emotional development. Nevertheless, post-colonial literature scholar Sara Grewal reminds us not to overlook orality, since "the dynamism, physicality, and embodiment, and contingency and ephemerality of rap as a performed, oral/aural genre are, I argue, essential to the 'street' aspects of its epistemology" (2020: 80).

Beat making also offers a highly engaging intervention approach because "near-instant gratification in the form of aural and visual feedback … means rapport can be rapidly developed in a fun and interactive way (Travis et al.: 749). Music production offers another appealing mode of self-expression (ibid.: 744), facilitated by recent efforts to democratize and decolonize production software (Nast 2001), improvements of open-source production software, and the general accessibility of quality production equipment.

The complexity of rap and hip hop's view of the construction of knowledge and its dissemination aims to highlight the plurality of experiences regarding self-expression within hip-hop culture, which talks back to different narratives on the evolution of hip-hop epistemology (Desfossés 2020; Marsh and Campbell 2020; Lamort 2017; Campbell 2014: 271). It is then not surprising to have seen the presence of hip-hop culture in school settings over the past decades (Crooke, Comte, and Almeida 2020: 19), as well as community center programs (Dimitriadis 2009). Dimitriadis explored how through hip hop, "contemporary youth are increasingly fashioning notions of self and community outside of school in ways educators have largely ignored" (2009: xi). These notions of self and community are often accompanied by political awareness, acting as a kind of counter to school: "rap, as I will show, proliferates in such sites, serving as a kind of alternative curriculum through which often intensely disaffected young people have produced and maintained notions of community, history, and self" (ibid.: 34). Similarly, Ladson-Billings (2015) points to the relevance of hip-hop-based programs for educating racialized youth because they offer the possibility of experiences outside, and sometimes challenge, Eurocentric music.

Playing with Identity through the Hip-Hop Alter-Ego

One aspect of hip-hop identities is the persona or alter-ego (Bradley 2018). In our research on youth well-being at NBS Studio, we became interested in the role the persona could play in fostering well-being.

The persona is not unique to hip hop. Popular music theorist Mickey Hess describes how as with "David Bowie performing as Ziggy Stardust or Garth Brooks performing as Chris Gaines, certain hip-hop acts perform a second artist persona. This phenomenon can take shape, through costumes, playfully evasive lyrics, and samples, as resistance to the material conditions of the musician" (2006: 298). According to music journalist Brent Bradley, these choices enable artistic freedom:

> The ability to recreate ourselves through the simplicity of adopting another persona allows us to explore areas of our personality that might not jive with what our peers would normally expect from us, so it makes sense why so many artists adopt alter-egos at various points in their careers. An alter-ego can work as a reset button on the expectations an artist carries, as well as serving as a fresh canvas for artistic freedom. (2018)

Creating a character offers the possibility of producing a distance from oneself allowing experimentation, imaginativeness, and vulnerability to interact from new angles. The alter-ego can become a tool by which the artist can explore their desires and create alternate realities. It can also involve choosing which facets of their identity to put forward, amplify, and share, and which not (Hess 2006: 298). This practice has been very widespread since the beginning of the movement for both MCs and producers and allows artists to explore different registers and themes (Williams and Stroud 2013: 19).

One of the most common strategies to shape an alter-ego is the "ego trip," which describes a "posture of the rapper praising his own qualities and performances" (Journet 2012). The ego trip is an example of hip-hop "braggadocio" (Williams and Stroud 2013: 19), a type of boastful behavior that glories the speaker and positions them as the best (Exantus 2022: 117; Fofana 2012). The ego trip can be traced back to rap battle culture and "comes from the fact that rap, nowadays, has become very competitive. Between clashes, battles, concerts, and other concepts, the rapper then finds himself obliged to promote himself" (Culturap 2021). In short, the ego trip is a technique of self-expression combining exaggeration and boasting, but also the possibility of dreaming; as such it opens the door to reinventing oneself. In this way, the ego trip can be a powerful technique to boost self-esteem and confidence and shows how artistic freedom can be transformative.

Studying NBS, Hip Hop, and Youth Well-Being

During Winter 2019, semi-structured individual interviews were conducted in French, English, or both, with nine participants from the NBS Studio aged 18 to 21. The sample was composed of six men and three women with origins from Chile, the Dominican Republic, France, Haiti, Lebanon, Madagascar, the Philippines, Senegal, and Vietnam. Five of them were born outside Canada, and all participants had moved at one point in their lives. They also all grew up in multilingual households, using a combination of their parents' native language and French and/or English. On NBS's website, the studio ethos is described as "an inclusive, safe space for young artists to grow their musical abilities and expand their knowledge of studio recording. We take a hands-on, practical approach to teaching youth about music production, recording, mixing, performance and writing songs" (NBS 2022). The youth center is mainly frequented by young people from the surrounding neighborhoods, but

NBS study participants also lived in each of the four major suburban regions outside the island of Montreal; that some are travelling up to ninety minutes by public transport to get to the studio is an indicator of NBS's popularity. The dedication of Jai Nitai Lotus, the studio coordinator and mentor, and of the youth mentors is worth highlighting when describing why the studio is so appreciated.

Our interviews with these youth indicated that going to the studio supports their well-being, alongside developing music creation and production skills. Support for well-being is grounded in four elements: community, criticality, self-expression, and performative identities.

1) Finding Community

To start, here is a participant describing an example of some alienation experienced in Quebec, but also in her family's country of origin:

> I cannot define a place where I can call home, because I feel different no matter where I go. Like when I'm here it's like you're not a Canadian Québécois because you're not pale. When I go to [country of family origin in Africa], well it's like I'm too pale to be from the place, and then I get dressed differently, I speak differently so that there is not really a place where I feel I belong." (Danielle, Laniel-Tremblay's translation)

This is an expression of not feeling at home in any national context, while the comments about skin color and language are a reminder of the ways race and language shape belonging and discrimination.

For youth involved in the study, their deep engagement with hip-hop culture is key to finding a place where they feel comfortable. The studio becomes an incubator for community connection. One participant explained, "Hip hop helped me get into a community, that's for sure. I started meeting more rappers and more people who share the same vision as me. I thought I was the only one, but in fact there are many who share the same vision as me about music" (Laniel-Tremblay's translation). Because hip-hop culture needs to be understood within the context of the Global Hip-Hop Nation[3]—and for many of the youth here, rap from France is a more important influence than rap from the US—connecting to hip hop allows the participants to recontextualize their identities, making links with communities outside Québec or abroad. For instance, the studio took part in the PHI_portal, a cross-border participatory installation at the multimedia center and gallery Phi Center in Montreal where artists were "invited to listening sessions with young artists from other cities, such as Milwaukee and Mexico City" (Lipset 2021). To a certain extent, the Global Hip-Hop Nation which materialized at NBS Studio represents an alternative to Quebec identity's narrative: first, by offering a place where their identities are not othered, and second by building bridges between members of the community and promoting their identities with a view to creating solidarities.

2) A Critical Voice and Self-Reflection

The participants all have different life trajectories, however, hip hop offers them a framework through which they can express and channel emotions and feelings. Ibrahima explains that "[Music] opened my mind, it allowed me to mentally move forward in life thinking like, yeah, you're not a kid anymore, and like when I was writing stuff and everything, I read it again and then I said to myself, like you know in real life, maybe you act this way, but you shouldn't."

This passage demonstrates how music and writing can become tools that enable people to reflect on their behaviors and promote personal thought processes. Ibrahima is also a Cégep[4] psychology student which gives him a different perspective on the relationship between music and the psyche. Along with Adjapong and Levy (2021: 6–10) and Travis et al. (2019), he concludes that "music is also a therapy." Another example re-

---

3   Alim (2009: 3) defines this concept as "a multilingual, multiethnic 'nation' with an international reach, a fluid capacity to cross borders, and a reluctance to adhere to the geopolitical givens of the present."
4   A college with pre-university and technical programs.

lated to the education field involves Jackson, who confides having improved his vocabulary and his writing thanks to his practice of rap:

> Now that I'm forcing myself not to... curse in my words, curse in my lyrics. It's a lot, it's a lot harder and it challenges my brain to be like okay, well hey, ok, you need to find another word that replaces that. Or you have to find another word that replaces that. That actually helps me with my vocabulary. So when I'm doing an English essay at school, I write super naturally and I write like sophisticated words.

By devoting themselves more to writing through hip hop, participants became more receptive to the power and impact of words, resulting in cognitive and political insights matched by a desire to surpass oneself.

Nick summarizes the powerful influence of hip hop when saying, "Hip hop taught me a lot of things about philosophy, how to deal with the world. You know, even if the music is not deep, the process behind it is, like the time spent in the studio, how to like help each other all the time."

Engaging with hip-hop culture provokes reflections on how social structures reproducing racial, economic, and social discrimination are affecting them:

> We are not little idiots. We don't make music just to promote bad stuff you know. We talk about it because, me of course, well I don't talk for myself because you know I have a good life, thank god...They [hip-hop artists] will talk, "Yeah I have dealed this I dealt that," after that you [the audience] it's up to you to make sure, by listening, to tell yourself, "ah shit these people they lived, they lived a nightmare and why not try to improve the situation of future generations." (Ibrahima)

Ibrahima reveals how through hip hop he makes connections with his life experiences and those discussed in artists' pieces. This process of self-reflection counters common concerns about the negative influence of hip hop's complex politics of representation, including violence, sexism, and consumerism, by depicting how people show discernment when analyzing rap. Precisely, this participant explains, why writing can be one of the last spaces of freedom and can raise awareness (Harper and Jackson 2018; Chang 2015). Ibrahima further explains how hip hop can give a voice to excluded people or communities such as "people who have a life that is a hassle, for example in HLM [*Habitation à loyer modéré*, meaning subsidized housing] in France, or in the ghettos of Harlem in the States, these people in their music claim their lives." Building on that, Nick declares that "society could learn about... open-mindedness because in hip hop there is a lot, a lot of open-mindedness. That, we accept everything, it's music and also, it's a lot of mutual aid between artists and everything. Society can learn to accept new, new people especially on the racial level."

Carlos Munoz, producer, and cofounder of a Montreal production label, points out that "guys who do rap are often like messengers of what is happening in the street" (Arbour-Masse 2018). Similarly, D'Amico describes rap as a kind of social documentary: "Rap provided practitioners with the possibility to describe, document and even critique urban realities; the surveillance, over-policing, and punishment of Black bodies; and the structures and strategies of domination that shaped their quotidian realities" (2019: 11).

As reports of racial profiling from the Montreal Police Service continue to make headlines (Schué 2019), there are social and political pressures facing racialized youth. In this sense, Ibrahima's words are particularly interesting. He continues by specifying how hip hop can be a catalyst for reflections of a political and social nature on the issues of systemic racism. His next example illustrates how the works of hip-hop artists made him realize that these stories should not be analyzed individually, but rather as multiple manifestations of deep social issues targeting racialized people:

> Lil Uzi Vert won't be able to talk to all the young people of future generations and tell them 'no, don't do this, don't do that,' because you know, he's a normal person, he won't be able go through every neighborhood and everything, so it's up to society to listen to this music, to accept it as it is...whether it was Donald Trump, whether it was Barack Obama, it doesn't matter, we have a problem in the

country [the USA] with the ghettos. Why not try to improve that and just make sure that these people live better, opening more jobs for young people.

The great popularity of hip hop allows artists to reach a very large audience, which represents an outlet for instilling awareness. Other themes appear in the discussion such as observations concerning gender stereotypes when Nick brings up the fact that "a problem in hip hop is that there is like, how to say that, a strong masculinity. It's really very masculine; it dictates how men have to act. Like the image of [a] thug, of [a] womanizer that creates toxic masculinity as such, and that needs to be changed."

These examples demonstrate how hip-hop culture can instigate political awareness by establishing connections between the audience and artists recounting similar experiences or by exposing youth to social issues. In sum, it encompasses the process of turning inward through a process of questioning and reflecting on different situations or problems, and outward by turning these into inspiration for creating.

3) Having a Public Diary: Expressing Feelings

Some participants describe themselves as introverts, drawing a parallel between writing lyrics and keeping a personal journal. This points to how hip hop encompasses a plurality of modes and variations of expression. In the following section, we will draw attention to the benefits of expressing feelings through hip hop and how this can translate into openness to others and gains in maturity. To start, Mark describes the value of having an outlet that matches his personality:

> Hip hop taught me about how to express myself. I'm like the type of dude I don't really like to talk as much. And it's like I have a way to express my feelings I'm pretty bad at expressing myself in words so if I make a song and people will understand how I feel, that's cool. That's why I like it a lot, and it kept me out of trouble; taught me how to communicate with people, it made me grow as

> a person, made me more mature. It's like having a diary, a public diary and it's like talking about how you feel and songs just like let it go.

This last quote testifies to the educational and therapeutic contribution of hip hop as a medium for gaining confidence, which supports Ibrahima's words regarding how rap helped him express himself. Clearly, the malleability of hip hop allows people to adapt it to their wants and interests. In addition, Mark emphasizes the importance of putting his emotions and thoughts in writing like a diary, and how it was beneficial for him to gain maturity. In his opinion, the public reception of his texts is a barometer to gauge if he has been able to formulate his message well. It is also relevant to note that hip hop and music have taken him away from problems, which challenges prejudices against hip hop that consider it to be inherently negative (Harper and Jackson 2018: 115). By devoting himself to hip hop, Mark tells us how this passion has become a way to channel his thoughts and emotions. Looking back, Mark acknowledges that hip hop had a direct impact on his personal development by allowing him to mature and helping him avoid problematic situations and contexts. These remarks underline the value of openness to others through words, and of connecting with yourself in a form of self-care (Travis et al. 2019: 748).

For other participants, the beat making and other musical aspects (rather than lyrics) are the central components through which they developed a connection that fostered their self-expression. Way and McKerrell (2017: 3) report that music can be semantically more ambiguous than an image or text; this seemed to open new modes of expression for some of our participants. For instance, Lamia expresses how creating beats for a song allows her to explore different emotions she cannot evoke with lyrics:

> These are things that I would just say when I make music. It's not something that I'm going to say, like, I'm not going to open up about that, it's more like, that's why I said it was like my escape, precisely with the words I feel that I don't express myself well. But

when it's done with the music, it comes, it flows, it comes more easily. So, like, that's why I manage to be more vulnerable when it's related to music.

This statement testifies once again to the multidisciplinary richness that hip hop offers and more specifically to the relevance of music which can be a medium for different possibilities, including accessing a range of other emotions. Mark agrees with this by adding how the emotions felt while listening to the music can be as, or even stronger than, the message of the lyrics: "I think the feeling is more important than what you're saying because some people don't know how to explain things so they know they don't need to express how do you feel but like not by words but just like by doing."

For introverts, hip-hop culture provides several elements which allow everyone to go at their own pace while respecting their limits and preferences. As Chantal summarizes: "In what I write, uh, it's more like philosophy, metaphors... it's a bit of everything, like what I see, what happens to me in life, situations that my friends experience." In short, writing or music creation represent avenues to make connections and give meaning to what the individual is experiencing by reformulating their thoughts using the multiple components of hip hop: lyrics, music, and knowledge. The multimodality at the heart of hip hop is ultimately a factor that makes it possible to highlight the different skills and preferences of young people, which is a great lesson in valuing and recognizing the plurality of skills and modes of expression. However, the benefits derived from writing lyrics and composing music are not exclusive to hip hop; it is the connection participants have with this culture that allows them to access tools to develop their self-expression, and other musical cultures could offer similar opportunities.

4) Gaining Confidence through Performance: Creating a Hip-Hop Persona

Given the importance of performance in hip hop, our participants described the time and dedication needed to develop and master the art and subtleties of emceeing. Participants expressed a desire not to have their style categorized for them, nor to have the usual stereotypes of young people doing rap applied to them. They don't want to be put in a box, or at least they want to create the box. However, we noticed an interesting tension: while many of the youth talked about the possibilities lyric writing and beat making offered for self-expression, they also described the importance of creating an artistic persona as part of the process of liberating themselves from some social expectations. For beginners in hip hop, the alter-ego technique can be appealing because it allows them to shape their MC character by subscribing to different codes of hip hop. It creates a space where it is possible to dream and give free rein to their imagination; metaphorically speaking, it opens doors and offers different opportunities.

Just as the Global Hip Hop Nation offers spaces of reference outside the limits of the Quebec nation, the alter-ego offers possibilities of taking on new identities. We argue that the concept of the alter-ego is anti-essentialist—identities are fluid, can be taken on and off, and are used for specific purposes in relation to particular audiences—and can be used to find an identity that fits. This rap practice offers a mental space to experiment with how identities play out in different circumstances. As with filters or effects on Instagram or TikTok that enable a person to change their appearance or voice, etc., the filter metaphor can apply to the alter-ego in hip hop, as artists use it to alter themselves or to reveal aspects of their identity and personality.

Almost all our participants have created a MC persona. The following excerpt from the interview with Jackson bears many similarities to Bradley's (2018) previous observations about the artistic and reinventive possibilities of the alter-ego:

> Édouard: So, when you rap, would you say that you are a different person?
> Jackson: Definitely... I just, I just feel like it represents me more. It's the one that doesn't, that doesn't like, who speaks about meaningful things. But JAY-jay, I feel like that's the person that I really wanna be. And then when I rap, I feel like I am that person...

Édouard: So, do you think that one day... you and JAY-jay will eventually merge?
Jackson: Actually, I hope that will happen very soon, right?... I feel like JAY-jay is just like waiting for me at a certain spot, and he's like, "aight, dude, I'm just waiting for you when you're ready to like stop, start, sorry, start speaking, speaking meaningful things." Yeah, JAY-jay, my persona, is very confident and doesn't have any problems speaking. But me as like... I'm confident when I speak to people, but sometimes I stumble on my words. And JAY-jay is totally different from that. So, so, so we're two opposites.
Édouard: It's a way for you to find confidence?
Jackson: Yeah. And ever since like, I came up with JAY-jay I became more confident, like, on my stuff... Yeah, so. It really helped me out.

For Jackson, his alter-ego "JAY-jay" is by his own admission an avatar of the individual he aspires to become. The alter-ego provides him confidence, particularly with regard to his slight speech impairment. For the participants, it seems that the possibility of creating a new or better version of themselves is what particularly appeals to them: fiction and the imaginary can become reality when they personify their alter-ego. In short, the possibility of embodying a persona or a renewed and improved version of oneself seems to allow young people to approach their daily life with more confidence and symbolizes a type of renewal.

As with Ibrahima, Mark explores the ways his alter-ego can open up new possibilities of expression for himself. He offers a new take, however, on the artistic persona, describing how his conveys emotions and moods: "I created something more like it's incognitoness [sic] it is just a shadow and like my main goal is to... I'm not a person, I'm just a mood...I think feeling is more important than what you're saying because some people don't know how to explain those things."

This perspective takes a very different approach to communication, focused on creating an atmosphere rather than narrative storytelling. Rather than build a new persona, his art helps him to partly disappear into his shadow, which means he is "incognito." This posture makes sense given that this same person had explained that he had difficulty finding the words to express his feelings. He also sees his creative process in terms of "movement," describing his style of writing as "abstract poetic movement" and how he is inspired by roaming in the neighborhood.

Mark's roaming alter-ego also seems to be an outlet for reconciling and channeling his multiple musical influences and allows him to evolve in different scenes and communities: "The way I move is kind of like I love a type of music where I'm in each different scene and I'm producing for like all these different types of scenes. Just like there's no difference, the only different thing is different people will have different taste of music. So like I love every type of music and so I have something to relate about every part of like a community."

Mark seems to value the simple things in life by privileging the feelings, senses, and desire to escape the more difficult aspects. He declares, "I mostly really talk about, the thing I see all the time, nature. I don't have to talk about drug dealing or the slum. It's not things I want to promote." This deliberate avoidance helps him move beyond the negative elements he may encounter:

> Édouard: Do you feel like by avoiding these topics it helps you?
> Mark: Yeah, because it helps you. I understand where you are trying to get. It helps you understand. I think the more you talk about something the more it gets real. It's like looking in the mirror and you're telling yourself "All you gonna do is bad," you gonna do bad. Then if you tell yourself "You gonna do good," you gonna do good. It's all mentality. It's how I see it.

In Mark's case, making music was one of the ways he helped himself out of the difficult contexts in which he grew up, specifying, "I had to break a path" trying not to repeat the same patterns present in his family. In the end, he mobilized different aspects offered by hip hop to develop a channel of his own to express his thoughts and feelings.

Up to now, participants have been discussing how confidence is a fundamental element of performance, and of hip hop in general. Presenting artwork and performing take courage and having some help can be welcome especially for beginner MCs. In this respect, the MC alter-ego can also enable another rap convention, the ego trip. Considering that participants are young adults exploring their identities and are quite new MCs, the ego trip is an appealing option because it can contribute to building a rapper's credibility in terms of following rap's codes while allowing to dare and experiment within its relatively defined structures. The ego trip is a great tool to boost one's confidence. Ibrahima says, "I do a lot of ego trips. That's to say, I value myself a lot as the person I am. That's to say, I talk a lot about myself, how I have confidence in myself and everything." Another participant, Moussa, gives us a very detailed description of his vision of the ego trip, in which he balances between exaggeration and authenticity:

> After all, there are certain codes that are linked to music in general, for example, the ego trip basically, it's something that is very much linked to rap... if it comes from art it's going to come out in art... it's not going to come out in my life every day. I'm not going to start hitting people because I heard such rapper or I said in my lyrics that so. Or in my lyrics, I appear, I can sometimes appear a little violent, but it's, it's ego trip, it's exaggerated. I'm not going to suddenly start hitting people, it's, it's stupid. But after, in rap, I try to rap what I am, I try to rap, to stay relatively true even if I can, I can mess around. Sometimes I mess around, I can go in all directions.

Moussa describes the need to use discernment and not take everything that is said at face value. He also shares how he tries to maintain a balance between exaggerated "messing around" and trying to stay "relatively true" to himself.

The alter-ego is one element in hip-hop's toolbox for exploring and experimenting with identity. In discussing their time at NBS Studio, participants have expressed being grateful for finding a community that supports their identities and allows them to connect with peers. They also mentioned that hip hop's introspective work fosters personal growth and political awareness. The analysis shows that creating raps allows youth to connect with their feelings. For some, writing lyrics is their gateway and for others, music production is a better outlet. For all, engaging with hip-hop culture brings possibilities to connect with and express their emotions. Finally, crafting their hip-hop alter-egos is an artistic strategy that fosters confidence through the option to reinvent yourself through projection and approach the creative process and performance from a less intimidating standpoint. The participants hope to transpose this confidence booster to other areas of their lives.

We also argue that on top of these other uses and benefits, the alter-ego has an anti-essentialist dimension that contrasts with the categories or stereotypes too often affixed to racialized youth. The youth use their personas to experiment, re-invent, and "mess around" with their identities; these are spaces of change, movement, and play. By opening new possibilities for themselves, the youth embody an anti-essential model of identity that contrasts with fixed, reductive, and exclusionary models of Quebec identity and belonging.

Conclusion

NBS Studio offers a welcoming environment propitious to youths' well-being and personal growth through engagement with hip-hop culture. This is in part due to hip hop's affordances, but also to the commitment to youth empowerment and positive development by the studio director and mentors. NBS' welcoming and supportive atmosphere and dynamic energy were reflected in the dedication and enthusiasm expressed by the participants during the interviews. They shared examples of how their passion helped them to become better people and create bonds within their community. They spoke about issues that matter to them, and how components of hip-hop culture such as rap, music production, and the alter-ego are helping them to achieve their goals, artistically and personally.

The youth's work can be observed in a series of videos called "We Out Here Live," presenting performances of the artists recording at NBS. As part of a week against racism, in collaboration with other community centers from the neighborhood, NBS produced a video in the Spring of 2022 (NBS Studio 2022). Young artists were invited to express themselves about their experiences with racism. This video is vibrant and poignant and displays several of the elements of youth well-being described in this chapter, such as political awareness, expressing emotions, and building community. It stands in stark contrast with the Quebec's Premier's continued refusal to recognize systemic racism. "We Out Here Live" embodies the community revolving around NBS Studio, including its contributions to youth well-being and growth, and is a strong example of hip hop's commitment to social justice.

References

Adjapong, Edmund, and Ian Levy. 2021. "Hip-Hop Can Heal: Addressing Mental Health through Hip-Hop in the Urban Classroom." *The New Educator* 17 (3): 242–263. https://doi.org/10.1080/1547688X.2020.1849884.

Alim, H. Samy. 2009. "Creating an Empire Within an Empire: Critical Hip hop Language Pedagogies and the Role of Sociolinguistics." In *Global Linguistic Flows: Hip hop Cultures, Youth Identities, and the Politics of Language*, edited by H. Samy Alim/Awad Ibrahim/Alastair Pennycook, 213–230. New York: Routledge.

Alvarez, Tomás T. 2012. "Beats, Rhymes, and Life: Rap Therapy in an Urban Setting." In *Therapeutic Uses of Rap and Hip Hop*, edited by Susan Hadley and George Yancy, 117–128. New York: Routledge.

Arbour-Masse, Olivier. 2017. "Comment le rap queb est-il devenu la musique de l'heure?" *RAD*, September 27, 2017. https://ici.radio-canada.ca/info/rad/serie/rap/6/comment-le-rap-queb-est-il-devenu-la-musique-de-lheure.

Arbour-Masse, Olivier. 2018. "Street rap – le son de la rue." *RAD*, November 8, 2018. https://www.rad.ca/dossier/rap/143/street-rap-le-son-de-la-rue.

Atséna Abogo, Marie-Thérèse. 2019. "Hip-Hop et pauvreté: entre résistance culturelle et créativité économique." *Reflets* 25 (1): 111–132. https://doi.org/10.7202/1064670ar.

Austin, David. 2013. *Fear of a Black Nation: Race, Sex and Security in Sixties Montreal*. Toronto: Between the Lines Press.

Banerjee, Sidhartha. 2020. "Francois Legault Sticks to Position That Systemic Racism Doesn't Exist." *National Post*, June 8, 2020. https://nationalpost.com/pmn/news-pmn/canada-news-pmn/francois-legault-sticks-to-position-that-systemic-racism-doesnt-exist-in-quebec.

Bouchard, Chantal. 2012. *Méchante langue: la légitimité linguistique du Français parlé au Québec*. Montréal: Presses de l'Université de Montréal.

Bouchard, Serge, and Marie-Christine Lévesque. 2014. *Ils ont couru l'Amérique: de remarquables oubliés, tome 2*. Montréal: Lux Éditeur.

Bradley, Brent. 2017. "Mask Off: A Brief Introduction to Alter-Egos in Hip-Hop." *DJBooth*, May 26, 2017. https://djbooth.net/features/2017-05-26-hip-hop-alter-egos.

Campbell, Mark V. 2014. "The Politics of Making Home: Opening Up the Work of Richard Iton in Canadian Hip Hop Context." *Souls* 16 (3): 269–282. https://doi.org/10.1080/10999949.2014.968978.

Chalet Kent. n.d. "We Are Here." Accessed January 2, 2024. https://chaletkent.ca.

Coulthard, Glen Sean, and Gerald R. Alfred. 2014. *Red Skin, White Masks: Rejecting the Colonial Politics of Recognition*. Minneapolis: University of Minnesota Press. https://doi.org/10.5749/minnesota/9780816679645.001.0001.

D'Amico, Francesca. 2015. "'The Mic Is My Piece': Canadian Rap, the Gendered 'Cool Pose,' and Music Industry Racialization and Regulation." *Journal of the Canadian Historical Association* 26 (1): 255–290. https://doi.org/10.7202/1037204ar.

Desfossés B, Félix. 2020. *Les racines du Hip-Hop au Québec (vol. 1)*. Rouyn-Noranda: Éditions du Quartz.

Dimitriadis, Greg. 2009. *Performing Identity/performing Culture: Hip Hop As Text, Pedagogy, and Lived Practice*. Rev. ed. of *Intersections in Communications and Culture*, V. 1. New York: P. Lang.

Dwyer, Janet Ingraham. 2005. "Kitwana, Bakari. Why White Kids Love Hip Hop: Wankstas, Wiggas, Wannabes, and the New Reality of Race in America. (Book Review)." *Library Journal* 130 (11): 86.

Exantus, Ludia. 2022. "Se construire en tant que femme dans le rap haïtien." *Revue temporalités et sociétés* 1 (1–2): 110–127. https://temporalites.charesso.org/index.php/ts/article/view/110-127-Exantus.

Faber, Tom. 2021. "Decolonizing Electronic Music Starts with Its Software." *Pitchfork*, February 25, 2021, https://pitchfork.com/thepitch/decolonizing-electronic-music-starts-with-its-software/.

Fofana, Dieynébou. 2012. "Génération hip-hop." *L'école des parents* 594 (1): 36–39. https://doi.org/10.3917/epar.594.0036.

Fortin, Andrée, Patrick Roy, and Serge Lacasse. 2006. *Groove: enquête sur les phénomènes musicaux contemporains: mélanges à la mémoire de Roger Chamberland*. Québec: les presses de l'Université Laval. https://doi.org/10.3917/epar.594.0036.

Hadley, Susan, and George Yancy. 2012. *Therapeutic Uses of Rap and Hip Hop*. New York: Routledge. https://doi.org/10.4324/9780203806012.

Harper, Kimberly C., and Hope Jackson. 2018. "'Dat' Niggas Crazy: How Hip-Hop Negotiates Mental Health." *The Western Journal of Black Studies* 42 (3–4): 113.

Heath, Travis, and Paulo Arroyo. 2014. "'I Gracefully Grab a Pen and Embrace It': Hip-Hop Lyrics As a Means for Re-Authoring and Therapeutic Change." *International Journal of Narrative Therapy & Community Work* 3 (3): 31–38.

Hess, Mickey. 2005. "Metal Faces, Rap Masks: Identity and Resistance in Hip Hop's Persona Artist." In *Popular Music and Society* 28 (3): 297–311. https://doi.org/10.1080/03007760500105149.

Hew, Alexander, Rachael Comte, and Cristina Moreno Almeida. 2020. "Hip Hop as an Agent for Health and Wellbeing in Schools." *Voices* 1. https://doi.org/10.15845/voices.v20i1.2870.

Howard, Philip S. S. 2020. "Getting Under the Skin: Antiblackness, Proximity, and Resistance in the Slāv Affair." *Theatre Research in Canada* 41 (1): 126–148. https://doi.org/10.3138/tric.41.1.126.

Journet, Nicolas. 2012. "Le rap, un genre élitiste?" *Les grands dossiers des sciences humaines* 3 (3). https://doi.org/10.3917/gdsh.026.0028.

Kassam, Iman, and Luca Caruso-Moro. 2022. "Rem Takes down Montreal Rapper's English-Language Promo Video." Montreal, CTV

News. August 29, 2022, https://montreal.ctvnews.ca/rem-takes-down-montreal-rapper-s-english-language-promo-video-1.6046330.

Laabidi, Myriam. 2012. "Représentation scolaires et culture hip-hop: expériences et trajectoires." PhD diss., Université Laval.

Laabidi, Myriam. 2006. "Culture Hip-Hop Québécoise et francophone, culture identitaire." In *Groove: enquête sur les phénomènes musicaux contemporains: mélanges à la mémoire de Roger Chamberland*, edited by Roger Chamberland, Serge Lacasse, and Patrick Roy, 167–177. Québec: Presses de l'Université Leval.

Lafortune, Gina, and Fasal Kanouté. 2019. "Récits d'expériences de jeunes issus de l'immigration en situation de décrochage: Quand l'école « ne marche pas » ou est un bad trip." *Éducation et Francophonie* 47 (1): 131–148. https://doi.org/10.7202/1060851ar.

Laniel-Tremblay, Édouard, and Bronwen Low. 2022. "De- and Reterritorializing Identities: The Global Hip Hop Nation at Work in a Youth Hip Hop Recording Studio." In *Critical Approaches Toward a Cosmopolitan Education*, edited by Carl E. James and Sandra R. Schecter, 86–100. New York, NY: Routledge. https://doi.org/10.4324/9780429327780-8.

Lamort, Kapois. 2017. *Les boss du Québec: R.a.p. du fleur de lysée (analyse socio-historique et sociologique du hip-hop dans la société Québécoise)*. Deuxième édition. Montréal: Production noire inc. (Noirs au travail).

Leavitt, Sarah. 2022. "Transit Agency Cuts Montreal Rapper's Promotional Video over Use of English | CBC News." *CBCnews, CBC/Radio Canada*, August 26, 2022. https://www.cbc.ca/news/canada/montreal/rem-pulls-rapper-anglophone-promo-video-1.6563614.

LeBlanc, Marie Nathalie, Alexandrine Boudreault-Fournier, and Gabriella Djerrahian. 2007. "Les jeunes et la marginalisation à Montréal: la culture hip-hop francophone et les enjeux de l'intégration." *Diversité urbaine* 7 (1): 9–29. https://www.erudit.org/fr/revues/du/2007-v7-n1-du1814/016267ar/.

Leppänen Sirpa, and Elina Westinen. 2018. "Migrant Rap in the Periphery Performing Politics of Belonging." *Aila Review* 30 (1): 1–26. https://doi.org/10.1075/aila.00001.lep.

Lepore, Stephen J., and Joshua M. Smyth. 2002. *The Writing Cure: How Expressive Writing Promotes Health and Emotional Well-Being*. Washington, DC: American Psychological Association. https://doi.org/10.1037/10451-000.

Lesacher, Claire. 2012. "Quand le rap dit la ville: perceptions sociolinguistiques des rap-peuses de Montréal." In *Actes du colloque dynamiques sociolangagières de l'espace: Mémoire des lieux et mise en mots de l'habitat populaire*, edited by Lounici Assia, and Nabila Bestandji, 137–159. Paris: L'Harmattan.

Lesacher, Claire. 2014. "Rap, langues, « québéquicité » et rapports sociaux de sexe: pratiques et expériences de rappeuses Montréalaises d'origine Haïtienne." *Diversité Urbaine* 14 (2): 77–95. https://doi.org/10.7202/1035426ar.

Levy, Ian P., Amy L. Cook, and Christopher Emdin. 2018. "Remixing the School Counselor's Tool Kit: Hip-Hop Spoken Word Therapy and YPAR." *Professional School Counseling* 22 (1). https://doi.org/10.1177/2156759X18800285.

Levy, Ian P. 2019. "Hip-Hop and Spoken Word Therapy in Urban School Counseling." *Professional School Counseling* 22 (1b). https://doi.org/10.1177/2156759X19834436.

Lipset, Michael. 2021. "NBS Studio: A Duty to Sound: Arts & Society: Phi Antenna, the Blog." February 18, 2021. https://phi.ca/en/antenna/nbs-studio-a-duty-to-sound/.

Low, Bronwen, Marilyn Steinbach, Maryse Potvin, David Lefrançois, Stéphanie Tremblay, Emmanuel Doré, and Stéphanie Demers. 2021. "The effects of law 21 on Education faculties in Quebec: 'We don't want people like you here.'" *The Monitor*, June 7, 2021. https://monitormag.ca/articles/the-effects-of-law-21-on-education-faculties-in-quebec-we-dont-want-people-like-you-here/.

Low, Bronwen. 2011. *Slam School: Learning through Conflict in the Hip-Hop and Spoken Word Classroom*. Stanford, CA: Stanford University Press. https://www.degruyter.com/document/doi/10.1515/9780804777537/html.

Magnan, Marie-Odile, Fahimeh Darchinian, and Émilie Larouche. 2017. "Identifications et rapports entre majoritaires et minoritaires. Discours de jeunes issus de l'immigration." *Diversité urbaine* 17: 29–47. https://doi.org/10.7202/1047976ar.

Marsh, Charity, and Mark V. Campbell, eds. 2020. *We Still Here: Hip Hop North of the 49th Parallel*. Montreal: McGill-Queen's University Press.

NBS Studio. n.d. "About." Accessed September 29, 2023. https://www.nbsstudio.ca/.

NBS Studio. 2022. "We Out Here Live." Accessed January 2, 2024. https://www.instagram.com/p/Cbx-cA8JtYa/.

Néméh-Nombré, Philippe. 2018. "Le hip-hop avec des gants blancs." *Liberté* 322 (322): 39–44.

Nerestant, Antoni. 2022. "Legault Says Accepting More than 50,000 Immigrants in Quebec per Year Would Be 'a Bit Suicidal.'" CBC News, CBC/Radio Canada, September 29, 2022. https://www.cbc.ca/news/canada/montreal/labour-minister-caq-immigration-1.6598558.

Pagliarulo-Beauchemin, Marc. 2016. "Les 'musiques émergentes' à l'heure du web 2.0: étude de cas du 'post rap' de Québec à Montréal." Master's thesis, Université du Québec à Montréal.

Renaud, Philippe. 2021. "Les leçons de la polémique du Franglais dans le rap Québécois." *Le Devoir*, March 29, 2021. https://www.ledevoir.com/culture/597799/serie-devoirs-de-francais-les-lecons-de-la-polemique-du-franglais.

Sarkar, Mela, and Lise Winer. 2006. "Multilingual Codeswitching in Quebec Rap: Poetry, Pragmatics and Performativity." *International Journal of Multilingualism* 3 (3): 173–192.

Sarkar, Mela, Bronwen Low, and Lise Winer. 2007. "'Pour connecter avec le Peeps': Québéquicité and the Quebec Hip-Hop Community." In *Identity and Second Language Learning: Culture, Inquiry, and Dialogic Activity in Educational Contexts*, edited by Miguel Mantero, 351–72. Charlotte, NC: IAP.

Saddik, Annette J. 2003. "Rap's Unruly Body: The Postmodern Performance of Black Male Identity on the American Stage." *Tdr* 47 (4): 110–27.

Savard Morand, Marie-Rose. 2019. "Gesamtkunstwerk de Dead Obies: posture, esthétique et poétique." Masters thesis, Université du Québec à Montréal.

Travis, Raphael. 2016. *The Healing Power of Hip Hop: Intersections of Race, Ethnicity, and Culture.* Santa Barbara, CA: Praeger.

Travis, Raphael, Elliot Gann, Alexander H.D. Crooke, and Susan M. Jenkins. 2019. "Hip Hop, Empowerment, and Therapeutic Beat-Making: Potential Solutions for Summer Learning Loss, Depression, and Anxiety in Youth." *Journal of Human Behavior in the Social Environment* 29 (6): 744–65. https://doi.org/10.1080/10911359.2019.1607646.

Way, Lyndon C. S., and Simon McKerrell, eds. 2017. *Music As Multimodal Discourse: Semiotics, Power and Protest.* Bloomsbury Advances in Semiotics, 10. London: Bloomsbury Academic.

Williams, Quentin, and Christopher Stroud. 2013. "Multilingualism Remixed: Sampling, Braggadocio and the Stylisation of Local Voice." In *Stellenbosch Papers in Linguistics* 42 (1): 15–36. https://doi.org/10.5774/42-0-145.

White, Bob W. 2019. "Franglais in a Post-Rap World: Audible Minorities and Anxiety About Mixing in Québec." *Ethnic and Racial Studies* 42 (6): 957–974. https://doi.org/10.1080/01419870.2019.1559943.

Wohlchies, Romane. 2021. "Le colonialisme comme processus patriarcal de dominations. La place des femmes et des féminismes dans le processus de décolonisation." Institut du Genre en Géopolitique, November, 2021. https://igg-geo.org/wp-content/uploads/2021/11/Le-colonialisme-comme-processus-patriarcal-de-dominations-3.pdf.

Chronicling New York Reggae and Hip Hop's Crossroads, and Community Media as Historical Archives from the Ground Up

James Barber

Abstract *In this chapter, I first establish some historical background concerning reggae's arrival and subsequent reception in New York. Thereafter, I illustrate details of the "Hip Hop x Dancehall Takeover" event, which took place at the VP Records Retail store on Jamaica Avenue, Queens, on April 23, 2022, during one of my extended research stays in New York. I use this as a starting point to highlight the activities of two longstanding New York-based archivists, ambassadors and activists of reggae and hip-hop culture in attendance: Ralph McDaniels, founder of landmark hip-hop television show, Video Music Box, established in 1983; and Shaun Walsh, who in the following decade founded Flatbush, Brooklyn-based community media channel Whatz Up NY TV.*

Introduction

My wider doctoral research addresses Jamaican mass migration to New York after 1965, and the subsequent spread of Jamaican culture and reggae music: first across the famed megalopolis, and later elsewhere in the US and internationally. I trace how the establishment of New York as an additional regional and global hub of Jamaica's diaspora, reggae music, sound system and dancehall culture, would lead to a reciprocal dialogue between reggae and hip hop across the following decades in the latter's birthplace. While some scholars have recognized that reggae took some time to "percolate" into wider African American cultural practice, reggae and hip hop's entanglements are considerably more substantive than their current representation would suggest (Marshall 2006: 215; Patterson 1994).

Across the 1980s, reggae's percolation "through African-/American, urban cultural practice" and in hip-hop culture especially was realized through contributions from pioneering figures primarily, though not exclusively, from the New York reggae and hip-hop scenes, a phenomenon both transnational and translocal in its entanglements. While I focus specifically on the arrival and distillation of Jamaican culture into wider New York popular music culture, I also highlight the fact that spreading reggae to a wider popular audience in the US megalopolis, and laying the foundations for its eventually prolific dialogue with local hip-hop culture, did not come about solely through the contributions of Jamaicans. Reggae's wider reception in New York would establish musical connections that traversed genres, music cultures, and communities.

Aside from Jamaicans and Jamaican Americans, key contributions to reggae's spread and crossover with hip hop in New York came from individuals of other Caribbean ancestries including (in no particular order): Trinidadians, Haitians, Bajans, Bahamians, Antiguans, alongside native New Yorkers born and raised beside their Caribbean neighbors, reflecting a diverse pan-Caribbean, "musical multiculture" of individuals from a cross-section of ethnicities, diasporas, and New York neighborhoods (Peth 2018; Marshall 2006: 215; Patterson 1994: 108; Melville 2020: 3). From the turn of the 1970s onwards, reggae would become increasingly audible in New York City's soundscape, resonating through the sound system sessions in the city's streets, dancehalls and nightclubs, on the mixtapes that blared from home and car stereos, and eventually on New York radio, soundtracked and facilitated by a community of *selectors* (DJs), singers, *deejays* (MCs), producers, sound system owners and operators, studios, record labels, record shops and distributors, and radio DJs (Kenner 2005).

My wider enquiries are principally informed by ethnographic research and personal interviews carried out between 2019 and 2023, in addition to wider literature and other secondary historical accounts and multimedia materials. Although somewhat suspended in time by the impact of the global pandemic, I spent a total of almost six months in New York City, with two extended visits, the first between October–December 2019, not able to resume my enquiries in person until the first half of 2022. Both stays focused on building up a picture of the key individuals, spaces and sites—primarily, though not exclusively—in the reggae and hip-hop scenes that contributed to reggae's emergence and spread in New York and the proliferation of its dialogue and eventual fusion with hip hop from the 1980s through the 1990s. Taken together, the primary and secondary accounts and materials gathered across the course of the research, serve as an initial attempt at providing a more substantial "mapping" of the emergence of reggae music and culture in New York and its ensuing intersections with a nascent hip-hop culture (Melville 2020: 3–7).

Through initial referrals from my existing contacts in the reggae and hip-hop scenes internationally, in particular the UK and Germany, while in New York I established a network of research participants on a word-of-mouth basis, otherwise known as "clustering" or snowball sampling (Kasinitz 1992: 12). The participants were some of the aforementioned groups of actors who shaped the development of the music and cultures of reggae and hip hop in New York from the 1970s and 1980s onwards, both in parallel and in their intersections, or in other cases local specialists and contemporaries of these individuals. The research also highlights the emergence across the 1980s of a subgenre of New York reggae and hip-hop fusion, sometimes referred to as raggamuffin hip hop,[1] which merged the sounds, styles and practices of the two cultures, particularly in terms of musical production, language and lyricism, and the

---

1   One of the earliest recordings to use the term was the 1988 album "Raggamuffin Hip-Hop" by London-based artists and proponents of the "fast-chat" deejay style Asher D and Daddy Freddy. When I spoke to several of my research collaborators in New York about the term, however, they were sometimes unfamiliar and even sceptical of the label, suggesting it probably had more to do with the commercialization, marketing, and commodification of 1980s and 1990s reggae and hip-hop fusion by the major labels who sought to market and capitalize on it.

visual style, fashion, and aesthetics of reggae and hip-hop culture (Marshall and Foster 2013).

I conducted both formal and informal semi-structured interviews with some of the central architects of this crossover and fusion in New York, attending reggae and hip-hop stage shows and DJ and sound system events where my research participants or other relevant artists to this historical era were performing. In addition, secondary research materials were gathered in public library archives, attendance at documentary screenings and panel discussions and through further enriching informal conversations on these overlaps in day-to-day settings around the city. Aside from the time spent in New York, despite the challenges of conducting fieldwork during a global pandemic, I remain in touch with many of the artists, producers, DJs, record shop owners, and archivists who I talked with along the way, individuals I seek to forefront in the representation of these historical developments. In early summer 2023, I was even fortunate enough to make a brief research visit to Jamaica, once more bringing the enquiries about reggae's spread to New York, and intersections with hip-hop culture, full circle.

This chapter functions as a selected illustration of some of the key sites and contributors to this popular music history that I spent time and spoke with during my research stays in New York. I walk the reader through a partial overview of reggae's migration to New York and its subsequent spread and eventual intersections and dialogue with hip-hop culture, especially during the latter's Golden Era. The first part of the article focuses on some historical background regarding reggae's arrival in New York and the increasing "visibility" and "audibility" of Jamaican culture and reggae music in the US metropolis (Marshall 2006: 218). The second part of the chapter, the dub version, or B Side, focuses on a significant event that occurred during my second extended research stay in New York in Spring 2022, the "Hip Hop x Dancehall Takeover" taking place at the VP Records Retail store on Jamaica Avenue, Queens.

First drawing on details from the event, including a series of panel discussions, the article highlights a selection of reggae and hip hop's intersections in New York, before focusing on the contributions of two important New York-based archivists, ambassadors, and activists of reggae and hip-hop culture in attendance. The host of the discussion panels for the day, Ralph McDaniels, or "Uncle Ralph," founder of the landmark hip-hop television show, Video Music Box (VMB). Next door in the store's yard where an all-vinyl reggae sound system session completed the event's program, I connected with community media organizer and archivist Shaun Walsh, founder of Whatz Up NY TV (WUNYTV), a Flatbush, Brooklyn-based community media channel.

Locating these two individuals' positions in the relevance of reggae and hip hop's parallel and shared histories in New York, the article illustrates how a chance meeting with these two figures furthered an understanding of the significance of these community media organizers and grass roots archivists in establishing an audiovisual history of the music cultures of reggae and hip hop in New York from the early 1980s up to the present day. Moreover, the article details how the very idea of taking a video camera into New York's underground music cultures began with Ralph's documentation of hip-hop culture, acting as a blueprint for representing hip hop and many other underground Black and marginalized popular music sub- and multi-cultures and scenes in New York. In the final section of the article, several extended conversations with Shaun are drawn upon to highlight his efforts in bearing the torch for reggae and Caribbean culture in the decade following VMB's establishment. Finally, the article reflects on the legacy of these two individuals, who have done so much at a grass roots level in terms of elevating reggae and hip-hop culture and establishing archives that document their historical development in New York, both in parallel and in their perpetual intersections, reciprocal influence, and fusion.

Hip Hop's Semi-Centennial, Godfather Herc, and Jamaica's Second Mass Migration

Across the course of 2023, a wealth of celebrations and commemorations took place in hip hop's birthplace, across the US and globally, for the culture's fiftieth birthday. Already documented within the dominant historical narrative of hip-hop's emergence and evolution are the founding contributions of its Jamaican-born godfather DJ Kool Herc (Clive Campbell), and the parties he hosted together with his sister Cindy at 1520 Sedgewick Avenue, The Bronx, in the late summer of 1973 (Chang 2007: 67). Having moved to the US from Kingston six years prior, age twelve, Herc has spoken about the impressions made upon him by his early exposure to reggae sound system and dancehall culture in Kingston (ibid.: 68–72). The influence of practices pioneered by the early Jamaican sound system *selector* (DJ) who would chat or *toast*[2] vocal improvisations live over a record in a dancehall session, a form of proto-rapping, and the innovations of Jamaican sound system and recording technologies, are all acknowledged as having shaped the emergence of hip-hop culture in The Bronx (Perry 2004: 13–15; Gilroy 1993: 33; Snapes 2021). Herc and others' recognition of the influence of these central aspects of Jamaican sound system culture on hip hop's emergence is further echoed by a host of other architects of New York's hip hop and reggae scenes, illustrated throughout.

Reggae's reception in New York, and its subsequent growing dialogue with hip-hop culture, was crucially facilitated through the migration and establishment of the Jamaican sound system (technological medium) and dancehall (space) nexus, mobile discotheques and sites of musical creation and innovation (Barber 2024: 129). Sound system scholar Julian Henriques' research highlights the role of the Jamaican sound system engineer in crafting an "exemplary apparatus" of subaltern, "non-epistemic" knowledge production, which, through its central musical and technological "repurposing" practices beginning in the 1950s, have propagated innovations in the dancehall that have in turn had a significant impact on global popular music cultures (Henriques 2021: n.pag.). Anthropologist Normal Stolzoff's historical reading of the dancehall suggests that it has been "a space of cultural creation and performance since the slavery era," noting the ongoing, global significance of Jamaican dancehalls as "cultural counterworlds," spaces that since

---

2 Toasting would later become known as deejaying and is referred to hereafter as the latter, not to be confused with the disc jockey (DJ), who in Jamaican sound system culture is more commonly known as the selector.

their formation have facilitated "the syncretic blending of African and European cultural forms" among Jamaica's lower classes (Stolzoff 2000: 3–4).

What academic and popular representations of Godfather Herc's founding contributions to the culture often tend to omit is the striking number of other hip-hop pioneers of Jamaican, West Indian, and Caribbean descent. Furthermore, there tends to be a failure of situating the arrival of these foundational figures and their families in New York within the context of the historical significance of the US' 1965 Hart-Celler Immigration Act. The law's passing "opened the proverbial gates" for a subsequent wave of wider mass migration to the US from the Caribbean, which in the Jamaican case signified the advent of the island's "second mass migration" (Greer 2018: 14; Patterson 1994: 107). As hip hop spread across the five boroughs and beyond during its "Golden Age" from the 1980s through to the mid-to-late 1990s, reggae practice, sounds, and stylings could be seen and heard more explicitly in hip-hop productions, language, lyricism, and fashion (Duinker and Martin 2017). This period coincided with the establishment of a "critical mass" of New York's Jamaican, and wider Caribbean population outlined below, in the boroughs of The Bronx, Queens, and perhaps Brooklyn especially, and the neighborhoods of Flatbush, East Flatbush, and Crown Heights (Marshall 2006: 2015). Resultingly, reggae, sound system, and dancehall culture was acutely resonant in these areas (Serwer 2016).

Reggae's Reception and the Increasing Audibility and Visibility of Jamaican Culture in New York

From the early 1970s, reggae music became increasingly "audible" in New York City's soundscape as the influx of Caribbean people, many of whom had moved to the metropolis in search of better economic prospects and greater sociopolitical stability, brought their music with them (Kenner 2005; Marshall 2006). Jamaicans moving to New York from reggae's homeland sought to establish their new home in the Empire State as a hub for reggae music and culture, with a host of both aspiring and established artists, producers, studio engineers, record shops, record labels, sound system owners, operators, and DJs migrating to New York. Elsewhere in the United States, smaller though nonetheless notable concentrations of Jamaicans would eventually settle in Miami, Atlanta, and urban centers across the Eastern Seaboard (Marshall 2006: 308).

Several figures central to reggae's wider reception in New York were guided by a musical vision and mission to spread their beloved reggae music from the island of Jamaica to the world (Hinrichs 2011: 12). One notable example is Philip Smart, music producer and owner of HC&F Studio, founded in Freeport, Long Island in 1982: "arguably the most significant and longest-running reggae studio in the US," with Smart at the helm until his retirement in 2013, sadly passing the following year (Serwer 2005). Born in Kingston in 1953, Smart had grown up in close company with reggae royalty and several other late masters of Jamaican music. His close teenage friend and collaborator was the producer and mystic melodica virtuoso, Augustus Pablo (Horace Swaby), while in the early 1970s, Smart would graduate as a sound engineer and producer from the studio of Jamaican dub pioneer King Tubby (Osbourne Ruddock), in Kingston's Waterhouse district (Meschino 2014). In 1976, Smart moved to New York to pursue studies in audio engineering. On settling in Brooklyn, he found an already "well-enough established network of Jamaican producers and sound systems," which as well as creating demand for reggae recording studios locally also kept him in work as a freelance engineer alongside his studies (Kenner 2013). Studios such as VP Records in Queens, Wackies in The Bronx, and Jah Life Outernational in Brooklyn. On establishing his studio, Smart set about realizing his ultimate motivation to make "New York known as a reggae town" (ibid.).

The Jamaican in New York: Early Tensions and "Shifting Significations"

Reggae's reception, and that of Caribbean culture more broadly, took some time to establish itself in New York, however. Many accounts from New York Caribbean reggae and hip-hop luminaries and otherwise reiterate the idea that being Caribbean in New York City in the 1970s could sometimes be a "liability," with Kool Herc recalling how West Indians arriving in this decade became a "target" for local gangs in The Bronx (Chang 2007: 72; Marshall 2006: 213). In cultural terms, at this point in time Jamaicans specifically were too "outsider" to be fashionable, their patois dialect unintelligible to their neighbors, and reggae too 'foreign' for Herc's early hip-hop DJing, with many new arrivals preferring to "conceal" their cultural heritage (Marshall 2006: 213–215).

As previously indicated, across the 1980s, however, this picture changed dramatically as 213,805 Jamaican citizens alone, 9 percent of the island's total population, moved to the United States, with almost half this number heading to New York (Waters 1999: 36; Manuel 1995: 241). Over the same period, a "critical mass" of the population was achieved, with New York's Caribbean population as a whole surpassing two million residents, making New York "the biggest Caribbean city and the second biggest Jamaican, Haitian and Guyanese city" globally (Marshall 2006: 215; Manuel 1995: 241). In turn, cultural significations also shifted. Reggae's wider reception in New York, and the US at large, was precipitated by a number of key transnational and translocal social, cultural, and political developments across the 1980s.

Musically speaking, back in Jamaica this decade saw the eventual dominance of the reggae 'dancehall' sound, which had reigned supreme in the dancehalls of Kingston since the turn of the decade. In 1985, producer King Jammy (Lloyd James) and artists Noel Davy and the late Wayne Smith, also Waterhouse residents, started a digital reggae revolution when they stumbled across a Casio MT40 keyboard pre-set (Trew 2019). The pre-set was deployed as a bassline on Smith's smash hit "Under Mi Sleng Teng," setting about yet a further revolution in reggae music: in its production techniques, lyrical content, and aesthetics (ibid.). The visibility of Jamaican culture in New York in this era was also heightened, though wider representations of Jamaicans were at equal turns "demonizing and lionizing," the former perpetuated by images in US media of the increasingly notorious Jamaican *posses*, or *yardies*, infamous drug-running gangs "set loose from political patronage by the profits of the drug trade" in Jamaica, who now "cornered the markets of Brooklyn and the Bronx and the greater Tri-State area" (Marshall 2006: 218). These and other factors taken together set about "shifting significations" of Jamaican culture and reggae music in New York across the 1980s, which became increasingly visible and audible in the city's streets, dancehalls, clubs, and radio network, and elsewhere in wider US popular culture (Marshall 2006: 213–221).

With the digital dancehall explosion in Jamaica quickly spreading to New York, particular practices and tropes of reggae culture began to show up more explicitly and prolifically in hip hop, and also vice versa, including the sampling and remixing of reggae *riddims* (rhythm tracks or instrumentals) in hip-hop productions, the adoption and increasing audibility of Jamaican language in rap music, the fusion of rap with dancehall deejay stylings, and the visibility of dancehall fashion in hip-hop style. Jamaican culture and reggae music resonated with New York hip hop's aesthetics at this moment, with the emergence of dancehall reggae bringing "Jamaican music closer to the production values of American hip-hop" (ibid.; Katz 2005: 85). Bridging the practices and aesthetics of the two cultures, in turn led to the fusion of New York reggae and hip-hop music and style and the emergence of the raggamuffin hip-hop subgenre (Marshall and Foster 2013).

Throughout the rest of this chapter and elsewhere, I forward the idea that reggae and hip hop's eventual fusion crossover in New York in the 1980s and 1990s, can in fact be thought of as the closing of the circle in a continuous "socio-sonic circuitry," or circularity, between Jamaican and African American popular music culture and practice, beginning with transnational cultural flows in and between Jamaica and the United States during the foundation of a national popular music culture in Jamaica in the 1950s (Marshall 2006; Patterson 1994: 108).

Dubbing Reggae and Hip Hop's Shared New York History: VP Records and Video Music Box Present "Hip Hop x Dancehall Takeover"

Figure 1: VP Records Retail Store, 170–19 Jamaica Avenue, Queens

(Author Photo, 2022)

VP Records Reggae Journey from Kingston, Jamaica to Jamaica, Queens

On April 23, 2022, the "Hip Hop x Dancehall Takeover" event took place at the VP Records Retail store, Jamaica Avenue, Queens, as part of international Record Store Day.[3] The event's co-host was Patricia Chin, aka

---

3   Founded in 2007, Record Store Day is an annual global celebration of independently owned "brick and mortar" record shops and record store culture. Further information can be found at recordstoreday.com.

Miss Pat, co-founder of VP Records and reggae's "matriarch" (Peru 2022). The article "VP Records – A Reggae Journey, Four Decades And Counting," drawn upon throughout this segment, describes how Miss Pat, together with her late husband Vincent 'Randy' Chin made their first entry into the music business when they established Randy's Record Mart, a second-hand record store in downtown Kingston, in the late 1950s (VP Records: n.d.). Since then, musical seeds first planted in Jamaica would go on to become VP Records, as it is known today, the world's biggest reggae record label, retailer and distributor, and largest independent record label outright, with a 25,000-strong catalogue of recordings.

Figure 2: VP Records Co-Founder Patricia Chin aka Miss Pat

(Author Photo, 2022)

Back in Jamaica, the Chin's enterprises had started out during a critical moment in the island's history. Not only did they witness the birth of the island's first indigenous pop music, ska, across the 1950s, but by the following decade, with Jamaica's independence from British colonial rule imminent, they lived through ska's emergence as the soundtrack to Jamaican independence. The popular craze for ska was eventually so great it precipitated demand for a domestic recording industry, which the Chins would soon become a central part of. Demand for Jamaican recordings was further stimulated by the first mass migration of the island's population to the UK beginning in 1948, which established the first significant global export market and hub for Jamaican music and culture (Patterson 1994: 107). By 1962, the Chins had moved their enterprises to Randy's now legendary site of 17 North Parade, Kingston, where within a few years they had also established their first studio, alongside the many other now-iconic Jamaican recording studios that emerged during this period. From 1968 up to the mid-1970s, Randy's Studio 17 would establish itself as one of the island's finest early studios, recording many of the greats of this musically fertile era including Bob Marley and The Wailers, Dennis Brown, and Gregory Isaacs.

As the initial optimism of independence quickly faded, Jamaica's social environment going into the 1970s presented many challenges, not least for the Chins and their aspirations to reach newly emerging global markets. As a result, the couple set their sights on New York City, "with its growing Jamaican community and access to the world's largest market for recorded music" and in 1977 relocated to Jamaica, Queens, where they established VP Records, retailer, manufacturer, and distributor of reggae music at their first location at 170–03 Jamaica Avenue (VP Records, n.d.).

Instrumental in spreading the early dancehall sound of the 1980s, they would also establish an important connection with arguably the leading Jamaican producer of this era, Henry "Junjo" Lawes, via the New York-based reggae producer Hyman "Jah Life" Wright. This triangle of the Kingston-New York connection helped to elevate the exposure of early dancehall stars such as Yellowman, Johnny Osbourne, and Barrington Levy. VP Records would go on to release seminal titles from dancehall stars of the post-1985 digital era, such as Shabba Ranks, Super Cat, Capleton, Buju Banton, Beenie Man, and Bounty Killer, who had first emerged as deejays and singers in Kingston's dancehalls, before establishing significant in-roads for Jamaican artists and reggae music; first, in New York City and later to wider audiences and markets in the

US and internationally (VP Records 2022: 01:57:59). This was further perpetuated by the crossover of these artists into New York hip-hop culture, with all the above collaborating in classic examples of 1990s reggae and hip-hop fusion, including: Shabba Ranks ft. KRS-One "The Jam" (1991), Bounty Killer ft. Jeru the Damaja "Suicide and Murder" (1995), and Capleton & Method Man "Wings of the Morning" (1995).

"Hip Hop x Dancehall Takeover" Panel Discussion: Four the Hard Way

The four-way panel discussion billed as the day's centerpiece featured several central figures of New York reggae and hip-hop culture and global popular music history, period, primarily addressing reggae and hip hop's New York entanglements in the 1980s and 1990s. In order of appearance were DJ and producer Kenny Dope (Kenny Gonzalez), born to Puerto Rican parents in Sunset Park, Brooklyn, who through his early exposure to music at home and in the streets began his music career in 1985, aged fifteen, working at a local record store (Lawrence 2006). He is perhaps best known as one half of the iconic New York production duo Masters at Work, together with DJ and producer 'Little' Louie Vega, Salsa King Héctor Lavoe's nephew (Louie Vega, n.d.). Their near forty-year partnership as a production team is recognized as "one of the most influential, long-running and prolific relationships in dance music history" (Lawrence 2006).

Alongside Kenny Dope was Kool DJ Red Alert (Frederick Crute), known within the community as "Uncle Red," a founding father of hip-hop culture, born in Antigua before moving with his family to Harlem as a child (Education Through Music 2022). Attending high school in The Bronx, he would witness hip hop's emergence as an attendee at Kool Herc's early 1970s house parties, and by the end of the decade had honed his own skills as a DJ, bringing him to the attention of Afrika Bambaataa (Lance Taylor) and his Universal Zulu Nation (Red Bull Music Academy 2017). From 1983 up to the mid-1990s, Red Alert would cement his legendary status on his weekly Kiss FM "Dance Mix Party" show, one of the first rap shows on commercial radio. True to the New York DJing style of this moment, his revered sets were famous for the diverse musical tastes they traversed (ibid.).

The third central figure in conversation was Brooklyn-born Sting International (Shaun Pizzonia), another renowned New York club DJ who began e of five. At sixteen years old, his reputation as a DJ led to his invitation to play at the WBLS FM Christmas party held at the iconic Studio 54 nightclub (Meschino 2018). With an extensive cross-genre knowledge of music, by the late 1980s, as well as being one of the most in demand club DJs in New York, he also focused his attentions on music production, with his passion for reggae leading to his mentorship under the late Philip Smart at his HC&F studio. A two-time Grammy award winning producer, he would also launch the careers of numerous notable Jamaican-born reggae artists in New York, including Shaggy (Orville Richard Burrell), "the only diamond-selling dancehall artist in music history," Red Fox (Gareth Shelton), and Screechy Dan (Robert Stephens), all four members of the wider Brooklyn-based reggae collective Ruff Entry Crew, a prominent musical force in New York's dancehalls of the Biltmore Era[4] in the late 1980s and 1990s (Meschino 2018; Wasserman Music, n.d.; Serwer 2013).

At the turn of the 1990s, Kenny Dope would release the first in a series of reggae and hip-hop fusion experiments, beginning with Masters At Work "Blood Vibes," where Dope took the vocal from Jamaican reggae artist Junior Reid's international hit "One Blood" and "mashed it up" with the drums from A Tribe Called Quest's "Bonita Applebum" (VP Records 2022: 00:36:53). These recordings began as "trial and error" experiments, "blends" or "transition records" that enabled New York DJs to "segue" between different musical styles in their sets (ibid.: 00:37:04). Like many up-and-coming producers of this era, Dope would hand over these

---

4   Named after the legendary reggae sound system sessions and stage shows that took place in and around the Biltmore Ballroom on Church Avenue, Flatbush.

recordings as exclusives on reel-to-reel tapes, not having the resources to press them onto *dubplates*[5] (ibid.: 00:42:30; Stolzoff 2000: 58).

After he handed "Blood Vibes" to Kool DJ Red Alert to play on his Kiss FM show, the reception on the radio and in the clubs for this reggae and hip-hop fusion was so well received, that Dope's experiments would give Red Alert the "ammunition" to "program (reggae) to the massive" (VP Records 2022: 00:42:47). Meanwhile, in 1990, Sting International also secured a DJ residency on Kiss FM, on the Hip-House Reggae show hosted by the prominent Barbados-born radio personality Dahved Levy. In parallel to Red Alert's efforts on the airwaves, Sting International's partnership with Levy would establish a "previously unavailable mainstream platform for reggae, dancehall and soca," as part of his "three-pronged strategy" to broaden reggae's reception beyond its core audience, with many of his productions becoming "important records... embraced by hip-hop and club DJs...," reflecting a unique "New York hybrid dancehall sound" (Meschino 2018).

Chronicling the Sites, Sounds, and Scenes of New York Reggae and Hip-Hop Culture's Evolution

"Uncle Ralph" McDaniels and Video Music Box: An Audiovisual Blueprint

The final member of the discussion was host Ralph McDaniels, "affectionately known" as "Uncle Ralph," born in Bed Stuy, Brooklyn in 1962 to part-Trinidadian parentage, a DJ, VJ, video producer, and founder of the landmark hip-hop television show VMB introduced earlier (Video Music Box, n.d.; Jones 2021: 00:11:46). Since founding the pioneering show in 1983, four decades of interviews, music videos, live footage from club nights, concerts, and events, today make up the Video Music Box Collection (VMBC): "the largest visual history of hip-hop culture" in the world,

---

5   Recordings pressed onto vinyl acetate as exclusives for a particular DJ or selector.

spanning from hip-hop's "metamorphosis" in its birthplace, up to the present day (Video Music Box Collection, n.d.).

VMB's story began in the early 1980s when McDaniels, completing his college studies, interned as an engineer at WNYC-TV Channel 31. In 1983, he was able to secure airtime for his hour-long show, which was broadcast six days a week. Alongside selected music videos, of equal importance to the show's eventual stature were the live footage and interviews captured on camera at events and nightclubs across the five boroughs (Stelloh 2012). In establishing the first hip-hop TV show, VMB set the blueprint for what the format of a hip-hop TV show would even look like, emphasizing a documentation of the culture at a street level, and providing an early platform for the very visibility of hip hop and Black American culture on US television: "Video Music Box was us showing us" says rapper DMC (Darryl McDaniels) of the pioneering Queens rap group Run DMC (Jones 2021: 00:53:38).

VMB's scope was not confined to hip hop alone, with documentation of the nascent and evolving New York R&B, house, reggae, and salsa scenes today totaling over 20,000 hours of rare footage and music videos (Video Music Box Collection, n.d.). In this regard, VMB has also played an important role in broadcasting an audio-visual introduction of other New York music cultures and scenes to a wider local audience. Regarding McDaniels' connection to reggae culture, the Puerto Rican, Bronx-raised hip-hop luminary Fat Joe highlights, "Ralph used to play the Caribbean stuff, the reggae stuff, before we even knew Jamaicans" (Jones 2021: 00:32:38). Furthermore, in McDaniels' work as a film and music video producer, during the 1990s he produced and directed music videos for Shaggy, Red Fox, Super Cat, and Shabba Ranks, all artists generally acknowledged to have 'opened the gates' for reggae's wider reception in New York and beyond (VP Records 2022: 01:49:35).

Uncle Ralph's role in documenting and representing the history of New York's music cultures highlights the importance of grassroots community media actors in chronicling the evolution of these scenes. When McDaniels began his activities in the early 1980s, both reggae and hip hop remained predominantly underground scenes, receiving little to no visual documentation or representation outside of the musical communities themselves. In establishing a visual format for the representation of the nascent New York hip-hop and reggae scenes in particular, Uncle Ralph and Video Music Box played a highly significant role in bringing hip hop and reggae to a wider, eventually international audience in the birthplace of the former, as many of the key figures attending the day's interviews attested.

Archiving Caribbean Culture in New York with The People's Cameraman: Whatz Up New York TV

As the main panel discussion drew to a close inside, Uncle Ralph would host a series of further discussions with a veritable roll call of figures central to reggae's wider New York reception and subsequent hip-hop fusion from the 1980s up to the present day. In no particular order, Ralph was joined by reggae veterans Johnny Osbourne, Mikey 'Mack Daddy' Jarrett, and Nadine Sutherland; Jamaican-born hip-hop pioneer Don Baron of 1980s rap group Masters of Ceremony; dancehall dons Red Fox and Screechy Dan; and contemporary champions of New York reggae culture, DJ Pee Wee of Pretty Posse Sound, DJ Slick of Nexxt Level Sound, selector Empress Breeze, and DJ Max Glazer of Brooklyn's Federation Sound.

With the rest of the panel discussions in full swing in VP's function room next door, guests browsed the store's extensive catalogue of Caribbean music recordings and related merchandise. Outside in the back yard, on a bustling sunny afternoon on Jamaica Avenue, an all-vinyl reggae sound system session was in full swing. In true Jamaican sound system style, high power bass vibrations frequently submerged the interviews inside, not to mention shaking the physical foundations of the neighborhood. Some of the guests would pass through to greet and talk with Uncle Ralph, before stopping by at the sound system session to touch the mic and bestow musical blessings on the occasion. Together with some of the legendary individuals in this all-star cast, I observed and soaked up the sound system atmosphere and situation outside in the yard, "where the real action was happening" (Walsh 2022).

Figure 3: Shaun Walsh interviews the artists Screechy Dan (left) and Red Fox (right)

(Author Photo, 2022)

I was briefly and graciously introduced to a string of central figures in reggae and hip hop's shared and respective New York histories, past and present, before at some point being struck by how many camera crews were in attendance, representing New York community media platforms, social media channels, and music news websites, documenting all aspects of this event and celebration of reggae music and culture, and reggae and hip hop's historical dialogue. Together, artists and other attendees basked in the spirited occasion of this commemoration.

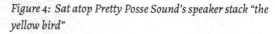

Figure 4: Sat atop Pretty Posse Sound's speaker stack "the yellow bird"

(Author Photo, 2022)

Red Fox and Screechy Dan joined another interview outside with Shaun Walsh, "the people's cameraman" and WUNYTV founder, and out of my curiosity as to his activities I introduced myself. During my remaining time in New York, Shaun and I would engage in several further extended conversations, which alongside an ongoing correspondence, form the basis of the discussion outlined in this section (Walsh 2022). In parallel to VMBC's extensive hip hop and multi-genre music and culture archive, by Shaun's own humble estimations the live concert and event footage and interviews with prominent music, community, and political figures he and his team have captured, represent the biggest historical archive of Caribbean culture in New York City: "I archive everything, you know [he laughs]. I got hundreds, man, hundreds of tapes[6] [cassette recordings] for the culture, you know, so I've archived from tapes to flyers, now to the video... all of that stuff I've archived" (Walsh 2022). Further reflecting on Ralph McDaniels and VMB's legacy, Shaun describes how when he first started taking a video camera to community events in 1997, prior to establishing WUNYTV as a Public Access television show in 2001, he was directly inspired by and emulated the format and blueprint pioneered by Uncle Ralph.

Shortly after Shaun and I's first meeting, WUNYTV was gearing up for its twenty-first anniversary event. On June 11, 2022, Shaun was joined by Red Fox and Screechy Dan in receiving honorary proclamations from the State of New York, presented by State Assembly member Brian Cunningham and Senator Kevin S. Parker in recognition for the three's respective and collaborative contributions from the 1980s up to the present day in elevating reggae music and Caribbean culture in New York, and in turn, elsewhere in the US and globally. All three were recognized primarily for their contributions to the community and local culture in Flatbush, heartland of New York's Caribbean community and the epicenter

---

6   Shaun is referring to predominantly live recordings of reggae sound system sessions, radio shows, and mixtapes made by DJs and producers, that circulated in and between Jamaica and the communities of its global diaspora. With regards to reggae, Kingston, New York, Toronto, and London and other active satellites of Jamaican and Caribbean diasporas were central hubs that propagated these exchanges. The importance of the culture of mixtapes, in a pre-internet age especially, is another central consideration with respect to the global spread and intersections of many underground music cultures in the 1980s and 1990s, not least reggae and hip hop.

of reggae dancehall culture during the Biltmore Era. Pointing to the importance of documenting and archiving this era, Shaun talks about the central Brooklyn sites in which reggae's creative cultivation in the 1980s and 1990s would occur, in venues such as The Tilden Ballroom, The Ark and Club Illusion, prior to its wider New York and US reception. Speaking of the venues of this era, he adds, "what I'm doing (archiving), what you're doing [my research], at least you can say it existed... they're parking lots and malls nowadays."

Born in the UK in 1970 to Jamaican parents, at six-months old Shaun went to live with his maternal grandmother in Albion Mountain, in the Jamaican parish of St. Mary, joining his older brother and sister who had already made the move prior to Shaun's birth. In 1978, the family emigrated again, settling in East Flatbush, by now home to a well-established and prominent Caribbean community. Arriving at the turn of the decade, New York City and the streets of its "outer boroughs—Brooklyn, the BX, Queens, Shaolin, even parts of Strong Island—ran red hot. Between Reaganomics, AIDS and the crack epidemic," the pressures of the city sometimes weighed heavy, and often even more acutely for new arrivals (Kenner 2013: n.pag.). The hostilities that Jamaicans and others faced in New York City, and the "shifting significations" of Jamaican culture across the 1980s, are further reflected in Shaun's experiences. He recalls, "I remember asking my parents, 'When will I be able to speak like the rest of the kids?' Trying to speak like, you know, American style, right? ... When we all came here, we all wanted to be American... that's what everyone was doing at that time, like we wanted to kinda assimilate into American culture." A key aspect of 'assimilating' into American culture for Shaun and others on first arriving in New York City was embracing the dominant youth culture of the moment, hip hop: "I was Run DMC's biggest fan, because we were all like hip-hop heads, you know? ... So, I was a Run DMC fan, everybody in the hood was a Run DMC fan, everybody... Every single person" (Walsh 2022).

Shaun was "too young" to have been exposed to reggae dancehall culture at this early age. But while many Jamaicans and other new arrivals to New York City attempted to assimilate, in terms of dress, speech, and the music they identified with, Shaun highlights how others, who he refers to as the "hardcore" dancehall people—in some cases Jamaicans who were more established in New York—had kept reggae culture alive within the community. As I introduced earlier, this was in fact an entire network of reggae activists, who kept reggae culture bubbling away in New York's Caribbean communities, in the streets, in underground clubs, dancehalls, and other community spaces.

Referencing the veteran, Jamaican-born, New York-based reggae singers and deejays, Mikey 'Mack Daddy' Jarrett, who began voicing recordings for Wackies and Jah Life as early as 1979, Reverend Badoo and Ranking Joe, Shaun says, "if it wasn't for the likes of those guys—those guys kept it—so for people like me now, we [had] something to go to" (Walsh 2022). In 1982, a respected member of the Jamaican community in Brooklyn known as Squire Dread (Howard Anthony Small) passed away. After the funeral, a memorial and tribute were hosted on Clarkson Avenue, Brooklyn, by the Jamaican-born, New York-based reggae sound system Third World Hi Fi. On the mic were deejays and singers Mikey Jarrett, Reverend Badoo, Willow Wilson, and Sammy Levi. Cassette recordings from this session soon circulated and, via his sister, one fell into Shaun's hands; something he identifies as one of his first entry points in reconnecting with reggae music and Jamaican culture and further the advent of his passion for archiving all aspects of the culture he came across.

This moment also represented a shifting tide for Shaun musically speaking, the waves of which were spreading throughout New York's Jamaican community across the 1980s. Shaun would begin to reconnect with his Jamaican roots, turning his back entirely on hip-hop and 'American' culture, and embracing the burgeoning reggae dancehall scene, which was quickly spreading from Jamaica to the world, not least through the spread of sound tapes. By now a transcontinental phenomenon, recordings of the latest big reggae dances taking place in Jamaica, and increasingly in the global hubs of the diaspora in the UK, US, and Canada, achieved legendary status through their international circulation. For New York-based Jamaicans, the in-flow of sound tapes and vinyl recordings were "even more important than hip hop... [as] each week's deluge of fresh vinyl served as a kind of broadband connection to their island homeland, transmitting high bit-rate signals in both directions about... how the yard massive was living in Jamaica and inna Babylon" (Kenner 2005).

In the mid-1980s, as the digital dancehall revolution took hold in Jamaica, Shaun had begun to go deep into reggae culture and would hone his lyrics and delivery in a reggae deejay style together with his peers, experimenting and imitating the leading Jamaican and New York dancehall artists of the day on the sound systems kept at his friends' houses, or at small parties. Several years later, Shaun started studying at New York's Stony Brook University, where over the next two years he began to perform on stages at college parties as the artist Bellymus (his childhood nickname back in Jamaica), alongside his friend Horsehead (David Duncan) aka H-Diggy. With time, he began to perfect his craft, and other emerging artists gave him and his deejay partner segments of their time slot to perform. On one such occasion in 1990, he shared the stage with Red Fox and another prominent Brooklyn-based reggae artist of that era, Naturalee. Headlining was the hip-hop group Leaders of the New School, which featured a young Busta Rhymes (Trevor Tahiem Smith Jr.), another East Flatbush native of Jamaican descent, and an outspoken commentator on the lack of recognition given to reggae music and Jamaican dancehall and sound system culture and the formative influences it has had on hip-hop culture. The rapper has credited dancehall icon Shabba Ranks as a key influence on his own style, having stated that he imitated aspects of Shabba's voice, fashion, and dancing and brought that into his own artistry as a rapper and in turn into hip-hop culture (Gardner 2022). He has also attributed the fast-chat lyrical stylings of prominent 1980s Jamaican dancehall deejays Papa San and Lieutenant Stitchie as a principal influence on his rapping style (ibid.).

Another important milestone in Shaun's life, and the WUNYTV story, was his exposure for the first time to student politics and activism on campus. He recalls, "At the time there was a blood drive by the Red Cross. They said that Haitians couldn't give blood because they are AIDS carriers. So, I said, shit, ok, I took off one of the plaques and started walking around and screaming and all that, and that was the beginning of this politically motivated kind of attitude that I have" (Walsh 2022).

At the turn of the 1990s, Shaun dropped out of his college studies and took on a job as a transporter in a Manhattan hospital, continuing his activities as a music artist and event promoter. He performed at central reggae venues in Brooklyn—Club Rendezvous (formerly Dynasty), The Ark and Club Illusion—alongside other prominent Flatbush-based reggae artists such as Screechy Dan and Red Fox, whose recording careers at this moment were taking off in line with reggae's wider New York and US reception, already well underway. Shaun would also perform as a support act for iconic reggae elders Alton Ellis and John Holt, and the dancehall veteran Tiger.

Thereafter, Shaun focused his attentions on a full-time nursing career, working for the next fifteen years as a licensed practical nurse, with the demands of the job leading him to quit his activities as a reggae artist and stage performer fairly abruptly. With his life-long passion for music and reggae always present, however, just a few years later he resumed his musical activities as a sideline. At the end of the 1990s, gang violence and guns once again plagued New York's streets. Shaun wanted to create a safe space for young people in Brooklyn away from the violence in the streets and founded a music promotion for high school students billed as Sunday Afternoon Jams. He adds, "I have a history [and] I know the struggle in this thing, man," referencing a near-death experience a decade earlier, when the house party he was attending in Brooklyn was shot up by gunmen and Shaun, an innocent bystander, caught a stray bullet that pierced the top of his skull.

Shaun's motivation to document local culture and community life, he reiterates, had always been in him, and now equipped with his own video camera, he documented every single one of these Sunday sessions, mimicking VMB's format and speaking to the attendees queuing up in the line, greeting them New York style with a "whatz up?" before documenting the performances and action inside. The format of this documentation at the parties, sowed the seeds of WUNYTV. As the Sunday jams grew "exponentially," Shaun sought to create a TV commercial to promote them. At first, he paid someone else do this for him, but as he honed his skills on the camera, he began to do his own. All this came prior to having his own show: "We had a lot of parties, and I think VMB was on at that time also, so we would mimic what they were doing. I have my guy outside with the microphone with the people in the line, talking to them, and then the guy would go inside the club and talk to the people, and I documented *all* the parties—something told me to keep the documentation" (Walsh 2022; original emphasis).

Some years later, Shaun wanted to air a commercial for one of his party promotions and approached an acquaintance who already had a show on the Brooklyn Community Access TV station, a Public Access network available to Brooklyn residents. In 2001 WUNYTV was born, airing as a weekly half-hour show. Shaun's idea was to cover "some party stuff to get the people to think about politics," principally focusing on issues pertaining to the cultural, musical, and political life of New York's Caribbean community.

In the show's "Weh Dem Gone?" segment, a riff on VH1's "Where are They Now?", Shaun foregrounded one of the main niches he wished to push in the show's musical content. The segment focused particularly on interviews with some of the older 'foundation' reggae artists, whom Shaun could see were often going by unnoticed at some of the events he was attending in New York, eclipsed by up-and-coming artists, and sensed that it was imperative to do this before some of reggae's celebrated elders passed. In 2004, the show began to be broadcast in parallel on the New York City-wide cable TV channel, Caribbean International Network, the same year that by absolute chance Shaun captured perhaps one of his greatest scoops with regard to reggae and hip hop's circularity.

In a Manhattan nightclub, Shaun and one of his interviewers known as General, chanced upon the meeting of Kool Herc and "Daddy" U Roy (Ewart Beckford), aka "The Teacher" and "The Originator" of Jamaican sound system deejaying. Though not the first proponent of toasting, he is recognized as the first person to elevate the form from the sound system to the studio, having perfected his art on Jamaican dub pioneer King Tubby's Hometown Hi-Fi sound system in the late 1960s (Snapes 2021). In 2019, at an event in Queens, New York, U Roy was "crowned" the King of Dancehall by "The Emperor" of modern dancehall deejaying, Shabba Ranks (Rexton Rawlston Fernando Gordon), two years prior to The Originator's passing (Lindsey, n.d.).

In the footage that Shaun captured, Herc referred to U Roy as "my king," even getting down on one knee to honor the great reverence that Herc and others have for an artist who would 'set the foundation' from Kingston to New York. From the Jamaican deejay style that U Roy developed on the sound systems of Kingston, Jamaica, and the blueprint this established, a young Herc would absorb U Roy's vocal stylings, and the early ska music of The Skatalites and Prince Buster on the neighborhood sound systems and bring that with him to The Bronx. U Roy's response to this recognition was to highlight the foundational influence that African American music had on Jamaicans prior to the beginnings of the development of local imitations of in-flowing R&B, blues, and jazz styles that would birth ska music, citing the reverence Jamaicans had for artists such as Fats Domino, Louis Prima, and Louis Jordan.

U Roy's sentiments regarding reggae's African American "roots" and "routes" were also echoed in another highlight of Shaun's archiving activities, when in June 1990 he met another foundational figure of Jamaican music, Clement "Sir Coxsone" Dodd, founder and producer of reggae's first record label Studio One, the "Motown of Reggae" (Hall cited in Paul 2005: n.pag.; Stolzoff 2000: 48; The Music Origins Project, n.d.). In the 1980s, Dodd faced a similar fate to that of VP Records and the Chin family mentioned earlier. The monumental Studio One, which had always been located on 13 Brentford Road, Kingston, was attacked by gunmen, and Dodd duly moved his operations to 3135 Fulton Street, Brooklyn (Katz 2004).

Given the respect in the room for Coxsone, who Shaun noticed early on was referred to even by his elders as "Mr Dodd," a sign of utmost respect, Shaun did not feel it was appropriate to record the occasion, though he is able to recollect many of the details through his archival memory. The advantage of this, he adds, was that without the presence of a camera Mr Dodd felt at ease to talk freely, "he was just giving it" (Walsh 2022). Dodd "credited Black American music for everything.... and this is *Coxsone*... so Coxsone got it from here [the US]," a reference to Coxsone's stays in the US in the early 1950s, where he and other early sound system owners would travel to the southern states to work as farm laborers, meanwhile sourcing rare US R&B and jazz recordings to bring back to Jamaica in order to establish an edge over rival sound systems (Walsh 2002, original emphasis; Katz 2004). Shaun continues, "So, I guess it's like people are saying... you have Coxsone, the original, got his music and influences from America, right, developed this Jamaican art form and then people later on down the line got influenced by a guy that was influenced by Coxsone, Kool Herc, so the thing just kinda like came back to—it's a circle, you know?" (Walsh 2022)

Conclusion

In Shaun's case, and in the case of the blueprint established by Ralph McDaniels and VMB, the documentation and archiving of reggae and hip hop's parallel and shared histories established by these individuals are invaluable resources for our understanding of the people, spaces, places, mediums, and innovations that shaped the evolution of reggae and hip-hop culture in New York, not to mention other marginal, multicultural music scenes of this culturally monumental megalopolis. In his comment earlier, "at least we can say it existed," Shaun also reflects the extent to which the life works of these two individuals were carried out without realizing the historical significance of the moments they were documenting, instead being informed by their participation and love for the two cultures. The result of these efforts as of 2024 are, in Shaun's case, an archive of over twenty-five years of Caribbean culture in New York, with tens of thousands of hours of footage, alongside an extensive collection of sound tapes, flyers, photos, and memorabilia that have captured and chronicled reggae history in New York.

Perhaps Shaun's principal inspiration for the format and approach of his activities when starting out, Ralph McDaniels, has today established the VMBC Inc. as a non-profit organization and archive with more than 20,000 hours of rare, raw footage of New York City's nascent and evolving hip-hop, reggae, and other music scenes, which also archives many of the music videos of this period, including those produced and directed by McDaniels himself. Across his forty-year career, McDaniels has also worked with inner city youth teaching film, radio and TV, and in making the archive public has established an extensive historical and educational collection that has seen him work together with the NYC Board of Education, the NYC Department of Corrections, the Schomburg Center for Research in Black Culture, The Universal Hip Hop Museum in The Bronx, and a range of other educational and arts institutions, with the archive functioning as a medium of cultural preservation, education and research (VMBC, n.d.).

Shaun has similar aspirations for his own archive once he has completed the slow process of single-handedly digitizing his materials. For researchers, especially those such as myself who come from outside of the immediate communities they are documenting and representing, I am hopefully not alone in recognizing the paramount importance of honoring representations of these cultures from the documents and accounts given by those who lived, participated, shaped, and indeed, captured them. Shaun and Ralph's efforts to chronicle reggae and hip hop's parallel and shared histories, as well as actively participating in their creation and evolution, have established invaluable archives that provide extensive, multimedia databases that can help us to understand, commemorate and educate about the evolution of these cultures: their social and musical history, including the development of musical practices and recording discographies, the spaces and technologies that facilitated this, and an (audio)visual representation of these developments as they unfolded. For their role in this, Ralph, Shaun, and other grassroots archivists should undoubtedly be recognized and remembered within these histories.

Discography/Videography

A Tribe Called Quest. "Bonita Applebum" (Album Version). Jive Records, 1990, vinyl single.

Bounty Killer ft. Jeru the Damaja. "Suicide Murder" (Remix). Massive B, 1995, vinyl single.

Capleton ft. Method Man. "Wings of the Morning" (Dynamik Duo Mix). Rush Associated Labels, 1995, vinyl single.

DJ Ralph McDaniels Records. "Video Music Box Takeover with DJ Ralph McDaniels," VP Record. Premiered April 29, 2022. YouTube Video, 3:03:41. https://www.youtube.com/watch?v=h2nDdI2pfSE&ab_channel=VPRecords.Jones, Nasir, dir. *You're Watching Video Music Box*. New York City: Showtime Networks Inc, 2021, https://www.sho.com/titles/3503704/youre-watching-video-music-box.

Junior Reid. "One Blood." JR All Stars, 1989, vinyl single.

Kenner, Robert J. "Five Borough Fire: Digital Dancehall NYC Style," In Philip Smart. *5 Borough Fire: Philip Smart Productions from the New York Dancehall*. Street Platinum & Gold Productions 1 83599 00012 2, 2005, Liner notes.

Kool DJ Red Alert. "Kool DJ Red Alert talks The Bronx, Grandmaster Caz and DJing." Red Bull Music Academy. Posted on August 23, 2017. YouTube Video, 1:23:11. https://www.youtube.com/watch?v=Aap7Vkdp3pM.

Masters At Work. "Blood Vibes." Cutting Records, 1991, vinyl single.

Shabba Ranks ft. KRS-One. "The Jam." Epic Records, 1991, vinyl single.

Wayne Smith. "Under Mi Sleng Teng." Jammy's Records, 1985, vinyl single.

References

Barber, James. 2024. "Shinehead's 'Jamaican in New York': The Circularity of Jamaican and African American Cultural Practice and Reggae's Resonance in Hip Hop from The Bronx to Brooklyn and Beyond." In *From Broadway to The Bronx – New York City's History through Song*, edited by edited by Veronika Keller and Sabrina Mittermeier, 126–139. Bristol: Intellect.

Chang, Jeff. 2007. *Can't Stop Won't Stop: A History of the Hip-Hop Generation*. London: Ebury Publishing.

Claudia Gardner. 2022. "Busta Rhymes Says He Emulated Shabba Ranks' Style And Brought It To Rap Music." *Dancehall Mag*, December 9, 2022. https://www.dancehallmag.com/2022/12/09/news/busta-rhy

mes-says-he-emulated-shabba-ranks-style-and-brought-it-to-rap-music.html.

Christina. M. Greer. 2018. "Hart-Celler and the Effects on African American and Immigrant Incorporation," in "Caribbeanization of Black Politics," ed. Sharon D. Wright, special issue, *National Political Science Review* 19 (1): 14–28.

Duinker, Ben, and Denis Martin. 2017. "In Search of the Golden Age Hip-Hop Sound (1986–1996)." *Empirical Musicology Review* 12 (1–2): 80–100. https://emusicology.org/article/view/5410/4799

Education Through Music. 2022. "Kool DJ Red Alert." Posted on June 2, 2022, https://etmonline.org/person/kool-dj-red-alert/#.

Gilroy, Paul. 1993. *The Black Atlantic: Modernity and Double Consciousness*. London: Verso.

Henriques, Julian. 2021. "Black Knowledge, Sounding and Technology." Paper presented at Auralities Research Network, Cambridge CRASSH, Cambridge University, UK, February 10, 2021.

Hinrichs, Lars. 2011. "The Sociolinguistics of Diaspora: Language in the Jamaican Canadian Community." *Texas Linguistics Forum* (54): 1–22.

Kasinitz, Philip. 1992. *Caribbean New York: Black Immigrants and the Politics of Race*. Ithaca: Cornell University Press.

Katz, David. 2004. "Clement "Sir Coxsone" Dodd: Pioneering producer of Jamaica's reggae music scene and founder of Studio One." *The Guardian*, May 6, 2004. https://www.theguardian.com/news/2004/may/06/guardianobituaries.artsobituaries.

Katz, David. 2005. "Sleng Teng Extravaganza: King Jammy and the Dawning of Jamaican Music's Computer Age," *Wax Poetics* 13: 84–90.

Kenner, Robert J. 2013. "Philip Smart: New York Reggae Foundations." *Red Bull Music Academy*, June 4, 2013. https://daily.redbullmusicacademy.com/2013/06/philip-smart-new-york-reggae-feature.

Lawrence, Tim. 2006. "'Kenny Dope: Choice.' Azuli Records, 2006." *Tim Lawrence*, July 16, 2013. https://www.timlawrence.info/articles2/2013/7/16/kenny-dope-choice-azuli-records-2006-29-january-2006.

Lindsey, Flair. n.d. "Shabba Ranks 'Crowns' U-Roy King in Queens: Irish and Chin Salute Living Legend at 10th Anniversary of 'Reeewind'."

Acclaim PR. Accessed November 3, 2023. https://madmimi.com/s/4 98fcf.

Louie Vega. n.d. "Grammy award winning DJ, Producer, Musician: About Me." Accessed February 22, 2023. https://louievega.com/.

Manuel, Peter. 1995. *Caribbean Currents: Caribbean Music from Rumba to Reggae.* Philadelphia: Temple University Press.

Marshall, Wayne. 2006. "Routes, Rap, Reggae: Hearing the Histories of Hip-Hop and Reggae Together." PhD diss., University of Wisconsin–Madison.

Marshall, Wayne, and Pacey Foster. 2013. "Hearing Raggamuffin Hip-hop: Musical Records as Historical Record." *Ethnomusicology Review*, October 1, 2013. https://ethnomusicologyreview.ucla.edu/content/hearing-raggamuffin-hip-hop-musical-records-historical-record-wayne-marshall-and-pacey.

Melville, Caspar. 2020. *It's a London thing: How rare groove, acid house and jungle remapped the city.* Manchester: Manchester University Press.

Meschino, Patricia. 2014. "Philip Smart, Celebrated Reggae Producer/ Engineer, Dead at 61." *Billboard*, March 14, 2014, https://www.billboard.com/music/music-news/philip-smart-celebrated-reggae-producerengineer-dead-at-61-5937500/.

Meschino, Patricia. 2018. "Sting International, Shaggy's Longstanding Producer, Reflects on His Pioneering Career (And Working With the Other Sting)." *Billboard*, August 16, 2018. https://www.billboard.com/music/music-news/sting-international-shaggy-producer-interview-8470447/.

Patterson, Orlando. 1994. "Ecumenical America: Global Culture and the American Cosmos." *World Policy Journal* 11 (2): 103–117. https://www.jstor.org/stable/40468616.

Paul, Annie. 2005. "Culture Is Always a Translation (Interview with Stuart Hall)." *Caribbean Beat* 71 (January/February). https://www.caribbean-beat.com/issue-71/culture-always-translation#axzz6y9oqrVMl).

Peru, Yasmine. 2022. "Miss Pat of VP Records receives York College's first Presidential Medal of Honour." *Jamaica Gleaner*, June 5, 2022. ht tps://jamaica-gleaner.com/article/entertainment/20220605/miss-pat-vp-records-receives-york-colleges-first-presidential-medal.

Perry, Imani. 2004. *Prophets of the Hood: Politics and Poetics in Hip Hop.* Durham, NC: Duke University Press.

Peth, Simon. 2018. "What is translocality? A refined understanding of place and space in a globalized world." *Transient Spaces and Societies,* September 25, 2018. https://www.transient-spaces.org/blog/what-is-translocality-a-refined-understanding-of-place-and-space-in-a-globalized-world/.

Serwer, Jesse. 2005. "From Cocoa Tea to T.O.K., Philip Smart's HC&F Studio is New York's Reggae Central." *Jesse Serwer*, November, 2005. http://jesse-serwer.com/music-culture/philip-smart-hcf-studio/.

Serwer, Jesse. 2013. "LargeUp Interview: On the Loose with Red Fox." *Large Up*, November 21, 2013. https://www.largeup.com/2013/11/21/largeup-interview-red-fox-on-fiyah-fox/.

Serwer, Jesse. 2016. "Playlist of the Week: Listen to "Brooklyn in the '90s" on Apple Music." *Large Up*, September 15, 2016. https://www.largeup.com/2016/09/15/playlist-week-listen-brooklyn-90s-apple-music/.

Snapes, Laura. 2021. "U-Roy, legendary reggae toaster, dies aged 78." *The Guardian*, February 18, 2021. https://www.theguardian.com/music/2021/feb/18/u-roy-legendary-reggae-toaster-dies-aged-78.

Stolzoff, Norman. 2000. *Wake the Town and Tell the People: Dancehall Culture in Jamaica.* Durham, NC: Duke University Press.

The Music Origins Project. n.d. "Studio One Was the Cradle of Reggae, Dancehall, Ska and Most Jamaican Music." Accessed November 7, 2023. https://www.musicorigins.org/item/studio-one-jamaican-music/.

Trew, James. 2019. "How Casio accidentally started reggae's digital revolution: The real story behind the mysterious 'sleng teng' riddim." *engadget*, July 19, 2019. https://www.engadget.com/2015-12-04-casio-and-the-sleng-teng-riddim.html.

Video Music Box. n.d. "You're Watching... Video Music Box." Accessed February 22, 2023. https://videomusicbox.com/.

Video Music Box Collection. n.d. "About VMBC." Accessed February 22, 2023, https://www.videomusicboxcollection.org/about.

VP Records. n.d. "A Reggae Journey, Four Decades and Counting." Accessed February 22, 2023. https://www.vprecords.com/a-reggae-journey/.

Walsh, Shaun. Interview with author, Flatbush, Brooklyn, May 2, 2022.

Wasserman. n.d. "Shaggy: Exclusive Booking Agency for Shaggy." Accessed October 22, 2023. https://www.teamwass.com/music/shaggy/#:~:text=As%20the%20only%20diamond%2Dselling,four%20in%20the%20top%2040.

Waters, Mary. 2001. *Black Identities: West Indian Immigrant Dreams and American Realities*. Cambridge: Harvard University Press.

Contributors

James Barber, MA, is a PhD candidate in the "Hip Hop as a Transcultural Phenomenon" research project at the University of Bern, Switzerland. His essay, highlighting Shinehead's song "Jamaican in New York" (1992) as an example of reggae and hip hop's wider intersections and fusion appears in the edited collection *From The Bronx to Broadway – New York City's History through Song* (Intellect, 2024). James is a music enthusiast, educator and sometime DJ, organizer, and promoter of music events, based in Berlin.

Martina Bratić received her PhD in 2022 from the Institute of Musicology of the University of Graz, where she currently works as a university assistant. She holds a Master's degree in musicology and history of art (Zagreb-Budapest). From 2012 to 2015, she worked as an associate musicologist at the Croatian Academy of Sciences and Arts in Zagreb, and was a Chief Curator at Inkubator Gallery in Zagreb. Martina is also a graduate of a one-year training program in women's studies.

Christian Büschges, PhD, is professor of Iberian and Latin American History at the Historical Institute and the Center for Global Studies of the University of Bern, Switzerland (since 2013). His main research interests include questions of ethnicity, social movements, and identity politics, as in his 2012 publication *Demokratie und Völkermord. Ethnizität im politischen Raum*. He is co-editor of the interdisciplinary journal

Iberoamericana. España – Portugal – América Latina and the Campus book series *Historische Politikforschung*.

Amy Coddington is an assistant professor of music at Amherst College, where she teaches classes on American popular music. Her book *How Hip Hop Became Hit Pop: Radio, Rap, and Race* (University of California Press, 2023) explores how rap broke through to a White mainstream audience in the 1980s and 1990s through programming on commercial radio stations. She has published related essays in *Journal of the Society for American Music* and *The Oxford Handbook of Hip Hop Music*.

Kevin P. Green, PhD, has over thirty years of experience as a freelance musician, music educator, and emerging scholar. His areas of emphasis include: hip-hop culture; jazz; the music of Cuba, Jamaica, and Brazil; music pedagogy; and US marching music ensembles. Green is currently assistant professor of Music, at California State Polytechnic University, Pomona. His duties include teaching music history lecture-based courses, and he is developing the Cal Poly Pomona Black Music Ensemble course to debut in Fall of 2024.

Kevin C. Holt is an assistant professor of Critical Music Studies at Stony Brook University (SUNY). His work broadly focuses on race, class, gender, and sexuality as they are negotiated/expressed in US popular culture. His current monograph project, *I Bet You Won't Get Crunk!* discusses Atlanta hip-hop party culture as performative resistance to systems of oppression and hypersurveillance in the US South.

Eliseo Jacob is a faculty member in the Department of World Languages and Cultures at Howard University with a PhD in Spanish and Portuguese from the University of Texas at Austin. He specializes in Latin American street literature, urban popular culture, and digital humanities. In 2022, he was a Fulbright scholar in Brazil where he developed a digital humanities project on the role of activism in cultural arts and writing communities from São Paulo's urban periphery.

Terence Kumpf is a native New Yorker who holds a PhD in Transnational and Transatlantic American Studies from the University of Dortmund. His interests in bi and multilingualism, music, and transculturation come from his experiences living and working in Germany, Amsterdam, and China. A member of the European Hiphop Studies Network, which he co-founded in 2018, Terence currently teaches English at the DPFA Regenbogen Schule in Rabenau, Germany.

Édouard Laniel-Tremblay is an educator and independent scholar intertwining education, sociolinguistics, and community-building initiatives in his practice. His research focuses on popular culture in Quebec and Canada, specifically on hip hop, and how it fosters identities and belonging for youth. He is a French immersion teacher for adults and is also involved in the digital arts community.

Bronwen Low has been leading and participating in research, knowledge dissemination, and program and curriculum development projects with a primary focus on how to best support socially marginalized young people underserved by traditional schooling models and practices. Her expertise lies in multi-sectoral partnerships, as well as in community arts and wellbeing, youth culture, popular poetics and hip-hop education, community music, and digital critical literacies.

Martin Lüthe is assistant professor at the John F. Kennedy Institute for North American Studies at Freie Universitaet Berlin and Einstein Junior Fellow. Lüthe published the monographs *"We Missed a Lot of Church, So the Music is Our Confessional": Rap and Religion* (Lit Verlag, 2008) and *Color-Line and Crossing-Over: Motown and Performances of Blackness in 1960s American Culture* (WVT, 2011).

Dianne Violeta Mausfeld is a research fellow at the Center for Inter-American Studies at the University of Bielefeld. She obtained her PhD in History at the University of Bern in 2022 as part of the SNFS-funded project "Hip Hop as a Transcultural Phenomenon," directed by Christian Büschges and Britta Sweers. Her case study focuses on Mexican

American and Latino artists and the emergence of the genre Chicano rap in Los Angeles during the 1980s and 1990s. She has published first research findings in *Popular Music History* (2019), *Norient* (2020), and *Lied und Populäre Kultur/ Song and Popular Culture* (Waxmann, 2021).

Britta Sweers, PhD, is professor of Cultural Anthropology of Music at the Institute of Musicology and the Center for Global Studies of the University of Bern, Switzerland (since 2009). A central focus of her research has been the transformation of traditional music cultures in a global context, including her publication *Electric Folk: The Changing Face of English Traditional Music* (Oxford University Press, 2005). She is co-editor of both the *European Journal of Musicology* and the Equinox book series *Transcultural Music Studies*.

www.ingramcontent.com/pod-product-compliance
Lightning Source LLC
Jackson TN
JSHW011420110225
78875JS00006B/67